Principles
of Expository
Preaching

Principles
of Expository
Preaching

by
MERRILL F. UNGER, Th.D., Ph.D.

ZONDERVAN

B. McCALL BARBOUR
28 GEORGE IV BRIDGE
EDINBURGH EHI IES, SCOTLAND

OF THE

PRINCIPLES OF EXPOSITORY PREACHING
Copyright 1955 by
Zondervan Publishing House
Grand Rapids, Michigan

Thirteenth printing   July 1978

ISBN 0-310-33411-X

Printed in the United States of America

DEDICATED TO MEN
CALLED OF GOD
TO PREACH THE WORD

CONTENTS

Contents

Contents

Chapter I

THE NEED OF EXPOSITORY PREACHING

It is difficult to exaggerate the far-reaching and beneficent influence the Christian pulpit has exerted on human society throughout the twenty centuries of its history. Careful unbiased study and reflection disclose that much of the moral, spiritual and social progress of our day is the direct result of centuries of Christian preaching. America, in particular, with its enviable heritage of freedom and individual opportunity owes an incalculable debt to the Christian pulpit. Perhaps no other one factor has been more potent in molding our democracy and in shaping the development of our free institutions than the voice of the man of God preaching the Word of God from the pulpits of our land.

The glory of the Christian pulpit is truly an illustrious glory, breathing the atmosphere of a higher world, and calling men from the sordidness of sin to God. But the glory of the Christian pulpit is a borrowed glow. As the God-imparted radiance that shown upon the face of Moses, when the ancient lawgiver came out from the divine presence, was a reflection of God's glory (Ex. 34:29), so the glory of the Christian pulpit is a reflection of the glory of the Word of God, which is the source of its message and the inspiration of its ministry. The exposition and authoritative declaration of the Word and will of God as revealed in the Holy Scriptures must ever remain the splendor of the Christian pulpit. Where such exposition and authoritative declaration are abandoned, "Ichabod, the glory is departed" (I Sam. 4:21) must be written over the preacher and over the pulpit from which he preaches.

To an alarming extent the glory *is* departing from the pulpit of the twentieth century. The basic reason for this ominous condition is obvious. That which imparts the glory has been taken away from the center of so much of our modern preaching and placed on the periphery. The Word of God has been denied the throne and given a subordinate place. Human eloquence, men's philosophies, Christian ethics, social betterment, cultural progress and many other subjects good and proper in their place have captured the center of interest and have been enthroned in the average pulpit in the place of the Word of God.

1. THE PREVAILING LACK OF A BIBLE-CENTERED EMPHASIS IN THE PULPIT

No fact of current religious life indicates quite so force-fully the need for preaching the Bible in our day as this. The pivotal injunction to every Christian minister to "preach the word" (II Tim. 4:2), urged so solemnly by the great Apostle upon young Timothy, has been ignored to a large extent by the ministry of our day. Instead of "preach the word" present-day pulpit practice would rather render the passage: "preach ethics, social betterment and cultural prog-ress, using the Word as a springboard."[1]

But there is a vast difference between preaching the Bible and using the Bible as a springboard from which to jump into a discussion of one's own thoughts. It is one thing to utilize the Bible as a sourcebook to furnish the content of the message. It is quite another thing to employ it as a mere "textual repository" to supply germinal ideas to develop hu-man impressions and opinions. There is a chasm, too, be-tween preaching the Bible and discoursing *about* the Bible. Strictly speaking, the contrast between the pulpit procedure is the difference between preaching and lecturing.

Moreover, there is a difference between preaching and teaching. Teaching may be about the Bible or may deal with the content of the Bible itself. But true preaching, al-though it involves teaching, goes beyond it, enforcing with unction and power the claims of the Word of God upon the needs of the hearers.

---

[1] Cf. Andrew W. Blackwood, "What Is Wrong With Preaching Today?" *The Asbury Seminarian* (Winter 1953), p. 12.

Much of current pulpit ministry consists in lecturing or discoursing about the Bible, rather than in preaching. But lecturing and pure teaching properly belong to the classroom, not the pulpit. Preaching is the glory of the pulpit and when men behind the sacred desk abandon preaching for lecturing or pure teaching the glory fades.

There can be no substitute for the authoritative declaration of the Word and will of God directed toward meeting human needs by the Spirit-chosen and Spirit-anointed man of God. This is true preaching.[2] This is the divine idea of the Christian pulpit, making it unique among the various religious platforms of our day. When ministers step down from this lofty eminence, they leave the divine idea of pulpit ministry, sacrifice the uniqueness that characterizes true Christian preaching, and become in greater or lesser degree on a par with those segments of Christendom which have largely replaced the simple teaching of the Scriptures with human ideas, traditions of men or the decisions of ecclesiastical councils. Those who carry such a tendency to its extreme become little different from protagonists and missionaries of the great non-Christian faiths.

2. THE CURRENT MOVEMENT TOWARD ECUMENICITY

This is, in fact, another salient indication of the pressing present-day need for preaching the Bible. A much publicized trend in contemporary church life, the modern Ecumenical Movement, "looks toward the visible unity of all Christendom,"[3] Catholic, Protestant and Greek Orthodox. Analyzed in the light of the Scriptures, it is found to be a radical departure from Biblical evangelicism and to be the direct result of the abandonment of preaching the Bible. Accordingly, the theology of the movement is unsound, the basis of the unity it advocates is faulty, and the very concept of the unity it advocates is confused and foreign to the New Testament.[4]

[2] For current definitions of preaching see Andrew W. Blackwood, *The Preparation of Sermons* (Nashville, Abingdon-Cokesbury Press, 1948), p. 13.

[3] René Pache, "Rome and The Ecumenical Movement," *Bibliotheca Sacra* (Jan., 1951), p. 53.

[4] René Pache (*The Ecumenical Movement;* Dallas, Texas, 1951) analyzes the movement in the light of Biblical evangelicism.

Leonard Hodgson, an ecumenist and a former secretary of the commission on Faith and Order of the World Council of Churches, like other leaders in the Ecumenical Movement, does not hesitate to advocate the necessity for a whole new vocabulary, set of values and theological concepts to insure the success of the movement in its aim to unite all Christendom in one undivided church, no matter how contrary such principles and procedures might be to plain Scriptural teaching.[5]

Whether through ignorance or unbelief and deliberate rejection of Scriptural truth, no tendency within the contemporary church illustrates more clearly the confusion into which men's thinking is thrown when the Word of God is set aside and no trend more definitely demonstrates the desperate need for strengthening the local pulpit by a return to preaching the Bible than the modern Ecumenical Movement. Unless there is such a return, an emasculated Christianity based on compromise such as modern ecumenicity fosters, will be powerless to stand before the lively and virile foes who threaten to stamp out its very existence.

3. THE WORLDLINESS AND POWERLESSNESS OF THE CHURCH

The far-reaching need for a return to preaching the Bible is also demonstrated by this obvious fact. In many churches where ritualism and formalism hold sway and the Bible is given no adequate place, there is little or no spiritual life. People who are not regenerated are admitted in wholesale fashion into church membership through routine ceremonies and ordinances, which are, however, powerless to regenerate apart from the Holy Spirit operating through the Word of God.

In many other churches people are saved, and the program may even be aggressively evangelistic. But the Word of God is not expounded from the pulpit. The bread and water of life are presented to the unsaved, and the sincere milk of the Word administered to the Christians, but believers are never fed the meat of the Word to bring them to full growth and maturity in Christ. Spiritually they remain babes.

[5] Leonard Hodgson, *The Ecumenical Movement* (Sewanee, Tenn., University Press, 1952).

As a result of failure to give the Word of God its full and rightful place in modern religious life, conditions are appalling. Lukewarmness and worldliness have swept into the Church, paralyzing its spiritual life and robbing it of its dynamic to challenge and appeal to the unsaved. Crime and immorality have increased by leaps and bounds. The divorce rate has skyrocketted, threatening to destroy the family and the foundations of our national life. The astronomical growth of the liquor traffic, flagrant desecration of the Lord's Day, and other national sins cry out for judgment. Only a return to the preaching of the Word of God is sufficient to meet the situation.

4. THE GROWTH OF SECULARISM AND THE THREAT OF COMMUNISM

The critical need for a revival of preaching the Bible at the present time is further evidenced by these ominous perils threatening our civilization. Nothing will avail to check the rapid secularization of our society except the ministry of the Word of God. A secularized society is soil prepared for the seeds of godless Communism. The ultimate weapon against this demon-impelled foreign ideology and the false-hood and slavery upon which it is built and by which it is propagated is the truth and freedom the Word of God brings. Rejection or neglect of God's Word is the best ally Communism ever had. The reason is simple. The Holy Spirit, the manifest power of God, operates through the Word of God, and in the final analysis truth energized by God's Spirit alone can overcome the lies of Communism energized by demon power.

The basic freedoms of the free world are the result of centuries of preaching the Bible. A church whose pulpit fails to "preach the word" becomes an easy prey to Communistic propaganda parading under the banner of truth. Church leaders who fail to give the Word of God its rightful place of centrality in the pulpit expose themselves to every type of deception and the subtle danger of unwittingly playing into the hands of the Communists.

Preachers who handle the Scriptures as a springboard to preach human morality and socialistic theories instead of a source-book for spiritual truth, who handle it as a repository of texts to be used in the discussion of human theories and opinions, rather than as *the Word itself*, to be studied verse by verse and chapter by chapter *to see what it has to say* — such preachers are frequently led to propagate doctrines that are contrary to the plan and purpose of God and which border perilously on the tenets of Communism.

Little wonder in our day Christian clergymen have frequently heaped upon themselves suspicion of actually espousing Communism and being Red agents. The fact that they perhaps are innocent of such intent and sincerely propagate their doctrines as truly Christian, does not minimize the danger of the situation. However, their conduct illustrates the tremendous need for preaching the Bible in our day and the evils and dangers to which both the pulpit and the pew are exposed when the Word of God is not enthroned behind the sacred desk.

Literature on the Need of Expository Preaching

Alexander, James W., *Thoughts on Preaching* (New York, Chas. Scribner, 1860), pp. 272-313.

Vance, James I., *Being a Preacher* (New York, Fleming Revell, 1923), Chap. II.

Dana, H. E., *Searching the Scriptures* (New Orleans, Bible Institute Memorial Press, 1936), Chaps. VI - IX.

Lowe, John, "The Recovery of the Theological Interpretation of the Bible" in *The Interpretation of the Bible*, ed. by C. W. Dugmore (London, Society for Promotion of Christian Knowledge, 1944), Chap. VII.

Wright, G. Ernest, "The Christian Interpreter as a Biblical Critic" in *Interpretation* (April, 1947), 1:131-152.

Rowley, H. H., "The Relevance of Biblical Interpretation" in *Interpretation* (Jan., 1947), 1:3-20.

Fritz, John H. C., *The Essentials of Preaching* (St. Louis, Concordia Publishing House, 1948).

Whitesell, Faris D., *The Art of Biblical Preaching* (Grand Rapids, Zondervan Publishing House, 1950), Chap. I.

Blackwood, Andrew W., "What Is Wrong With Preaching Today?" *The Asbury Seminarian* (Winter 1953).

CHAPTER II

THE CAUSES OF THE DEARTH OF EXPOSITORY PREACHING

The present condition in the pulpits of the land is to a degree reminiscent of the days of the boy-priest Samuel when he ministered unto the Lord before Eli at Shiloh. "And the word of Jehovah was precious (rare) in those days; there was no frequent (widely spread) vision" (I Sam. 3:1, ARV). As in Samuel's boyhood, so today such a scarcity of the Word of God is never a sudden development or a situation behind which there are not definite causes operating over an extended period. In those days contributory factors were the apostasy and anarchic confusion of the long period of the Judges and more immediately the shameful profligacy of the priests and the indulgent weakness of the high priest Eli. Today there are causes just as definite for the dearth of Biblical preaching.

1. THE REJECTION OF THE WORD OF GOD BY MODERN LIBERALISM

As the result of two centuries of radical destructive Biblical criticism, especially that of the Graf-Wellhausen School of Germany, the modernistic or so-called liberal segment of professing Christianity has experienced great growth and increased influence in the contemporary religious scene. This has eventuated in the rejection of the authenticity of many of the books of the Bible, the ruling out of the supernatural and the denial of the Word of God.

The remarkable discoveries of archeology, however, in the last century and a half, elucidating, illustrating and often

17

authenticating the Holy Scriptures, have compelled abandonment or drastic revision of many of the older theories of radical higher criticism that issued in complete spiritual bankruptcy, and have initiated a new, more constructive, tendency in Biblical studies. This newer trend, while substantially accepting the results of modern criticism, has attempted to harmonize the alleged discoveries of modern critical scholarship with a constructive approach to the Bible as a spiritual book demanding a "spiritual" as well as an "intellectual understanding" to its "full comprehension."[1] This movement, represented in criticism by H. H. Rowley and in theology by Barthianism and neo-orthodoxy,[2] rejects the older orthodox view of plenary-verbal inspiration of the Bible, and "reconciles" the alleged "assured findings" of modern criticism on the basis of the errancy of the Scriptures.[3]

Wholesale rejection of the doctrine of verbal plenary inspiration of the Scriptures in critical circles, with insistence that the Bible is subject to errancy and human limitation, has resulted in an inevitable reduction of its authority and a sharp decline in preaching it. If the Bible is considered merely to contain the Word of God, rather than actually to be *in toto* the Word of God, there is naturally a decreased sense of responsibility to study its text minutely, or to systematize its theology, or authoritatively to declare its message.

As a consequence liberally inclined seminaries are more and more abandoning the actual study of the Bible for studies *about* the Bible. Synthetic and analytical study of the Scriptures is, tacitly at least, considered to be unworthy of the academic level of the seminary and the graduate theological level, and it is relegated to the Bible institute. Requirements in the original languages of Holy Writ are aimed mainly to meet the needs of the critical scholar rather than to supply indispensable tools for the Biblical expositor. Training in principles of exegesis is neglected or frequently ignored altogether.

---

[1] H. H. Rowley, *The Relevance of the Bible* (New York, 1944), p. 19.

[2] For an exposé of the unsoundness of neo-orthodoxy see Chester E. Tulga, *The Case Against Neo-Orthodoxy* (Chicago, Conservative Baptist Fellowship, 1953), pp. 1-64.

[3] Rowley, *op. cit.*, p. 28.

Under such modern views of the Bible it can easily be seen how the literary and critical approach to Scripture is rapidly superseding the theological and doctrinal. Young ministers are sent forth trained in literary criticism, human philosophy, educational psychology, modern sociology and kindred disciplines, but too frequently are utterly unequipped for the supreme task of the Christian minister, that of declaring the Word of God with conviction and authority and expounding the Scriptures with understanding and spiritual insight as a coordinated body of revealed truth.

The outcome of this distressing condition is inevitable. The liberalistically trained minister is forced because of his ignorance of the scope and meaning of the Bible to use a Biblical text or passage as a mere springboard from which to discuss morality, sociology, current events or politics or to review the latest novel or current motion picture. The Christian pulpit is thus of necessity prostituted as a lecture platform instead of remaining a place where the Word of God is powerfully proclaimed and intelligently expounded.

2. THE LACK OF BIBLE-CENTERED EMPHASIS IN ORTHODOX CONSERVATISM

But the sad decline in Biblical preaching is not only evidenced in modern liberalism. There are ominous trends in the same direction in the professedly conservative wing of Christianity. Although the orthodox pulpit perhaps never becomes so spiritually bankrupt as to be converted into a lecture platform, yet there are a multitude of churches which are evangelistic and sound, growing and organizationally progressive, but which are, nevertheless, weak in preaching and teaching the Bible. While it is true souls are soundly converted by plain and effective gospel preaching, nevertheless the converts remain to a great extent babes in knowledge and experience.

This prevalent condition is largely due to the inability or failure of the pulpit to "preach the word" (II Tim. 4:2) in the sense of systematically expounding the Holy Scriptures and relating the believer to his position in Christ and to God's plan and purpose for the ages.

On the other hand, the failure of the orthodox pulpit to perform its complete task of not only discharging its ministry of evangelism but its important task of pastoral teaching as well is traceable to conservative seminaries, which train men for these orthodox pulpits. While the average conservative seminary includes some instruction in Bible, it is quite frequently incredibly meager, usually limited to a survey course in Old and New Testament. What is even more disappointing is that such a study embraces little more than the acquisition of scattered Biblical facts without connection with the over-all plan and purpose of God for the ages as revealed in the Bible as a whole. The result is that the student is unable to relate his knowledge of the factual content of Scripture to any systematic exposition of the sacred Book as a unified revelation.

Moreover, the curriculum of the average conservative seminary is geared to the apologetic rather than to the expositional approach. The student is taught to defend rather than declare the Word of God and to be able to answer the critical theories about the Bible rather than to know the Bible itself. In line with this procedure Systematic Theology, which is often extensively philosophical and psychological, finds a place on the curriculum rather than Biblical Theology, based strictly on the revealed Word of God. Courses in homiletics stress topical or textual sermons, with little attention to the vast importance of expository preaching. Work in Biblical Hebrew and Greek, if not seriously curtailed, is given little impetus for practical use in expounding the Word because of the lack of a Bible-centered emphasis in other courses.

3. THE WIDESPREAD ANTIPATHY TO THE PREMILLENNIAL-DISPENSATIONAL SYSTEM OF INTERPRETATION

The reason why many ministers do not attempt to preach the Bible verse by verse, chapter by chapter, book by book, systematically and comprehensively, with each part related to the whole, and the whole related to each part, is that they have never been taught that the Scriptures have a coherent plan and purpose and can be intelligently dealt with in a comprehensive way, both analytically and synthetically. Instead, seminary students are commonly given the impression that the Bible possesses no such coherency of structure and are actually warned against those who claim it does and who study it from this approach.

In line with this widespread agnostic attitude toward the Scriptures, often tacitly, at least, represented as the proper humble and pious approach to Holy Writ, many ministers and ministerial students are bereft of any true dynamic for studying the Bible as a coordinated whole and connected revelation of God's plan and purpose for the past, present and future. Texts and passages, it is true, are used to meet present needs of hearers, but the treatment is often pathetically superficial, with no attempt whatever made to relate the text or passage to the larger context of Scripture or to the over-all divine plan and purpose for the ages, or to solve difficulties or reconcile apparent discrepancies.

Such preaching of necessity fails to exalt the Word of God. The marvelous coherence of its subject matter, the wonders of its fulfilled prophecies, the splendor of its yet-to-be-fulfilled predictions, the consistency of its plan, the omnitemporality of its message and the sublimity of its purpose, are ignored or very inadequately held up to view.

But *an adequate system of interpretation is indispensable* if one is going to be an expositor of the Bible. Without such a system the Bible to a large extent is closed to orderly handling and intelligent understanding. Numbers of systems of interpretation exist. The most common are the premillennial, postmillennial or amillennial views based on whether the second advent of Christ will occur before or after a future literal millennium or whether the spiritual millennium is already here and Christ's advent will usher in the eternal state.

The question of which system of interpretation is to be accepted must be determined by the ability of the particular system selected to open up the Scriptures, to solve difficulties, explain things that differ, show the symmetry and harmony of the Scriptures and expound the whole under a unified plan. While careful, systematic *study of the Scriptures themselves* under any system of interpretation will make a man a stronger preacher, there are strong reasons to support the claim that the premillennial plan is manifestly superior to non-premillennial plans because of its marvelous ability to open up the Word of God, especially the prophetic portions, which comprise certainly not less than one-fifth of the Sacred Volume and which have such vital bearing on the rest.

Premillennialists are noted for their ability to expound prophecy, as well as the entire range of revealed Scripture. Most striking, perhaps, is their capacity to distinguish between things that obviously differ, such as the kingdom promised to Israel and the Church founded by Christ, and to avoid applying the great kingdom prophecies of the Old Testament to the Church of the New Testament, necessitating the most violent spiritualizing process to explain away the obvious resulting confusion of such a procedure.

But premillennialists are of necessity dispensationalists, at least to some extent. Indeed, a non-dispensational premillennialist is an anomaly. Because some have gone to extremes in this matter and have caused great harm and confusion to the Church, others have shied away altogether from sound dispensational distinctions, which are so obviously to be found in the Word. The result again is to incur serious disability in the matter of intelligently expounding the Sacred Oracles.

The growing hostility of some sections of the Church to premillennialism of the sound and thoroughly Scriptural variety based of necessity upon certain indispensable time distinctions is a sign of the times pointing to the widespread need for a return to Bible preaching. When men are grounded in any system of theology based squarely upon the Bible, they will have gone a long way toward becoming able expositors, whether they call themselves postmillennialists, amillennialists or premillennialists. It is our conviction, however, that the student trained in premillennial truth will have far greater advantage in expounding the Word in its fulness than men trained in non-premillennial systems. The rich prophetic and eschatological portions of the Bible (about twenty-five per cent of its actual content) will glow with light and challenge to the soundly instructed premillennialist. The remaining portions, too, will be suffused with new symmetry and meaning. Premillennial truth verily produces able expositors.

LITERATURE ON THE DEARTH OF EXPOSITORY PREACHING

Stevens, Abel, *Essays on the Preaching Required by the Times* (New York, Carlton and Phillips, 1856).

Blackwood, Andrew W., *Preaching From the Bible* (Nashville, Abingdon-Cokesbury Press, 1941).

————, "What Is Wrong With Preaching Today?" *The Asbury Seminarian* (Winter 1953).

Noyes, Morgan P., *Preaching the Word of God* (New York, Charles Scribner's Sons, 1943).

Ramm, Bernard, *Protestant Biblical Interpretation* (Boston, W. A. Wilde Co., 1950), pp. 36-47.

CHAPTER III

THE BENEFITS OF EXPOSITORY PREACHING

The greatest single need of the contemporary church is undoubtedly the strengthening of the local pulpit. This fact is not difficult to realize in the light of distressing present-day conditions in this phase of the Christian ministry and in view of the key place pastoral preaching holds in the carrying out of the divine program. The progress of God's work depends primarily on the local church, and the local pastor has the most strategic position for weal or woe in this important activity. In no way can the individual pulpit be strengthened for its momentous task than by a diligent return to the Biblical injunction: "Preach the Word." The benefits of such a ministry are incalculable.

1. EXPOSITORY PREACHING GIVES THE PREACHER AUTHORITY AND POWER

Holy Scripture as inspired of God, literally "God-breathed" (II Tim. 3:16), possesses a potent quality when preached by one who believes what he preaches is in truth the "Word of God." The authority and power, which the inspired oracles possess, become manifest in the pulpit ministry of the faithful expositor of the Bible. He speaks, yet the thrilling fact is true, God at the same time speaks through him. He is conscious of inadequacy, yet finds his task attended by divine authority. He is aware of weakness, but discovers the power of God operating in the Word he preaches, which is "living and active, and sharper than any two-edged sword . . . piercing even to the dividing of soul and spirit, of both joints and marrow, and quick to discern the thoughts and intents of the heart" (Heb. 4:12, ARV).

The Apostle Paul's experiences at Thessalonica furnish an inspiring example to every preacher how wonderfully effective a Bible-centered ministry can be. As a result of the faithful proclamation of God's truth, the Apostle could say "our gospel came not unto you in word only, but also in power, and in the Holy Spirit, and in much assurance. . . . And ye became imitators of us, and of the Lord, having received the word in much affliction, with joy of the Holy Spirit" (I Thess. 1:5, 6, ARV).

More than this the Apostle could say that as a result of the ministry of the Word the Thessalonian converts became exemplary believers, not only famous for their own consistency of life and testimony, but also for their missionary zeal in sending forth the word, which had wrought so blessedly in their own lives, to others. "Ye became an ensample to all that believe in Macedonia and Achaia. For from you hath sounded forth the word of the Lord, not only in Macedonia and in Achaia, but in every place your faith to God-ward is gone forth . . ." (I Thess. 1:7, 8, ARV).

This note of divine authority and accompanying power attending the preaching of the Word of God is not a benefit lightly to be esteemed by any minister. The blessings to himself and to the people to whom he ministers are so great that no preacher, if not out of consideration for himself, then in view of others, can afford to miss them. This is the glory and the excellency of the ministerial vocation. Losing this, the minister loses the "pearl of great price." Forfeiting this blessing both for himself and his hearers, like the Ephesian church, which had left its first love to Christ, the minister must remember whence he has fallen and "repent and do the first works" (Rev. 2:5).

But there is always a subtle temptation for the preacher to substitute human opinions and ideas for divine authority. Adhering closely to the Scripture will guard the preacher from the snare of the "springboard sermon," one that takes a text merely as a starting point to discuss something other than the Word of God and buttresses its arguments and reinforces its appeal with numerous citations of competent human authorities but with scarcely a quotation of corroborating Scripture.

There is also the perpetual peril of substituting human interest and human problems for divine power. While human interest is vital to good preaching and good preaching always addresses itself to the human problem, yet both become a liability instead of an asset when preachers depart from the Scriptural order and give secondary place or little place at all to divine power. Preachers who do not expound the Scriptures are exposed to this danger, while even preachers of the Bible who are not constantly alert in *stressing what the Word of God* stresses find themselves lopsided in their presentation of these matters.

For example, in the story of the paralytic let down through the roof and healed by Jesus (Mark 2:1-12) one might be sidetracked by the human interest of the account to dwell on Oriental architecture, paralysis as a type of sin, or the relationship between sin and suffering, and quite neglect the main point of the passage "that ye may know that the Son of man hath authority on earth to forgive sins" (ARV).

Again, in the account of Paul's "thorn in the flesh" (II Cor. 12:1-10), the human need might easily be dealt with in such a way, with profitless discussion about what the "thorn" was, that the truth emphasizing the divine power might be completely neglected. The important note to be sounded is that which rings the changes on the power of God. "My grace is sufficient for thee, for my strength is made perfect in weakness."

The divine authority and power which rest upon the true herald of the Word of God must be continually guarded against loss or diminution. The preacher of the Bible must ever be on watch against departing from the vantage point where what he says bears the authority of "Thus said the Lord." In the proportion that his sermons depart from this position and are watered down by men's thoughts and opinions, or featured by human interest and human problems to the point of relegating the power of God to a secondary place, in that proportion do they lose the note of divine authority and forfeit the manifestation of the divine power.

2. EXPOSITORY PREACHING PROVIDES AN INEXHAUSTIBLE STORE OF SERMONIC MATERIAL

Ministers who do not systematically "preach the Word," who have never been taught to "rightly divide its truth" and to set forth the wonders of its plan and purpose, are continually at wit's end how to get suitable homiletical material. Many a sincere pastor desperately scours the latest book of sermons by some successful pulpiteer, or depends upon Spurgeon or Jowett for any expository efforts with which he may occasionally regale his congregation. One does not have to go far to detect Truett or Talmadge being preached from the pulpit instead of the Word.

It must be confessed that Spurgeon or Jowett, Truett or Talmadge make good pulpit fare even when warmed over and served secondhand. But it is tragic that many ministers have not been trained or encouraged to come themselves to the same exhaustless fountain of truth and inspiration that these great preachers came to and to get their sermon material firsthand and fresh from God as they did.

The preacher who will honor the Word of God by believing that it has unity and coherence, that it actually unfolds the divine plan and purpose from eternity past to eternity future, and who will diligently study it in this attitude of reverent faith, will be more and more amazed at its wonders and find himself possessed of an ever-increasing store of thrilling and heart-warming truth which will furnish the basis of more sermons than he could preach in a lifetime.

There truly is no dearth of preaching material for the man who cultivates the study of the Word of God itself. The well is deep and the supply of refreshment unfailing. As the man of God ponders prayerfully over the sacred page, he will find himself less and less dependent upon human aids and more completely cast upon the tuition of the Spirit of God. It is as the man of God becomes more completely Spirit-taught in the things of God that his preaching rises to its greatest excellency.

The deeply spiritual student of the sacred page will find a freshness and a vigor in his message which will not require ceaseless searching for novel illustrations from men's pen. The Word will begin to suggest illustrations from its own pages, illustrations which will frequently be found to be more forceful than those gleaned from life and secular literature, although the latter, of course, will always have a legitimate place in sermonizing. True preaching of the Bible, however, will keep such illustrative material, often so excessive in some men's sermons, strictly in the proper place.

As the preacher strives to know and preach the Word, he will find such a wealth of inspiring Scriptural themes crowding in upon him for attention and treatment that he will covet his sermon time, whatever length it is, whether twenty or thirty minutes or more, to an ever-increasing degree for the presentation of Biblical truth illuminated by illustrations taken from the Bible itself. Non-scriptural material will be subject to more keen discrimination before it is admitted to the sacred domain of the pulpit.

Nothing like Bible study and Bible preaching can condition a true expositor to be discriminating in the choice of the type and quality of the illustrations he permits himself to use in his messages. The preacher of the Bible will find himself no longer taken up, as once he may have been, with the superficial ultra-emotional variety of story that is often of extremely dubious factual content. He will demand that illustrative material be on the same high level of spirituality and solidness that characterizes the holy truth he expounds.

3. EXPOSITORY PREACHING MEETS HUMAN NEEDS

The fact that the Christian pulpit in proclaiming the Word of God faces the realities of life and provides for the deepest needs of the human heart makes it a vitally necessary institution in a free world. As preaching the Bible declines, men degenerate morally and spiritually and become slaves to sin and self. When this happens, there is only an additional step to becoming slaves politically with the loss of free government to Communism, Fascism or some other foreign ideology.

One of the most fundamental needs of the human race is deliverance from the penalty and power of sin. The Bible sets forth in unmistakable terms both the reality of sin and the absolute need of deliverance from it. Biblical preaching, therefore, does not dodge this vital point, but meets it fully. Non-Biblical preaching, however, frequently denies or ignores the reality of human depravity and hence offers no adequate way of salvation. The result is that it fails the human soul.

Failing the human soul in its most crucial need of salvation from sin, humanistic preaching, the heralding of the "social gospel," or the proclamation of salvation by character or good works, or any other non-Biblical message, fails to meet the human need in all other important spiritual requirements. These messages give no assurance of salvation, guarantee no peace or joy for this life, nor offer any solid hope for eternity.

However, as the Christian preacher faithfully expounds the Word, all these and other important questions will be answered and a faith imparted which assures joy and satisfaction in this life and radiant expectancy for the life to come.

But the faithful preaching of the Word of God will not only meet the individual hearer's need. It will meet the need of the group, or the nation or the nations of the earth in their dealings with one another as well. The desperate confusion rampant in a distraught world today is due to the rejection of the Word of God by great segments of the world's population. A simple return to faith and obedience in the Word of God and its faithful proclamation from every Christian pulpit would do more to bring about rest and stability to a bewildered and war-torn world than all our panicky plans, the frantic deliberations of men, and the feverish build-up of armaments. The Word of God is the sure panacea for our national and international sickness.

4. EXPOSITORY PREACHING PRODUCES MATURE WELL-TAUGHT CHRISTIANS

It fills our churches with truly regenerated and Spirit-filled men and women, aggressive in the work of God, and joyous in Christian fellowship. In contrast, non-Biblical preaching results in the wholesale admission of unregenerate men and women into church membership. This sad condition is inevitable where the Biblical plan of salvation is not clearly set forth nor clear Scriptural truth presented on what the Christian life is and how it is to be lived.

Such a condition can mean only one thing. The church becomes largely a lecture hall for discourses on morality and character building, instead of a meeting place for the public declaration of the divine way of salvation and deliverance from sin. It partakes more of the character of a social club than an assembly of saints for fellowship in the Spirit. It assumes the character of an agency for promoting the selfish interests of its members rather than a missionary vehicle for carrying the Gospel to the uttermost part of the earth.

Having no clear understanding or experience of God's redemptive grace, the church which does not preach the Bible cannot be expected to carry the Gospel to the heathen. People must first experience the benefits of the Gospel themselves before they are willing to carry it to others.

However, there are numerous churches today that preach a clear message of personal salvation from the penalty of sin through faith in the atoning work of Christ and consist of truly regenerated members, but suffer great weakness because of lack of instruction in the Word. The result is that the believers are stunted in growth and experience. They have experienced the power of deliverance from the *penalty* of sin, but know practically nothing of deliverance from the *power* of sin and the Spirit-filled life of victory.

Over against this condition of weakness, Biblical preaching creates stalwart Christian character and produces strong spiritual churches aggressively evangelistic and world-wide in missionary outlook and outreach. It fortifies people with the truth of God and the power of God to withstand temptation and the strain of modern life. It sets men's affections on things above and not on things of the world (Col. 3:1-3), generates a love for God and man, and inspires a spirit of service and consecration.

In the light of the tremendous present-day need for preaching the Bible and in consideration of the widespread evils which prevail because of a lack of such preaching, together with the vast benefits which accrue both to preacher and hearers alike from a Bible-centered ministry, it is the purpose of this treatise to encourage every preacher to give himself more completely to this glorious work.

Every minister can be a preacher of the Bible if he will study to show himself approved unto God "a workman that needeth not to be ashamed, rightly dividing the word of truth" (II Tim. 2:15). Why should he not be such a preacher? "It is the preaching that God has bidden him preach. It is the preaching which draws down heaven's approval and counts for the most in time and eternity. Preaching the Bible brings the highest joy to the preacher, and does the most good for the hearers."[1] Brethren, let us preach the Word!

LITERATURE ON THE BENEFITS OF EXPOSITORY PREACHING

Alexander, James W., *Thoughts on Preaching* (New York, Chas. Scribner, 1860).

Dabney, R. L., *Sacred Rhetoric* (1870).

The Expository Times (Edinburgh, T. & T. Clark, monthly since 1889).

Jeffs, H., *The Art of Exposition* (Boston, The Pilgrim Press, 1910).

Patton, Carl S., *The Use of the Bible in Preaching* (Chicago, Willett, Clark and Co., 1936). Modern view.

Blackwood, Andrew W., *Preaching From the Bible* (Nashville, Abingdon-Cokesbury Press, 1941).

————, *The Preparation of Sermons* (Nashville, Abingdon-Cokesbury Press, 1948), Chap. VI.

————, *Expository Preaching For Today* (Nashville, Abingdon-Cokesbury Press, 1953), Chap. II.

Roach, Corwin C., *Preaching Values in the Bible* (Louisville, The Cloister Press, 1946).

Reu, M., *Homiletics* (Minneapolis, Augsburg Publishing House, 1950), pp. 319-324.

Whitesell, Faris D., *The Art of Biblical Preaching* (Grand Rapids, Zondervan Publishing House, 1950).

Stevenson, D. E., *A Guide to Expository Preaching* (Lexington, Ky., College of the Bible, 1952, booklet 10 pp.).

[1] Faris D. Whitesell, *The Art of Biblical Preaching* (Grand Rapids, Zondervan Publishing House, 1950), p. 160.

CHAPTER IV

DEFINITION OF THE EXPOSITORY METHOD

If one accepts the plain injunctions of the Bible in general and the exhortation of the Apostle Paul to Timothy to "preach the word" (II Tim. 4:2) in particular, it is quite obvious that *the principal task of the preacher is to proclaim the truth set forth in the Scriptures of the Old and New Testament.* To define "the main business" of the minister in these terms, as R. Ames Montgomery correctly does, however, is scarcely an "assumption," as he maintains,[1] but in the light of Scriptural testimony, a fact. Moreover, the fact suggests the basic reason of the importance of expository preaching.

But the importance of the expository method is not only suggested by the fact that it fits into the main business of the preacher. It also meets the supreme need of the hearer. No matter how scientifically enlightened or culturally progressive men may become, there will never be a diminution of their need for the Word of God. Especially this will not be the case in a time such as ours when the Bible is becoming increasingly unknown and misunderstood and the "day of Bible knowledge as our fathers understood it is quite gone, a loss that may entail deeper consequences in national life and outlook than any of us yet comprehend."[2]

Great contrariety of opinion and considerable confusion exist concerning the question precisely what expository preaching is. Many homileticians define it principally on the basis of the length of the passage or portion of Scripture expounded,

[1] *Expository Preaching* (New York, Fleming Revell, 1939), p. 36.
[2] James Black, *The Mystery of Preaching* (New York, Fleming Revell, 1924).

32

whether a verse or a number of verses, or a larger unit involving chapters or books. For example, Andrew W. Blackwood stipulates "a Bible passage longer than two or three consecutive verses."[3] F. B. Meyer specifies "the consecutive treatment of some book or extended portion of Scripture."[4]
However if a clear and unconfused definition is to be arrived at, the valid criterion, it would seem, is not the length of the portion treated, whether a single verse or a larger unit, but the *manner of treatment*. No matter what the length of the portion explained may be, if it is handled in such a way that its real and essential meaning as it existed in the mind of the particular Biblical writer and as it exists in the light of the over-all context of Scripture is made plain and applied to the present-day needs of the hearers, it may properly be said to be expository preaching.

1. Expository Preaching Is First and Foremost Biblical Preaching

It is emphatically not preaching *about* the Bible, but preaching the Bible. "What saith the Lord" is the alpha and the omega of expository preaching. It begins in the Bible and ends in the Bible and all that intervenes springs from the Bible. In other words, expository preaching is Bible-centered preaching. Whatever extra-Biblical material is employed — illustrations from human experience, history, archeology, philosophy, art or science — must be purely subsidiary and strictly fitted into one single aim: to elucidate the portion of Scripture chosen, whatever its length, and enforce its claims upon the hearers.
It is quite obvious that the popular "springboard sermon" which employs a passage from the Bible as a starting point for a discourse on morality or sociology, or some other worthy but not strictly Biblical subject, is not expository. The exceedingly common homiletical practice of our day of using the Bible as a mere textual anthology from which to choose seedling thoughts for sermons on current events or social

---

[3] *Expository Preaching For Today* (New York, Abingdon-Cokesbury Press, 1953), p. 13.
[4] *Expository Preaching* (London, Hodder & Stoughton, 1912), p. 29.

betterment is a far cry from expository preaching and is an indication of the spiritual superficiality of our age.

It is a tragedy of unparalleled proportions that many present-day ministers preach as if the Bible were little more than a collection of isolated religious aphorisms or anecdotes, unconnected to one another and to the general context out of which they are taken, or to the Bible as a whole.

2. EXPOSITORY PREACHING IS BIBLICALLY INSTRUCTIVE PREACHING

As Montgomery says, "the expository preacher purposes above everything else to make clear the teaching and the content of the Bible."[5] The average church member today, even in many churches that are otherwise soundly evangelistic and missionary, is a Biblical illiterate because of a lack of stimulating Bible instruction from the pulpit. People in the pew will not study the Bible if preachers in the pulpit do not study it and preach it. A love for the Word in the pulpit is bound to produce a love for the Word in the pew.

The Bible expositor must not only be a student of the Word; he must be a teacher as well. He must feed Christ's sheep (John 21:17). He must be like "a man that is an householder, which bringeth forth out of his treasure things new and old" (Matt. 13:52). In a special sense the pastor, who is located indefinitely in one place, must be a teacher. "And he gave some to be apostles; and some, prophets; and some, evangelists; and some, pastors and teachers" (Eph. 4:11, ARV).

It is clear that the gift of pastoring and that of teaching are closely associated. The pastor must be a teacher. If he is to be a faithful shepherd he must be a Bible expositor because his business is to teach the Scriptures. Yet the Bible expositor must be more than a teacher. He must be a preacher as well, for true expository preaching, although it consists to a large extent of teaching, goes beyond mere impartation of an intellectual comprehension of truth. In addition it embraces appeal to the emotions and the will.

[5] *Op. cit.*, p. 42.

The portion of Scripture to be expounded must be that "on which the preacher has concentrated head and heart, brain and brawn, over which he has thought and wept and prayed, until it has yielded up its inner secret, and the spirit of it has passed into his spirit."[6] With this essential preparation real expository preaching takes place, when the preacher with unction and power, clearly explains the meaning of the passage of Scripture dealt with and effectually presses its truths upon the needs of his audience. Then, and not till then, does teaching the Bible become expository preaching.

Expository preaching has been brought into disrepute in some quarters because it has occasionally been misrepresented. The teaching of the Bible in a purely analytical and abstract way, divorced from spiritual power and passion and unaddressed to human need, has paraded as preaching of the Bible. But teaching, no matter how Biblical in content, accurate in interpretation, or coordinated in its presentation is not expository preaching, if it does not bring the Word of God down to the plane where men live and with the unction and the power of the Holy Spirit challenge them with its claims.

Strictly intellectual teaching of the Bible may possibly have a place on the lecture platform, in the seminary classroom or in the Bible conference or where the need exists mainly for instruction in the letter, but even under these circumstances it is questionable whether spiritual fervor or concern for the needs of the hearers, which are vital elements of preaching, may be neglected. The very nature of Biblical truth and the constant necessity for its cleansing ministry in the human soul make the purely intellectual approach to it extremely hazardous.

The difference, therefore, between teaching of the Bible and expository preaching is one of degree, rather than of kind. In teaching there is a more pronounced appeal to the intellect with a larger degree of the didactic or instructional element and less appeal to the emotional and volitional faculties. In preaching, however, there is a greater appeal to

[6] F. B. Meyer, op. cit., p. 29.

the emotions and the will than is proper in pure instruction. But both *impart a knowledge of the Bible itself,* the former only more so than the latter. Moreover, both are inspirational and challenging to human conduct and action, the latter only more so than the former.

Proper understanding of what true expository preaching is would save many a church from a ministry that is ostensibly Biblical and expositional, but spiritually barren, and spare many a Bible conference from what might be called "intellectual curiosity" in the letter of Scripture without vital concern for the spirit. A correct conception of what Biblical teaching is, moreover, would keep many a seminary from becoming a spiritual "cemetery," where zeal and power are buried in the grave of theory and higher criticism, or even spiritless orthodoxy.

3. EXPOSITORY PREACHING IS PREACHING THAT EXPOUNDS THE SCRIPTURES AS A COHERENT AND COORDINATED BODY OF REVEALED TRUTH

The true expositor not only believes that the Bible is a unified whole with definite plan and purpose, but bends every effort to understand that over-all plan and purpose and to relate whatever portion of the Scripture he may be expounding, whether a single verse or large unit, to the whole.

While the expository method is not dependent upon the length of the passage expounded, as has been noted, the best work in this sphere is ordinarily done in systematic verse by verse, paragraph by paragraph, book by book exposition. "When you preach from the Bible," as Andrew W. Blackwood says, "deal with it as it was written, book by book, and as a rule paragraph by paragraph."[7] This wise counsel avoids conducting "a sort of Cook's tour through the Holy Scriptures."[8]

But even a "Cook's tour" becomes marvelously illuminating and spiritually edifying when it is conducted by a competent guide who not only has a close-up and detailed knowledge of Scriptural truths but who is also acquainted with a bird's

---

[7] "What Is Wrong With Preaching Today?" *The Asbury Seminarian* (Winter 1953), p. 18.
[8] *Ibid.*

eye view of God's revealed ways with man and is able to fit the more or less isolated truths of Scripture into the larger context of a coherent system of interpretation.

It is the necessity of an adequate system of interpretation, which will open up the Old and New Testament as a co-ordinated whole, that undoubtedly constitutes the chief barrier against expository preaching in the case of many ministers. Unless a pastor is taught such a system in seminary, which is extremely unlikely in the average theological institution today, he either remains unequipped for expository work as a result of this deficiency, or by sheer labor and searching of his own, fits himself for this important pastoral task.

While there have been great expositors of Holy Writ who have not been premillennialists, the premillennial system of interpretation, in the writer's opinion, gives impetus to exposition and offers the key that unlocks the meaning of the Bible, especially the extensive and important prophetic portions. This system solves the most difficulties, sets in bolder relief the marvelous coherency of plan and purpose of the Sacred Oracles, most glorifies the Word of God, and acts as the greatest incentive for systematic expository work.

Moreover, it is the writer's firm conviction that a thoroughly open-minded and unbiased study of the premillennial plan of interpretation by ministers at large, with the observance of sound Biblical dispensational distinctions, would do more than anything else to bring about a revival of expository preaching in the churches.

Wholesale spiritualizing of Old Testament prophecies to Israel by their application to the New Testament Church and vain attempts under non-premillennial interpretations to identify things that obviously differ, have involved so many difficulties and seeming discrepancies that many honest minds have given up any systematic exposition of the Bible altogether. A workable system of interpretation would effect wonders in stimulating interest and genuine effort in expository preaching.

LITERATURE ON THE EXPOSITORY METHOD

Porter, Ebenezer, *Lectures on Homiletics and Preaching* (New York, J. Leavitt, 1834), Lectures XVII-XX.

Pierson, A. T., *The Divine Art of Preaching* (New York, Baker & Taylor, 1892).

————, *The Making of a Sermon* (Gospel Publishing House, 1907).

Fiske, F. W., *Manual of Preaching* (New York, A. C. Armstrong, 1893), pp. 201-212.

Jeffs, H., *The Art of Exposition* (Boston, The Pilgrim Press, 1910), Chap. VII.

Breed, David R., *Preparing to Preach* (Chicago, W. P. Blessing Co., 1911), pp. 385-398.

Meyer, F. B., *Expository Preaching* (London, Hodder & Stoughton, 1912).

Evans, William, *How to Prepare Sermons and Gospel Addresses* (Chicago, Bible Institute Colportage Assoc., 1913), pp. 111-116.

Fosdick, Harry E., *The Modern Use of the Bible* (New York, Macmillan & Co., 1924). Modern view.

Haldeman, I. M., *A Review of Harry Emerson Fosdick's The Modern Use of the Bible* (Philadelphia, Sunday School Times Co., 1924).

Knott, H. E., *How to Prepare an Expository Sermon* (Cincinnati, Standard Publishing Company, 1930).

Maclaren, Alexander, *Expositions of Holy Scripture* (Grand Rapids, Wm. B. Eerdmans Publishing Co., 1937).

Morgan, G. Campbell, *Preaching* (New York, Fleming Revell, 1937).

Montgomery, R. Ames, *Expository Preaching* (New York, Fleming Revell, 1939).

Baughman, Harry F., "Books on Biblical Preaching," in *Interpretation* (October, 1950).

Coggan, F. D., *The Man of the Word* (London, Canterbury Press, 1950).

Traina, Robert A., *Methodical Bible Study* (New York, Ganis and Harris, 1952).

Blackwood, Andrew W., *Expository Preaching For Today* (Nashville, Abingdon-Cokesbury Press, 1953), Chap. VI.

CHAPTER V

ILLUSTRATIONS OF THE EXPOSITORY METHOD

Although expository preaching is always Biblical, as well as Biblically instructive, and expounds the Scriptures as a coherent and coordinated body of revealed truth, this type of discourse may assume a number of different forms of treatment.

1. THE RUNNING-COMMENTARY METHOD OF EXPOSITORY PREACHING

If one insists that a message must possess homiletical structure to classify as a sermon, this type of expository discourse would be excluded from the sermonic category as it reduces sermonic structure to a minimum or ignores it altogether. It focuses attention upon the Biblical text itself rather than upon outlines or upon logical development of the passage.

Although this is not the highest type of expository treatment, at least from a homiletical point of view, it may, however, validly be included as a method of expository preaching. It may possess all the requisite elements of a sermon except strict sermonic structure. The speaker makes explanations, uses illustrations and appeals to the intellect, emotions and will.

In the hands of a gifted expositor and thorough student of the Word, like the late Harry A. Ironside, whose world-wide preaching and writing ministry was based largely upon this type of expository approach, this method has great advantage and appeal. Skillfully cultivated, it lends itself admirably to freshness and spontaneity of treatment and freedom and versatility of presentation. The preacher is not held in constraint by the limitations of a rigid outline and can more easily adapt his message to a particular audience or need and more readily follow the promptings of the Holy Spirit. He is also spared artificiality of treatment by striving after rhetorical devices such as alliteration, catchy words or phrases, etc., which often detract attention from the Scriptural truth which is being expounded.

However, in the hands of men who do not have exceptional gifts or a profound grasp of Biblical truth the running-commentary method of exposition can be extremely unfortunate. The preacher who is not a diligent Bible student will find in it an easy substitute for hard work and will be tempted to put too little preparation into the message. If ill prepared, he will certainly ramble, and his comments are bound to be trite and colorless.

If he is an industrious Bible student but lacks the gift of vivid illustration or the ability to discern what is relatively important and unimportant, he will deal largely in trivialities and neglect major issues. Moreover, he will be inclined to distribute his comments poorly over the entire passage and will clutter up his message with too many Biblical facts. In this case the message will suffer, strangely enough, from being too Biblical.

One does not have to go far to find would-be expository preaching that fails in this vital point of allocation of material. The content of it is so loosely thrown together and so inadequately explained, illustrated and applied, that the result is a welter of disconnected Biblical facts that confuse rather than enlighten and edify.

Such handling of the Scriptures is an abuse of the expository method. A message that contains so much Biblical content that there is neither space nor time to employ the normal rhetorical devices of explanation, illustration, argumentation, application and exhortation is not properly a sermon at all, and is as out of place in the pulpit as it is in the classroom.

H. A. Ironside excelled in the running-commentary type of sermonizing because of his diligence as a student of the Bible, his remarkable powers of vivid illustration, and his ability to put first things first — never permitting himself to bog down in trivialities. Adhering to the important points of a passage, he was not sidetracked by lesser issues. Always he applied the truth to his hearers in earnest exhortation and dynamic appeal to heart and will.[1]

2. THE BIBLE-READING METHOD OF EXPOSITORY PREACHING

Somewhat akin to the running-commentary type of exposition is the Bible-reading method. Both lack homiletical structure, normally require less preparation than formal sermons and tend to grant greater freedom of presentation and delivery to the speaker. The procedures, however, differ in approach. Whereas the running commentary fastens attention upon the text, and is topical only insofar as the paragraph, chapter or book dealt with is topical, the Bible-reading method rivets attention on the topic itself. Usually a subject such as faith, prayer, soul-winning or service is chosen. The main Scriptures on the topic are selected from a concordance or work like Nave's Topical Bible, and the message is developed loosely without any particular thought to logic or sequence.[2]

This method is simple and useful in expounding the Scriptures and appeals to the beginner who does not have a grasp of the Bible as a whole or of homiletical procedure. D. L. Moody employed it in the early period of his ministry before he became acquainted with regular sermonic patterns. However, it is not a finished form either of the spoken or the written message and will not satisfy the logical thinker or the minister who aims at attaining the utmost in clarity of utterance.

For the preacher who is not satisfied with anything less than his best, the Bible-reading method of exposition will sooner or later be abandoned for the topical expository sermon. The latter will be much more demanding in thought

[1] For an example see his treatment of I John 2:1, 2 under the title of "Christ Our Advocate," *Addresses on The Epistle of John* (New York, Loizeaux Brothers, 1931), pp. 35-47.

[2] For treatment and examples of the Bible-reading method, see Faris D. Whitesell, *The Art of Biblical Preaching* (Grand Rapids, Zondervan Publishing House, 1950), pp. 39-44. See also Andrew W. Blackwood, *Preaching from the Bible* (Nashville, Abingdon-Cokesbury Press, 1941), Chap. IX.

and preparation, but much more rewarding in illuminating the Word of God. However, Bible-reading exposition can be a vehicle of great blessing if it is not overpacked with Biblical facts, but makes room for the normal rhetorical processes of explanation, illustration, application and exhortation. Without these homiletical aids, though, it fails to qualify for inclusion in the category of preaching at all and has no rightful place in the Christian pulpit.

3. THE PURELY EXPOSITIONAL METHOD OF EXPOSITORY PREACHING

In this type of expository work the teaching element predominates, sometimes to such an extent that classification under the category of preaching is practically precluded. The necessary elements of effective proclamation of Biblical truth to a normal audience, such as formal sermonic structure, illustration, application, argumentation and exhortation, are absent or reduced to a minimum. Stress is laid on setting forth the quintessential meaning of a paragraph, chapter or book.

This method of pure exposition, however, is not only to be differentiated from expository preaching; it is to be distinguished from the running-commentary type of exposition and the Bible-reading type as well. Whereas the running commentary does not have an analytical outline, the purely expository method does. But it is not a finished sermonic structure, with introduction and conclusion, with main points and subpoints containing alliteration, key words, parallel structure or other homiletical devices. It is rather a strictly bony skeleton, suggested purely by the analysis of the Biblical passage as it is broken up into its natural thought divisions. No attempt is made to balance, omit or rearrange. The aim is to set forth the meaning of the Sacred Text in the order and symmetry it possesses, not in the order and symmetry created by the expositor and superimposed upon the passage.

Pure exposition is differentiated from the Bible-reading method in that it is a verse-by-verse, chapter-by-chapter approach and is not topical. It is at its best when soundly exegetical, although it is more than exegesis.

The writings of G. Campbell Morgan (1863-1942), one of

the foremost Bible expositors of modern times, are good examples of the use of the method of pure exposition. His books on Jeremiah, the Gospels, Acts, and I and II Corinthians are strictly expository and predominantly didactic rather than sermonic. Although they lack the finished form of a sermon, and contain very few illustrations and other homiletical devices, the expository genius of the author and his mastery of the Bible commanded the rapt attention of large audiences everywhere. As he expounded a passage, the central theme and outline stood out clearly.

G. Campbell Morgan's treatment of I and II Corinthians illustrates his thorough exposition according to a carefully worked out analytical outline followed religiously throughout the exposition. He divides I Corinthians under two heads:[3]

    Introduction (I:1-8)
    A. Corrective: The Carnalities (I:10-XI)
    B. Constructive: The Spiritualities (XII-XV:57)
    The Final Appeal (XV:58)
    Conclusion (XVI)

His second point is developed in detail according to the following analysis:[4]

    B. Constructive: The Spiritualities (XII-XV:57)
      I. The Unifying Spirit (XII:1-31)
        1. The Creation of Unity (1-3)
          a. The Contrast (2)
          b. The Principle Implied (3a)
          c. The Power (3b)
        2. The Administration of Unity (4-7)
        3. The Realization of Unity (8-31)
          a. Gifts of the Spirit (8-11)
          b. Ministrations of the Lord (12-27)
          c. Workings of God (28-30)
      II. The Unfailing Law (XIII, XIV)
        1. The Law (XIII)
          a. Values (1-3)
          b. Virtues (4-7)
          c. Victories (8-13)
        2. The Law at Work (XIV)
          a. General Instruction (1-3)

[3] *The Corinthian Letters of Paul* (New York, Fleming Revell, 1946), p. 7.
[4] *Ibid.*, pp. 144-204.

b. Argument (4-25)
c. Corinthian Application (26-40)
III. The Ultimate Triumph (XV:1-57)
1. The Gospel of Christ's Resurrection (1-11)
2. The Importance of Christ's Resurrection (12-34)
3. Intellectual Difficulties (35-40)
4. The Assurance and Challenge (51-57)

4. THE SERMONIZING METHOD OF EXPOSITORY PREACHING

This is the highest type of expository work, demanding not only a clear understanding of the chosen passage but a logical and finished presentation and application of it in full sermonic form to the needs of the audience. The topic and the main divisions are drawn from the passage, and the treatment adheres in the closest possible manner to it in conscientious attempt to teach what the Spirit of God meant to teach by it.

The expository preacher will usually take a passage longer than a single verse, since he is paramountly interested in the message of God's revealed truth, and of necessity in its contextual relationship. Indeed, expository preaching is at its best when a book is expounded, section by section, in the best homiletical style. The preacher will do his finest work in this field when by illustration, argumentation and explanation he not only makes the meaning of the passage absolutely clear but when by application and exhortation he displays a distinct and dominating purpose to reach the will of his hearers to move it Godward.

W. H. Griffith Thomas, who excelled in expository preaching, correctly emphasizes three requirements for successful work in this field of ministry. Concerning an exposition of any passage he says:

(1) It should only concern the salient features. There are many details that must be resolutely omitted lest we are too long, and lest we blur the definite impression.

(2) It should mainly concern the spiritual meaning. Anything historical, or geographical, or Oriental, must be kept resolutely subordinated to the supreme issue; it is a sermon, not a lecture.

(3) It should always have a searching message. The application in an exposition should be emphasized and never omitted.[5]

---

[5] W. H. Griffith Thomas, *The Work of the Ministry* (London, Hodder & Stoughton, n.d.), pp. 229-230.

Alexander Maclaren (1826-1910), the famous preacher of Manchester, England, is perhaps the greatest exponent in modern times of the sermonizing type of expository preaching.[6] Almost every one of his through-the-Bible expositions is a masterpiece of beauty, clarity, simplicity and spiritual insight. Under his deft treatment the most complex passages unfold themselves in a flood of light.

Maclaren's outlines, always lucid and logical, usually have three points and are always faithful to the passage or text he is expounding. He never permitted himself to be diverted from the salient features or the spiritual meaning of the passage he was expounding and always aimed it as a searching message to the heart and conscience of his hearers.

Although his messages were frequently based more directly on one verse of a passage, he usually captured the essential meaning of the passage in his exposition of the verse. For example, consider the clarity of his threefold outline based on Hebrews 7:26: "Such an high priest became us, who is holy, harmless, undefiled, separate from sinners, and made higher than the heavens":

The Priest Whom We Need

I. We All Need a Priest, and We Have the Priest We Need in Jesus Christ.

II. We Need for a Priest a Perfect Man, and We Have the Perfect Priest Whom We Need, in Jesus Christ.

III. We Need a Priest in the Heavens, and We Have in Christ the Heavenly Priest Whom We Need.[7]

F. B. Meyer (1847-1929) of Christ's Church, London, also excelled in the sermonizing type of exposition. He customarily organized his message around a key verse through which he interpreted the whole passage he was handling.[8] Joseph A. Seiss in his magnificent expositions of the Book of Revelation deals with a passage as a solid whole, and conforms the

[6] See his classic *Expositions of Holy Scripture* (17 vols., Grand Rapids, Wm. B. Eerdmans Publishing Co., 1942).

[7] Vol. XV, pp. 10-20.

[8] For example, see his expositions of Hebrews, entitled *The Way into the Holiest* (New York, Fleming Revell, 1893; reprint, Grand Rapids, Zondervan Publishing House), pp. 9-277.

outline and structure of his sermon-lectures to the importance of the ideas in the passage.[9]

The method employed by Seiss, however, with emphasis upon a preaching rather than a lecturing presentation, is perhaps the best all-around approach to Biblical exposition. Dealing with a passage as a solid whole tends to encourage more careful exegetical work on it in its entirety. Conforming the outline and structure of the sermon to the importance of the ideas in the passage encourages a more balanced presentation of Biblical truth than grouping that truth around a key verse contained in the passage. If the preacher can remember to stress only the salient features of the passage and emphasize its spiritual meaning in urgent appeal to heart and will, this method is to be commended as the very best.

The following expository message by the present author on Philippians 2:12-16 will serve as an illustration of this method. The thought for the sermon is suggested by verse 15: ". . . among whom ye shine as lights [luminaries] in the world . . ." However, the main points of the message are derived from the passage as a whole.[10]

SHINING AS STARS

Introduction:
    (1) Beauty of stars at night.
    (2) Beauty of true Christians shining as stars in the night of sin.
    (3) How to shine as stars.

I. *Shining As Stars Requires We Work Out Our Inwrought Salvation Diligently* (vv. 12, 13).
    1. God works it in (13).
    2. We must work it out (12).

II. *Shining As Stars Requires That We Serve Our Lord Joyfully and Spontaneously* (14, 15).
    1. Without murmuring and contention (14).
    2. With blamelessness of character (15a).
    3. As an example in a dark and crooked world of sin (15b).

III. *Shining As Stars Requires That We Witness For Our Lord Faithfully* (16).
    1. By holding forth the Word of Life (16a).

[9] *The Apocalypse* (3 vols., Philadelphia, Approved Books Store, 1895; reprint, Grand Rapids, Zondervan Publishing House).

[10] Merrill F. Unger, *Pathways to Power* (Grand Rapids, Zondervan Publishing House, 1953), pp. 153-160.

2. The Word of Life a torch in a dark place (16b).
Conclusion: Let us be starlike Christians.

LITERATURE ON THE EXPOSITORY METHOD

Taylor, W. M., *The Ministry of the Word* (New York, Randolph & Co., 1883).

Pierson, A. T., *The Divine Art of Preaching* (New York, Baker and Taylor Company, 1892).

Lockhart, Clinton, *Principles of Interpretation* (Ft. Worth, S. H. Taylor, 1915).

Schodde, G. H., *Outlines of Biblical Hermeneutics* (Columbus, Lutheran Book Concern, 1917), pp. 137-186.

Knott, H. E., *How to Prepare an Expository Sermon* (Cincinnati, Standard Publishing Co., 1930).

Patton, Carl S., *The Use of the Bible in Preaching* (Chicago, Willett, Clark and Co., 1936). Modern view.

Ray, Jeff D., *Expository Preaching* (Grand Rapids, Zondervan Publishing House, 1940).

Noyes, Morgan P., *Preaching the Word of God* (New York, Charles Scribner's Sons, 1943).

Blackwood, Andrew W., *Preaching from the Bible* (Nashville, Abingdon-Cokesbury Press, 1941), Chaps. VII, XII.

————, *The Preparation of Sermons* (Nashville, Abingdon-Cokesbury Press, 1948), Chap. 6.

Stibbs, Alan M., *Understanding God's Word* (London, Inter-Varsity Fellowship, 1950).

Blocker, Simon, *The Secret of Pulpit Power Through Thematic Preaching* (Grand Rapids, Wm. B. Eerdmans Publishing Co., 1951).

Littorin, Frank T., *How to Preach the Word with Variety* (Grand Rapids, Baker Book House, 1953), pp. 47-107.

Evans, J. Ellwood, "Expository Preaching," *Bibliotheca Sacra* (Jan., 1954).

Perry, L. M. and Faris D. Whitesell, *Variety in Your Preaching* (New York, Fleming Revell, 1954).

Schroeder, Frederick W., *Preaching the Word With Authority* (Philadelphia, The Westminster Press, 1954).

CHAPTER VI

VARIATIONS OF THE EXPOSITORY METHOD

It is a mistake to impose too narrow a definition upon expository preaching. In the minds of many, this type of pulpit ministry consists simply of a series of sermons expounding some book or books of the Bible. While this is undoubtedly an important method of expository approach, it is only one. Moreover, the tendency closely to confine pulpit exposition inevitably leads to monotony of treatment, discouragement in the cultivation of the expository method, and eventual abandonment of it altogether.

There is no reason why true expository preaching should be confined to a single method of dealing with the Scriptures. To be the refreshing and adaptable vehicle for expounding the body of revealed truth that it ought to be, it should be unrestricted in employing all the standard homiletical procedures. The important consideration is that the expository sermon be not only Biblical, that is, based strictly on the Bible, but also Biblically instructive and challenging in the sense of expounding the Scriptures as a coherent and coordinated body of revealed truth and bringing that truth to grips with the human will and conscience.

If the homiletical discourse meets these essential requirements of being expository, there is no reason why it may not take the form of the topical or textual sermon, or the form of a Bible reading or running commentary, as well as paragraph-by-paragraph, chapter-by-chapter, book-by-book exposition.

1. THE TOPICAL SERMON AS A VARIATION OF THE
EXPOSITORY METHOD

Although much topical preaching strays from the Bible
and concerns itself largely with human sources of wisdom,
the topical sermon may be strictly Scriptural and expository.
The preacher may get his topic from the Bible and develop
it as the Bible develops it. In this type of Bible exposition
the topic determines the content of the sermon and the
Scriptures themselves determine the manner in which it is
developed.

Several kinds of expository sermons may be classified as
topical preaching. *Doctrinal sermons* of which there are entirely too few in these times, are topical in nature and furnish
an admirable vehicle for the highest type of expository discourse. The particular doctrine chosen becomes the topic.
Ordinarily a single Scriptural text presents only one aspect of
the doctrine, so that a number of key passages treated in
their contextual relationships and giving a comprehensive
view of the topic must be selected. The best work in this
field will carefully expound what the Scriptures themselves
reveal rather than what might be gleaned from books of
theology.

The following outline of a message on justification by the
eminent expositor W. H. Griffith Thomas illustrates a topical
doctrinal sermon treated expositorily. It justifies inclusion in
the category of the expositional message because it accurately
explains the doctrine of justification in proper focus upon the
full Scriptural revelation on the subject.[1]

JUSTIFICATION

Introduction.
1. Foundation doctrine of the Reformation.
2. Foundation of all Christian life and service.
3. Foundation in the Old Testament (Gen. 15:6, Ps. 143:2, Micah
6:6, Hab. 2:4, Job 4:17; 9:2, etc.).
I. What Is the Meaning of Justification?
1. Restoration of true relation to God lost by sin.
(a) Removal of condemnation by the gift of forgiveness.

1 W. H. Griffith Thomas, *Grace and Power* (reprint, Grand Rapids, Wm. B.
Eerdmans Publishing Co., 1949), pp. 74-83.

      (b) Removal of guilt by imputation of righteousness.
      (c) Removal of separation by the restoration of fellowship.
    2. Declaring righteous before the law (Ps. 51:4, Rom. 8:33-35).
      (a) Contrast with forgiveness.
      (b) Contrast with sanctification.
      (c) Contrast with Roman Catholic doctrine.
  II. What Is the Basis of Justification?
    1. Merit of the finished work of Christ.
    2. Not human merit (Gal. 3:10, Acts 13:39, Rom. 10:3).
 III. What Is the Method of Justification?
    1. Through faith.
      (a) In a fact (I John 5:1).
      (b) In Christ's Word (John 4:21).
      (c) In Christ (John 3:16).
    2. By Christ in Whom we believe.
 IV. What Is the Value of Justification?
    1. Basis of spiritual health.
    2. Foundation of peace (Rom. 5:1).
    3. Answer to the moral perplexities of original sin (Rom. 3:25).
    4. Secret of spiritual liberty.
    5. A Necessity for spiritual power.
    6. Secret of spiritual service.

Biographical sermons constitute another variety of the topical message. This type of discourse, which deals with the lives of Bible personalities, is best, however, when treated expositorily. Many Bible characters, especially those of the Old Testament, lend themselves to admirable treatment when their careers are interpreted around some central, unifying Scriptural truth which characterizes them and gives coherence and spiritual challenge to a biographical treatment of them.[2]

The life treated may be dealt with in a single sermon. In this case there is less opportunity for careful exegesis of pertinent key passages. If, however, a series of messages on an important character such as Abraham or Moses is prepared around a central, unifying theme, much wider latitude exists for accurate exegesis of key passages from the original language, and this will add freshness and originality to the treatment.

A. B. Simpson, a gifted and deeply spiritual expositor, founder of the Christian and Missionary Alliance, excelled in the bio-

---

[2] Cf. Frank T. Littorin, *How to Preach the Word with Variety* (Grand Rapids, Baker Book House, 1953), pp. 95-103.

graphical sermon, made coherent and compelling by organization around a unifying theme. He forcefully presents Old Testament characters under such sermonic titles as "Abel or Justifying Faith," "Enoch or Sanctifying Grace," "Noah or Separating Faith," "Abraham or the Obedience of Faith," etc.[3] Simpson's treatment of Isaac will serve as an example of the expository biographical sermon.[4]

Isaac — The Patience of Faith

Introduction:
1. Quiet, gentle man.
2. Chosen type of Christ.
3. Lesson of his life — death to self and the life of meekness, patience and lowliness.
I. Painful Trial As a Child.
   (a) Younger brother and rival of Ishmael.
   (b) Persecuted and scorned by him for his faith.
II. Severe Test As a Youth.
   (a) Yielding up himself on Moriah.
   (b) Type of Christ's death and ours.
III. Faithful Choice As a Young Man.
   (a) In matter of his affections, his marriage.
   (b) Far-reaching importance of this decision.
IV. Faith and Patience Toward the Trials of Life.
   (a) Famine.
   (b) Vexation from the Philistines.
   (c) His children.
Conclusion: Blessings and rewards of his patience and faith.

Another type of topical sermon is the *ethical discourse*. This should be expository and based strictly on Scripture. The topical message ought to expound specific Biblical passages and be addressed strictly to the saved. Indiscriminate preaching of morality to unsaved people may be positively injurious if it confuses God's plan of salvation and causes the unregenerate to rely upon human merit and good works for acceptance with God instead of on the finished work of Christ. Whether the particular Scripture dealt with is addressed to "Jew" (unsaved), "Gentile" (unsaved) or "the Church of God" (saved) (I Cor. 10:32) must be the very

[3] A. B. Simpson, *Standing on Faith* (Harrisburg, Pa., n.d.).
[4] *Ibid.*, pp. 30-36.

first concern of the expository preacher who aspires to be an able minister of "the new covenant" (II Cor. 3:6).

Topical sermons most readily suggest themselves for special days and events of the year. But the faithful Bible preacher must beware that the incessant clamor of special days and events of the year for recognition does not prove a temptation to lure him from true Bible exposition. Mother's Day, Father's Day, Children's Day, Independence Day, etc. plus an ever-increasing number of special days in many denominational programs — all tend to crowd out solid exposition of the Bible and to displace it with superficial preaching deficient in Biblical content and appeal. When special sermons are absolutely necessary, the aim should be to make them as expository and Biblical as possible.

2. THE TEXTUAL SERMON AS A VARIATION OF THE EXPOSITORY METHOD

Although much textual preaching, like topical preaching, strays from the Bible, *bona fide* use of this method will expound what the text or passage itself says, rather than what the preacher wishes to draw from it to give expression to his own thoughts or ideas. If the speaker expounds what the text or passage actually means, he is perforce compelled not only to break it up into its leading words or clauses and use these as the headings of his discourse, but he must relate the passage to its context in order to arrive at its accurate meaning. If the preacher does this, in a very definite sense he will be preaching an expository sermon, though of the textual variety. The only difference from a purely expository message, as commonly conceived, will be the shorter length of the passage elucidated.

Charles Haddon Spurgeon (1834-1892), pastor of the Metropolitan Tabernacle of London and one of the greatest preachers of the Christian pulpit, is usually classified as Biblical and textual in his sermonizings, but not expository.[5] While it is true Spurgeon did not always employ close exe-

---

[5] Faris D. Whitesell, *The Art of Biblical Preaching* (Grand Rapids, Zondervan Publishing House, 1950), pp. 156f.; cf. J. Ellwood Evans, "Expository Preaching," *Bibliotheca Sacra* (Jan., 1954), p. 56.

gesis and careful interpretation, he frequently did. The following message based on I Peter 2:24, 25 is an example of a textual expository message preached by this "prince of preachers":[6]

THE SIN-BEARER

Introduction:
1. The immediate context — part of Peter's address to servants (slaves).
2. Beautiful connection with the lowly Saviour as our Sin-Bearer.
3. Comfort of cross to all oppressed, enslaved by sin.

I. The Bearing of Our Sins By Our Lord.
(a) The scriptural fact is certain.
(b) Modern denials of it are criminal.
(c) The sin-bearing was continual.
(d) The sin-bearing was final.
(e) The sin-bearing was marvelous and miraculous.

II. The Change in Our Condition.
(a) Now legally dead to the punishment of sin.
(b) Actually made "dead to sins."
(c) Brought into life.

III. The Healing of Our Diseases.
(a) Of brutishness.
(b) Of proneness to wander.
(c) Of inability to return.
(d) Of readiness to follow other leaders.
(e) Of fear of sin, death and hell.

Conclusion: This wonderful work of grace wrought in us we owe not to the teaching or example of Christ but to His stripes — His substitutionary sacrifice.

Textual preaching worthy of the name, as in the case of Spurgeon's sermon from I Peter 2:24, 25, will in large measure be expository. This ought to be especially true of any sermon when the text is chosen from the doctrinally rich passages of the New Testament. On the other hand, if a text is selected out of the narrative, poetic or didactic sections of the Old Testament, which would be much less doctrinally concentrated, the content of the message would normally decrease in expository content. However, such a sermon ought at least to be thoroughly Biblical, if not strictly expository.

[6] *Great Pulpit Masters* (New York, Fleming Revell, 1949), Vol. II, pp. 137-149.

In choosing a text in which the context suggests little or nothing to aid in its development, as a passage from Proverbs or parts of Job, the preacher who is a diligent student of the Bible will be rescued from the temptation to fill out the sermon with un-Biblical ideas or illustrations.

Spurgeon's remarkable sermon "Songs in the Night,"[7] suggested by Job 35:10, is an example of a textual message based upon a thought of intriguing beauty which is developed almost completely apart from its context and in which the text itself is somewhat altered. Instead of developing the question, "Where is God my Maker, who giveth songs in the night?" Spurgeon abandons the inquiry and simply dwells upon the striking thought put in declarative form, "God my Maker, who giveth songs in the night."

Some would question the validity of such a treatment of the text itself and would criticize the preacher for ignoring the context. But here where the context offers so little, the messenger is justified in abandoning this method of development in favor of elucidating and illustrating his germinal thought by a general marshalling of Biblical truth and illustration. The result is a sermon of haunting beauty and power with a large Biblical content. Even in a message of this character Spurgeon demonstrates that he is a "Bible preacher" and expounds his text by appeal to the Bible itself. It is therefore incorrect to deny a large expository element in a message of this type which is commonly classified as purely textual.

LITERATURE ON VARIATIONS OF THE EXPOSITORY METHOD

Harvey, G. W., *A System of Christian Rhetoric* (New York, Harper & Brothers, 1873), pp. 302-360.

Hoppin, James M., *Homiletics* (New York, Funk & Wagnalls, 1883), pp. 444-525.

Fiske, F. W., *Manual of Preaching* (New York, A. C. Armstrong, 1893), pp. 39-244.

Breed, David R., *Preparing to Preach* (Chicago, W. P. Blessing Co., 1911), pp. 375-446.

Meyer, F. B., *Expository Preaching* (London, Hodder & Stoughton, 1912).

[7] For an analysis of this sermon see Ozora S. Davis, *Principles of Preaching* (Chicago, University of Chicago Press, 1924), pp. 123-151.

Broadus, John, *A Treatise on the Preparation and Delivery of Sermons* (New York, Harper and Brothers, 1926), pp. 300-316.

Blackwood, Andrew W., *Preaching from the Bible* (Nashville, Abingdon-Cokesbury Press, 1941).

Jones, Bob, Jr., *How to Improve Your Preaching* (New York, Fleming Revell, 1945), pp. 9-31.

Littorin, Frank T., *How to Preach the Word with Variety* (Grand Rapids, Baker Book House, 1953), pp. 79-124.

Evans, J. Ellwood, "Expository Preaching," *Bibliotheca Sacra* (Jan., 1954).

CHAPTER VII

THE SPIRITUAL QUALIFICATIONS OF AN EXPOSITOR

There is no requirement more essential for one who would expound the Word of God than the spiritual. Since "all Scripture is given by inspiration of God," that is, is "God-breathed" (II Tim. 3:16), the Book of God can only be comprehended through the teaching ministry of its divine Author, the Holy Spirit, who resides in the believer. He who inspired the Word is alone able to illuminate its meaning to the preacher of the Word. Adjustment to the laws according to which the Holy Spirit operates in the believer is therefore a *sine qua non* of the Bible expositor.

Despite the paramount importance of the spiritual element in the life and ministry of the preacher of the Word, it is amazing how little stress is laid upon this aspect of the minister's equipment in our modern day. In many circles, conservative as well as liberal, the necessity of humble dependence upon the Holy Spirit for a proper understanding of the Holy Scriptures and cultivation of the spiritual life are neglected or lost sight of altogether in the prevailing emphasis on other phases of ministerial equipment. But the fact remains that no matter what other training a minister may have, if his proper relation to the Holy Spirit has been ignored, the chief element in his competence as a preacher of the Bible has been missed. As a result he will be seriously deficient in the most crucial area of his preparation.

1. THE EXPOSITOR AS A REGENERATED BELIEVER

It seems scarcely necessary to mention such an obvious fact as this: One who handles the Bible needs above all else to be spiritually renewed. Yet so frequently for one reason or another do men who have never experienced salvation enter the ministry and attempt to preach and teach the Word of God, that the absolute necessity of this fundamental spiritual requirement needs to be emphasized.

It is quite apparent from the Word of God that an unregenerate man "is sensual (natural), having not the Spirit" (Jude 19). As a consequence, no matter how brilliant or gifted he may be, he lives only in the realm of physical sense. There, is nothing in him to respond to the Spirit's teaching or to understand Spiritual truth. The Holy Spirit does convict the unrenewed man "of sin, and of righteousness, and of judgment" (John 16:8) but as a "natural man," not indwelt by the Holy Spirit as every regenerated man is (I Cor. 6:19; Rom. 8:9), he "receiveth not the things of the Spirit of God: for they are foolishness unto him: neither can he know them, because they are spiritually discerned" (understood only by the Spirit) (I Cor. 2:14).

The basic prerequisite of anyone who would understand the Word of God (and he must understand it before he can preach or teach it) is that he enjoy the Holy Spirit's tuition. This can only be the case as one is regenerated and is thus indwelt by the Holy Spirit, the divine Teacher Himself. "Now we have received, not the spirit of the world, but the spirit which is of God; that we might know the things which are freely given to us of God" (I Cor. 2:12).

There is a twofold reason revealed in Scripture why anyone who would expound the Word of God must enjoy the benefits of the teaching ministry of the Holy Spirit. The first is that the Holy Spirit alone *knows* the things of God. The second is that the Holy Spirit alone can *teach* the things of God. That the Spirit alone knows the things of God is clearly taught in the Bible. "For what man knoweth the things of a man, save the spirit of man which is in him? even so the things of God knoweth no man, *but the Spirit of God*" (I Cor. 2:11).

Any truth of the divine revelation, even the simplest and most elementary, must be Spirit-revealed. This at one stroke

shows the grave danger to which the unregenerate or the
merely technical scholar is exposed in approaching the Word,
and warns of his complete incompetence to understand the
spiritual content of Holy Writ, no matter what his other
credentials of education or ability may be.

But the Spirit of God not only alone knows but alone
can teach "the things of God." "Which things also we speak,
not in the words which man's wisdom teacheth, but *which
the Holy Ghost teacheth*" (I Cor. 2:13). The divine wisdom,
which the Holy Spirit teaches, in this sense is the Word of
God. "Comparing spiritual things with spiritual" (I Cor. 2:13)
'is the apostolic directive for the realization of the full-orbed
benefits of the Spirit's instruction in the things of God. The
entire body of revealed truth, moreover, is the medium through
which the Holy Spirit instructs the believer.

2. The Expositor As Spirit-filled and Spirit-taught

It is not sufficient that the preacher of the Bible be a regenerated believer. To enjoy the full, untrammeled teaching
ministry of the Spirit he must also be yielded to God's will,
adjusted to God's purpose, and under the full control of the
Spirit's wisdom and power. Although a renewed man has
a new nature and is indwelt by the Spirit, he still possesses
his old Adamic nature, and is constantly under pressure to
allow it to work through his physical members, making him
a carnal Christian. Whenever he does, the Spirit of God is
grieved (Eph. 4:30), and His ministry of instructing the carnal believer is seriously curtailed.

It is evident, therefore, why the Holy Spirit can only fully
discharge His teaching ministry in the spiritual believer. He
is emphatically the *Holy* Spirit, and employs the cleansing
power of the Word (John 15:3) in His beneficent instruction. When the Christian persists in an unholy walk, he
thereby automatically rejects the Spirit's instruction in refusing to walk according to the Word of God.

In the Upper Room Discourse (John 14-16), just before
His death, our Lord had much to say concerning the advent
of the Holy Spirit to reside in the disciples and undertake

His teaching ministry in and through them. "Howbeit when he, the Spirit of truth is come, he will guide you into all truth; for he shall not speak of himself; but whatsoever he shall hear, that shall he speak: and he will shew you things to come" (John 16:13). Guidance into "all truth" comprehends being led into paths of practical holiness as well as into spheres of spiritual knowledge, especially comprehension of the prophetic Scriptures.

The Apostle Paul likewise connects being Spirit-taught with being Spirit-filled, "Wherefore be *ye not foolish,* but *understand* what the will of the Lord is. And be not drunken with wine, wherein is riot, but *be filled with the Spirit*" (Eph. 5:17, 18, ARV).

3. The Expositor As Divinely Called and Commissioned

In addition to an experience of regeneration and spiritual fullness resulting in the enjoyment of the Spirit's unobstructed teaching ministry, the Bible expositor must possess the settled conviction that God has called and separated him to the Gospel ministry as a life work. This call and commission have been the portion of all God's prophets and apostles throughout Old and New Testament times.

Moses was called in the desert (Ex. 3:1-12), the child Samuel in the Tabernacle (I Sam. 3:1-18), Isaiah in the Temple (Is. 6:1-13) and Paul in the city of Damascus (Acts 9:17). Jeremiah had such a constraint to preach the message of God that it was in his heart "as a burning fire" shut up in his bones and he was "weary with forbearing" and could not stay (Jer. 20:9). Paul cried out, "Woe is unto me, if I preach not the gospel!" (I Cor. 9:16).

There are many ways in which the call may come — directly or indirectly, through circumstances. But come it must! Preaching God's Word is important work. God does the selecting, the calling and the empowering for this momentous task.

Laymen may preach and teach the Bible and do it well. But when God calls a man to give his full time to the ministry of the Word, that man ought to know he is divinely called and commissioned for this sacred occupation.[1] Moreover, God intends that he should know and graciously extends His call, so that no preacher ought to be without this divine assurance.

4. THE EXPOSITOR AS A MAN OF EXEMPLARY CHRISTIAN CHARACTER

That a preacher of the Bible must be Spirit-filled, Spirit-taught and divinely commissioned presupposes, of course, that he possess sound Christian character. Yet so often are Biblical terms theologized and made merely abstract concepts devoid of practical meaning and divorced from concrete experience that emphasis must be continually laid on the necessity of the preacher practicing what he preaches.

No other qualification is quite so important to the success of the preacher of the Bible as consistency of conduct. What a man is, in a sense, is more important than what he says. Unless the silent sermon of a godly life is present to preach effectually, the spoken sermon never will.

People may forgive many deficiencies in preachers of the Bible, but inconsistency of Christian character *never!* The preacher's life and testimony must be the channel of truth to men. Life is to be communicated as well as words conveyed. The water of life must flow through cleansed channels. The bread of life must be broken and dispensed with clean hands. The power of the Spirit must be manifested through empty and yielded vessels. The truths of the Word of God must become "living and personal in living persons."[2]

The necessity of practical godliness in the servant of Christ is everywhere emphasized in the Scriptures. Paul took every precaution that he might be able to say to the Corinthians, "Be ye followers of me, even as I also am of Christ" (I Cor. 11:1). He was able to write to the Thessalonians, "Ye are witnesses, and God also, how holily and justly and unblameably we behaved ourselves among you that believe" (I Thess. 2:10). He solemnly enjoined the young man Timothy to be

---

1 Cf. Faris D. Whitesell, *The Art of Biblical Preaching* (Grand Rapids, Zondervan Publishing House, 1950), pp. 65f.
2 A. Vinet, *Homiletics* (New York, Ivison & Phinney, 1854), p. 20.

"an ensample to them that believe, in word, in manner of life, in love, in faith, in purity" (I Tim. 4:12, ARV).

5. THE EXPOSITOR AS A MAN OF PRAYER

This qualification of a Bible expositor is so obviously essential that the very mention of it seems trite. Yet, strangely enough, it is apparently in the realm of prayer that the greatest failure occurs among ministers. It takes a long while for many otherwise able expositors to discover this simple fact. Others never realize it. As a result their ministry is characterized by intellectuality rather than spirituality. The letter of Biblical truth is illuminated, but not properly combined with the spirit and power of the Word.

There can be no substitute for definite and stated times of fellowship with God. This exercise of soul is indispensable. It is the source of power and blessing. It is the gateway to enlarged spheres of service. It is the time when God speaks through His Word to His servant that His servant by lip and life may speak to his needy fellow man.

Any time may be given to prayer, but the best time for this holy exercise and the period that every minister ought to guard jealously for this purpose is the "morning watch."[3] This is the best hour of the day. The mind is clearest, the body strongest, the spirit most responsive after a night of refreshing sleep. This best hour of the day ought to be dedicated to the highest privilege of man — communion with God.

> O Jehovah, in the morning
>   shalt thou hear my voice;
> In the morning will I order my prayer unto
>   Thee, and will keep watch (Ps. 5:3, ARV).

6. THE EXPOSITOR AS A STUDENT OF THE WORD

Too much stress can scarcely be laid upon this requirement for one who would excel in exposition of the Bible. If the Bible is to be expounded, one must know the content of the Sacred Scriptures. Accordingly, H. Jeffs lists "intimate

[3] For the vast benefits of the morning devotional hour see the present author's *Pathways to Power* (Grand Rapids, Zondervan Publishing House, 1953), pp. 7-16.

familiarity with the Book" as "first among the qualifications
of the expository preacher."[4]

The other spiritual qualifications enumerated in this chapter indeed are prerequisite to this paramount requirement
and must underlie the true expositor's knowledge of God's
Word. But when a Bible preacher stands behind the sacred
desk it is his vital and experiential knowledge of the Scriptures that most immediately comes into use. This knowledge
must be clear, comprehensive and accurate. It must be an
apprehension of divine truth that is coordinated with the
divine plan and purpose for the ages as revealed in the Bible
as a whole. But more than this historic and prophetic grasp
of Scripture there must be an understanding of the Biblical
message in terms of the needs of everyday life and in the
light of the contemporary world scene.

Such a mastery of the Bible can only come as a result
of Bible reading, or through what G. Campbell Morgan described as "persistent study of the Word on the part of the
minister."[5] The expositor must live in his Bible. Other books
he must read, but the Word of God must be his daily food
and drink. He must study it, meditate upon it day and night
like the Psalmist (Ps. 1:2) and ever delight in its power and
freshness. His theology must be a Biblical theology drawn
vital and fresh from the pages of Holy Writ and thus geared
to human need.

7. The Expositor As a Man of Spiritual Gift

Closely bound up with a man's call to preach the Word of
God is the divine bestowment of a spiritual gift or gifts for
the ministry. God assuredly does not call without bestow-
ing the necessary spiritual talents for the discharge of the
ministry to which he calls.

The gift, moreover, is not to be confused with the Holy
Spirit who bestows the gift. The gifted men themselves are
Christ's gifts to the Church. "And he gave some, apostles;
and some, prophets; and some, evangelists; and some, pastors

[4] H. Jeffs, *The Art of Exposition* (Boston, The Pilgrim Press, 1910), p. 28.
[5] *The Ministry of the Word* (New York, Fleming Revell, 1919), p. 203.

and teachers" (Eph. 4:11). But the gifted men are endowed with ministerial talents by the Holy Spirit. Some ministers, of course, have greater talents than others. But all have some gift. The Apostle writing to the Corinthians emphasizes the fact that "there are diversities of gifts, but the same Spirit," but that "the manifestation of the Spirit is given to every man to profit withal" (I Cor. 12:4, 7). The expository preacher must be a man endowed with "the word of wisdom" and "the word of knowledge" by the Holy Spirit (I Cor. 12:8). The Spirit must not only fill him and teach him, but furnish the dynamic for the effective exercise of the talents He has bestowed upon him as a servant of the Lord and as a member of the body of Christ. With his spiritual talents thus exercised and under Spirit control, the expository preacher is bound to be a great blessing wherever he ministers.

LITERATURE ON THE SPIRITUAL QUALIFICATIONS OF AN EXPOSITOR

Vinet, A., Homiletics (New York, Ivison & Phinney, 1854), pp. 203-250.

Stalker, James, The Preacher and His Models (London, Hodder & Stoughton, 1891), pp. 31-235.

Kelly, George, The Divine Idea of Preaching (London, A. H. Stockwell, 1901).

Terry, Milton S., Biblical Hermeneutics (New York, Methodist Book Concern, 1911), pp. 28-30.

Jeffs, H., The Art of Exposition (Boston, The Pilgrim Press, 1910), Chap. III.

Evans, William, How to Prepare Sermons and Gospel Addresses (Chicago, Bible Institute Colportage Assoc., 1913), Chap. II.

Brown, Elijah P., Point and Purpose in Preaching (New York, Fleming Revell, 1917), pp. 120-172.

Morgan, G. Campbell, The Ministry of the Word (New York, Fleming Revell, 1919), pp. 176-222.

Brown, Charles R., The Art of Preaching (New York, Macmillan & Co., 1922).

Vance, James I., Being a Preacher (New York, Fleming Revell, 1923), Chap. V.

Black, James, The Mystery of Preaching (New York, Fleming Revell, 1924).

Oman, John, Concerning the Ministry (New York, Harper & Brothers, 1937).

Stewart, James S., *Heralds of God* (New York, Charles Scribner's Sons, 1946).

Spann, J. Richard, ed., *The Ministry* (Nashville, Abingdon-Cokesbury Press, 1949). Symposium.

Eberhardt, C. R., *The Bible in the Making of Ministers* (New York, Association Press, 1949).

Guffin, Gilbert L., *Called of God: The Work of the Ministry* (New York, Fleming Revell, 1951).

CHAPTER VIII

THE TECHNICAL EQUIPMENT OF AN EXPOSITOR

Although there is no requirement more essential for one who would expound the Word of God than the spiritual, there is another requirement which is also vitally necessary and must not be neglected. This is the educational and technical part of a preacher's training. It is not enough that the expositor be a regenerated believer, Spirit-filled and Spirit-taught and divinely called and commissioned. Nor is it sufficient that he be a person of exemplary Christian character, a man of prayer, a diligent student of the Word and endowed with spiritual gifts. The Bible expositor needs in addition to these qualifications a thorough training in the technicalities and disciplines that underlie competent handling of the Holy Scriptures.

While it is possible that men of unusual gifts by dint of diligent work and self-application may become eminent Bible expositors and Bible preachers without much formal education, and such names as John Bunyan, Charles Spurgeon, G. Campbell Morgan, H. A. Ironside and Lewis Sperry Chafer may be cited as examples, yet these names are definite exceptions to the rule. In the preponderating majority of cases excellence in the field of Bible exposition presupposes a thorough academic and theological training in addition to the spiritual.

1. THE EXPOSITOR AS A MAN OF BROAD GENERAL EDUCATION

There are vast benefits to be derived from a comprehensive course in the arts and sciences by every prospective minister. Such a program of generalized study, leading to what has been commonly called the bachelor of arts degree, ought to be included in the training of every Biblical preacher. It furnishes an indispensable intellectual and cultural background for the presentation of the Gospel, and no minister can omit it from his general preparation without serious loss.

The value of a broad academic training on the college level lies in the fact that it teaches men "to think for themselves and to think their way through."[1] This ability is of the utmost importance in dealing with spiritual truth. Unless the mind is well trained in its approach to Biblical truth, it will be in danger of doing bungling work. The simplicity of the Gospel of Christ will be in peril of being misconstrued as superficiality or obscured as a hard-to-be-understood complexity. Discipline of the mind to think clearly, to analyze keenly, and to evaluate accurately is one of the great assets that comes to the well educated man.

Besides furnishing mental discipline, broad academic training supplies a fund of useful knowledge. This varied information is not only of the greatest value indirectly in giving a cultural background to the expository preacher, but it is directly useful in suggesting illustrations from many spheres of knowledge for the elucidation and application of spiritual truth.[2]

In view of the far-reaching advantages of comprehensive academic preparation for the Gospel minister the present-day trend in conservative circles toward the Bible college, often with a heavy emphasis on Bible and theological subjects to the crowding out of the arts and sciences, is to be regretted. Men who look forward to full-scale seminary training ought to be careful to avail themselves of a standard course in the arts and sciences as the best possible preparation for the specialized study toward which they are looking.

Fundamental in pre-theological study is a thorough and accurate discipline in the field of English language, including composition, literature and speech. Above all other skills the minister needs to be able to speak and write his native

[1] G. Campbell Morgan, *The Ministry of the Word* (New York, Fleming Revell, 1919), p. 185.
[2] *Ibid.*, p. 187.

tongue with fluency and finish. Deficiency in this basic realm will seriously cripple the student throughout his seminary course and his future ministry. Many seminarians wage a losing battle with the Biblical languages because they are compelled to learn English at the same time they are attempting to master Hebrew and Greek.

Important also for the pre-theological student are courses in ancient and modern history, psychology, philosophy, the natural and social sciences, and foreign languages. Especially valuable is a classical course including Latin and non-Biblical Greek. In the writer's opinion nothing would do more to contribute to the cultural background of seminary students and raise the general level of their academic proficiency than a sound college discipline in ancient Greek and Roman languages and cultures.

2. THE EXPOSITOR AS A STUDENT OF THEOLOGY

The preacher who merely uses the Bible as an anthology of seedling thoughts to suggest sermons which are largely his own ideas on philosophy, morality and religion, may perhaps afford to neglect the study of theology. This also may be the case with the preacher who attempts "to preach the Bible" but who does so superficially, never trying to expound it systematically as a coordinated body of truth or to wrestle with problems of interpretation. But this can never be the case with the true expositor. He must not only have a system of theology. His system must be both comprehensive and thoroughly Biblical. It must not only cover the entire gamut of doctrinal revelation set forth in the Bible; it must also adhere with the utmost rigidity to the truths set forth in that doctrinal revelation. In proportion as a system of theology fails to be comprehensive and thoroughly Biblical, to that extent it will hinder the expositor from attaining the maximum degree of proficiency in expounding the Sacred Oracles.

There is little doubt that the absence of an adequate Biblical theology among many preachers is to a large degree responsible for the neglect and low ebb of expository preaching in the pulpit of the present day. In many seminaries the courses in systematic theology are preponderantly philosophic and apologetic, and appeal to the head rather than the heart. This type of theology may produce ministers who preach *from* the Bible and who in a limited sense preach *the Bible*. But it can never produce real Bible expositors. Only a theology that is strictly Biblical and Biblically comprehensive, one which appeals to the heart as well as the head and addresses itself to man's deepest needs, as Scriptural truth always does, can accomplish this.

However, there is a vexing question which has caused endless disagreement and embarrassed progress in the development of interest in expository preaching and hindered cultivation of this type of pulpit ministry. The question is this: Is it possible to arrive at an authoritative, consistent, systematic theology that is not only strictly Biblical but Biblically comprehensive, which covers the whole range of revelation from eternity past to eternity future? In short, can the theology of the Bible be reduced to a coherent system in which seeming discrepancies disappear, difficulties and problems are explained, and order and symmetry appear?

Many preachers flatly deny that such an exhaustive, coherent and self-consistent Biblical theology is possible, or even desirable. They stress the fluidity and practicality of pulpit theology rather than its Biblical comprehensiveness and accuracy.[3] Others balk at the necessary distinctions which must be made in things that obviously differ, such as law and grace, the church and the kingdom, salvation and rewards, etc., in order to formulate such a system.[4] Others are openly hostile to distinguishing various ages in redemptive history, refusing to grant that God has dealt in different ways with man in different time periods and under different conditions.[5] Others are satisfied with a mere systematic philosophic or apologetic theology which is only Biblical to a limited extent, and fails

[3] H. Jeffs, *The Art of Exposition* (Boston, The Pilgrim Press, 1910), pp. 49-62.
[4] Oswald T. Allis, *Prophecy and the Church* (Philadelphia, Presbyterian & Reformed Publishing Co., 1945), pp. 16-54. For a contrast to this incorrect position see *Things that Differ (Essential Principles and Discriminations for Biblical Interpretation)* by W. H. Rogers (New York, Loizeaux Brothers, 1940), pp. 1-70.
[5] George L. Murray, *Millennial Studies* (Grand Rapids, Baker Book House, 1948), pp. 11-41.

to wrestle with essential doctrinal problems of the Bible. Still others, frightened away from seeking a sound Biblical system of theology by the Babel of unsound systems that exist, have shied away completely from an attempt at systematic formulation of Bible doctrine.

The result of this neglect or opposition to a comprehensive Biblical theology that deals as thoroughly, for example, with prophecy and eschatology as with soteriology and ecclesiology are systems of doctrine so partial or fragmentary that they offer little impetus to Bible exposition. They leave so many phases of revealed truth untouched, so many problems of interpretation unsolved, and so many Scriptural difficulties unexplained that the preacher trained in them is discouraged from attempting to embark on a Bible expository career.

On the other hand, the preacher who aspires to be an expositor must not only be thoroughly persuaded that an exhaustive, coherent and self-consistent system of Biblical theology is possible, but must bend every effort to discover that system, relentlessly test it in the crucible of God's revealed truth, master it, and make it a vital part of his life and service. Above all he must use it constantly in ministering the Word of God to the deepest heart needs both of the saved and unsaved, to whom he is called to preach.

3. THE EXPOSITOR AS A STUDENT OF BIBLICAL LANGUAGES

The preacher who aims to be an authoritative expositor, thoroughly equipped for his task, must be a student of the original languages in which the Bible is written. This fact is apparent from several simple considerations. In the first place, the accurate interpretation of any literary production, whether sacred or secular, depends upon an understanding of the original language in which it was written, and the Bible is no exception. In fact by the nature of its inspiration in which each and every word of its text is inspired in a manner distinct from any other piece of literature, the comprehenison of the original is of special significance.

In dealing with the sacred volume the careful student cannot proceed far without encountering fine points of exegesis. He is soon called upon to distinguish between subtle shades of meaning, or to decide on some important points of syntax, or to handle some difficult problems of text or interpretation. In such cases the original tongue constitutes the final court of appeal.

Without a knowledge of the original languages an expositor is entirely dependent upon secondary sources for his knowledge of what the Scriptures teach. This is the case inasmuch as only the original is the primary source. To the extent that the expositor is ignorant of the meaning of the original, he is denied access to the final court of appeal and the authoritative and trustworthy decision it is able to render.

This situation, however, does not mean that revealed truths cannot be acquired through the medium of a translation. They, of course, can. On the other hand it does mean that an expositor without a working knowledge of Hebrew, in which practically all of the Old Testament is written except small portions in Aramaic (Daniel 2:4 - 7:20; Ezra 4:8 - 6:18), and without a grasp of Hellenistic Greek, in which the entire New Testament is recorded, lacks the necessary tools to perfect his work and guard himself against inaccuracy of statement or conclusion or what is worse, to shield himself against falling into positive error.

Many of the popular errors that flourish in Christendom, as well as lopsided truths and doctrinal hobbies that furnish the basis for new sects and divisions in the professing Church, are due in large part to the activity of teachers and leaders deficient in their knowledge of the Hebrew and Greek Scriptures. Unable to subject their tenets to the test of the inspired original, they have in many instances popularized what might be called "translational theology." This type of doctrinal aberration, to the danger of which all teachers and preachers deficient in a knowledge of Hebrew and Greek are exposed, is based upon ambiguous and frequently erroneous renderings of the original languages rather than upon sound exegesis of the original languages themselves.

In the light of the tremendous responsibility which rests upon the preacher not only to preach the Word, but to preach it accurately and fully, it is nothing short of a moral duty for one who would handle the Scriptures to gain a mastery of the original Bible languages, if at all possible.[6] To refuse to take advantage of such an opportunity is to miss the chance to gain a knowledge of the use of tools that are indispensable for the fully qualified expositor.

The teacher who can not only feed the flock of God sound Scriptural truth but protect himself and those under his pastoral care from unsound doctrines as well, must be able to go to the primary source of truth in the original Hebrew and Greek Scriptures. If he is unable to do this, he is shut up to translators, commentaries and other secondary sources, which, for all he can prove, may be inaccurate and misleading. Knowledge of the original involves the very fountainhead of truth and is fundamental to the technical equipment of an expositor.

4. THE EXPOSITOR AS A STUDENT OF RELATED THEOLOGICAL DISCIPLINES

Although a working knowledge of the original languages of Scripture, together with the mastery of a comprehensive system of Biblical theology based squarely upon the careful exegesis of the original text, is the basic technical qualification of an expositor, other important areas of training are essential for the highest success in this field, beside a knowledge of the Bible itself.[7] Important among these is the field of ancient history and archeology.

Good expository preaching from the aspect of the technical equipment required demands more than knowledge of the letter of the Sacred Text. There must be also a grasp of sufficient background material to give proper interest and appeal and to illuminate the Scriptural passage. Courses in ancient history, geography and archeology, which deal with Bible times, are indispensable to the expositor. Very frequently accuracy of interpretation hinges upon the understanding of some ancient custom or historical event or some difficulty illustrated by the discoveries of modern archeology.

---

[6] Cf. G. Schodde, *Outlines of Biblical Hermeneutics* (Columbus, Ohio, Lutheran Book Concern, 1917), p. 154.
[7] Cf. Morgan, *op. cit.,* pp. 184-197.

If the expositor is ignorant of Biblical backgrounds, his exposition may not only run the risk of lacking color but also may incur the danger of being inaccurate.

Closely akin to the field of history and archeology in furnishing necessary background for exposition of the Bible is the department of ecclesiastical history, including the history of missions and Christian doctrine. With a comprehension of the development and expansion of the Church through the Christian centuries, together with a survey of the various doctrinal movements and developments in the various periods, the expositor is supplied with a valuable aid in interpreting the Scriptures to the present generation.

In the light of the example of twenty centuries of Church history, the student is able to see the constructive outworking of truth in the Church as well as the destructive effect of error. He is thus placed in a strategic position to embrace the one and avoid the other. In surveying the blessings of missionary activity as it has been manifested in the Church, he is enabled to enrich his expository ministry with the proper Biblical emphasis on world evangelism.

Other courses essential to a fully rounded preparation of the expositor for his work of expounding the Scriptures are Old and New Testament Introduction. These phases of study also furnish background material for expository work, but in addition deal with the defense of the Scriptures against rationalistic attack. Coupled with these areas of training must be courses in apologetics, Christian evidences and philosophy.

While formal courses in apologetics and philosophy and kindred studies are necessary to the best work of exposition, the true expositor will never rely upon these helps as his main strength and appeal. These adjuncts and aids will be kept strictly in a subordinate position.

To the expositor who utterly believes the Scriptures and who delights in them and continually studies them, the preaching of the Word itself will be its own best defense. The able expositor will realize that the surest way to cut through the serried ranks of rationalism and unbelief is to lay bare the Sword of the Spirit, the Word of God, and skillfully wield it. To him the Biblical and expository approach will always transcend the philosophic and apologetic. His choice of a seminary will be determined by this approach, as well as his emphasis in his preaching ministry.

5. THE EXPOSITOR AS A STUDENT OF THE PRACTICAL PHASES OF MINISTERIAL WORK

Besides the more theoretical courses the expository preacher needs training in practical homiletics to prepare him in the actual mechanics of preaching expository sermons. Work in preaching, however, is necessarily twofold. There is the theoretical which is actually inseparable from the practical.

Concerning the theory of preaching the expositor should be thoroughly acquainted with all the standard homiletical procedures — how they have been used as well as abused in the history of preaching, and how they may be employed in their highest and best manner in true exposition of the Word of God. To this end it is necessary to present a clear definition of what expository preaching is.[8] It is also essential to study illustrations of the expository method as it has been employed by outstanding expositors in the history of the Church[9] and to appreciate the possibilities of this type of preaching for challenging and holding the interest of audiences by the use of the various homiletical procedures to which the expository method is adapted.[10]

In addition to sound theory the expositor needs actual practice. If a man is called to preach, he ought to preach at once — not wait till he is trained. He ought to be preaching before he is trained and during his training, as well as after. G. Campbell Morgan's conviction is certainly sound: "I think no greater mistake can be made than to neglect preaching for a number of years."[11]

But the student preacher needs wise and sympathetic oversight in his pulpit ministry. He needs assistance perhaps most

---

[8] See Chapter IV.
[9] See Chapter V.
[10] See Chapter VI.
[11] *Op. cit.*, pp. 193f.

urgently immediately after his call to preach. Every pastor
should do his utmost to give encouragement and help to
young men in his congregation who fit this category. He can
do this by furnishing them occasional opportunity to exercise
their gift in some public service of the local church and by
stimulating them to attend the seminary that will best fit
them for a Bible-preaching ministry.

The seminary can perhaps do the most for the student
preacher in the matter of practice preaching. The work in
the sermon class is undoubtedly helpful, but preaching before one's class is at best speaking under somewhat artificial
conditions. Certain technicalities can no doubt be acquired
and faults and failures corrected in this manner but the
greatest assistance a seminary can offer its students in this
field is-to have an efficient public relations department designed to secure openings for student preaching and teaching during the academic year, as well as during vacations.

Such student preaching, in which the principles learned
in class may be put into practice under favorable conditions,
is highly beneficial in every way and is needed by every
seminarian. The theological student who does not preach
fairly regularly during his seminary career and who consequently does not have opportunity to put into practice what
he learns in the classroom, particularly in his courses in homiletics, labors under a very serious handicap, from which he
may suffer later on in his formal ministry. In the matter of
preaching, the best learning is done by ministering. The
only way to learn to preach is to preach. The only way to
learn to preach expositorily is to begin to expound the Word.

There are other practical phases of ministerial work, however, beside the homiletical. An expositor, if he is to be a
pastor, must be trained also in practical psychology, in human relationships, in Christian education, in church and
church-school organization and administration, and in all the
practical phases of the life of a good minister of Christ.

It is a tragedy to see an able pulpiteer and expositor, thoroughly trained in the art of exposition, whose education in
the other practical phases of church administration and ac-

tivity has been neglected. Able to do an outstanding work in expounding the Bible, but unable to enlist and put to work the people who crowd his services, his church severely suffers organizationally.

On the other hand, it is even more tragic to see a minister who has been thoroughly trained as an administrator and organizer build up a magnificent organization, but who has never been trained as an able expositor of the Word. The people whom he enlists he is unable to teach and lead on in the Christian life. If he has a saving message, he is unequipped to give the spiritual babes the meat of the Word that they might grow into Christian adulthood.

The ideal aim of every seminary ought to be to train adequately in both important areas — the area of preaching and that of administration. Then people will not only be attracted to the public services, but will be regenerated and built up in the Christian life as a result. What is also of great importance, as strong Christians they will be enlisted in strategic places of leadership.

LITERATURE ON THE TECHNICAL EQUIPMENT OF AN EXPOSITOR

Davidson, Samuel, Sacred Hermeneutics (Edinburgh, 1843), pp. 252-319.
Fairbairn, Patrick, Hermeneutical Manual (Edinburgh, T. & T. Clark, 1858), pp. 63-166.
Muencher, J., Manual of Biblical Interpretation (Gambier, Ohio, 1865), pp. 145-173.
Immer, A., Hermeneutics of the New Testament, ɩ.anslated by A. H. Newman (Andover, 1877), pp. 159-183.
Adams, John, Sermons in Syntax (Edinburgh, T. & T. Clark, 1908), Chaps. I, II.
Angus, J. and S. G. Green, The Bible Handbook (New York, Fleming Revell, 1908; reprint, Grand Rapids, Zondervan Publishing House), pp. 201-215.
Terry, Milton S., Biblical Hermeneutics (New York, Methodist Book Concern, 1911), Chap. II.
Burnham, Sylvester, Elements of Biblical Hermeneutics (Hamilton, N. Y. Republican Press, 1916).
Schodde, G., Outlines of Biblical Hermeneutics (Columbus, Ohio, Lutheran Book Concern, 1917), pp. 154-179.
Scroggie, W. Graham, Know Your Bible (London, Pickering & Inglis, 1940), Vols. I and II.
Berkhof, Louis, Principles of Biblical Interpretation (Grand Rapids, Baker Book House, 1950), pp. 67-166.

CHAPTER IX

THE BASIC DOCTRINAL PREREQUISITES OF AN EXPOSITOR

A preacher, it is true, does not have to subscribe to an elaborate system of doctrine before he can start out on a career as an expositor, but he does need certain fundamental convictions concerning the Bible. Unless he believes this book is unique, unlike any other literature, either ancient or modern, he will have neither the motive nor the desire to undertake the rigorous program of preparation necessary for the difficult task of expounding the Scriptures. Moreover, unless he is persuaded this book is reliable historically, archeologically, scientifically, textually and doctrinally, he is not likely to take great pains to give a serious and comprehensive account of its message.

If the minister is an extreme liberal and the Bible is to him little more than a fallible collection of ancient religious traditions, often discordant and contradictory, and inspired only in the sense that all great literature is inspired, why should he attempt to expound it systematically, or expect to see in it doctrinal detail, or divine plan and purpose? Or if one revolts against the extremism of modern liberalism with its inevitable spiritual superficiality (in some cases bankruptcy), and adopts more mediating views of the Bible and inspiration such as are represented by so-called neo-orthodoxy or Barthianism and similar movements in the direction of conservatism, one may to some degree avoid the superficiality of extreme liberalism, but he will not yet have reached the sound position necessary for true Bible exposition.

Neo-orthodoxy, for instance, in accepting the essential conclusions of destructive higher criticism and empirical science, rejects an infallible Bible and berates what it calls "the literalism of fundamentalism."[1] In rejecting an infallible Bible protagonists of this movement necessarily reject that which is closely connected with an infallible Bible — plenarily and verbally inspired Bible.[2] The result is that, if they are not completely robbed of ardor for genuine Bible exposition by their position, but seek to give a serious accounting of the message of the Scriptures, they take such unwarranted liberties that their interpretations are unsound and uncomprehensive doctrinally.

If a minister is to have the impetus to be an expositor and possess a solid foundation upon which to build a career as an exponent of divine truth, he must have certain definite convictions concerning the Bible as the Word of God. Without these as a starting point he is like the man whose house, built upon the sand, was swept away when the storm came (Matt. 7: 24-29).

1. THE EXPOSITOR MUST BELIEVE THE BIBLE IS A DIVINE REVELATION

Unless there is a firm conviction that God has disclosed His redemptive plans and purposes to man in written objective form in the Holy Scriptures, there can be little progress in the exposition of the content of that revelation. But when it is apprehended that in the pages of the Bible God has communicated to the mind of man truth that otherwise would be unknown and unknowable to the mind of man, the first step fundamental to Biblically correct interpretation is taken.

It is essential that the expositor become fully aware not only of the *necessity* of divine revelation, but of its reasonableness. If God created man in His own image and endowed him with capacity for divine communication, it is

---

[1] See Bernard Ramm's discussion of this approach in *Protestant Biblical Interpretation* (Boston, W. A. Wilde Co., 1950), pp. 41-47.

[2] See Otto Piper's attack on verbal inspiration in "Discovering the Bible," *Christian Century* (Feb. 1946), 63:266 and in "The Authority of the Bible," *Theology Today* (July, 1949), 6:159-173. For Emil Brunner's attack see throughout his volume *Revelation and Inspiration*.

natural to expect that the Creator would communicate Himself and His mind to his rational creature. If unfallen man needed divine revelation and instruction (Gen. 2:16, 17; 3:8), how much more fallen man, completely incapacitated by sin.

The expositor must also come to understand the progressiveness of God's revelation. The divine self-disclosure as it pertains to the written objective revelation contained in the Scriptures had a beginning and an ending in time. "Between these termini, separated by many centuries, God revealed His doctrine, plans and eternal purpose gradually, progressively, unfolding the revelatory bloom petal by petal."[3] Not only must the progressiveness of these unfoldments be realized, but because of this fact, systematic study of them "is necessary for the acquirement of a balanced knowledge of the Truth."[4]

Further, there must be a clear comprehension of the *orderliness* in the progress of God's plans and purposes. There can be little advance in genuine exposition of Biblical truth until the fact is seen that God has revealed a definite sequence of events through which his eternal purpose for man and the earth is to be accomplished. Nothing is more detrimental to expository handling of Sacred Scripture than to deny God has revealed such an orderly plan or to doubt that this divine purpose may be known and followed as the foundation of systematic dealing with revealed truth.

When the student comes to the conviction that the Bible, as God's revealed truth, does contain the orderly plan of the divine purpose for man and the earth from eternity past to eternity future, and that this plan may and ought to be known, he is at once set on the right path which leads to the fullest possible knowledge of God's ways with men. In addition, he is orientated in God's programmed purpose in the matter of his testimony and service in the particular age or time period of the history of redemption in which he lives.

On the other hand, lack of conviction that the Bible does

[3] Rollin Thomas Chafer, *The Science of Biblical Hermeneutics* (Dallas, *Bibliotheca Sacra*, 1939), p. 34.
[4] *Loc. cit.*

outline a definite divine plan for man and the earth not only bars the student from a career as a Bible expositor by restricting him to superficial and disconnected handling of Scripture, but also exposes him to the attacks of negative criticism and destructive interpretation. By being blinded to the various periods or ages in which God deals in a particular way with man according to certain revealed conditions, the student is placed in a sphere which admits a wide scope of mere human opinion. The result is hopeless confusion. Things different are identified as being the same, and things that are identical are made to differ. Not only are common matters of Biblical revelation such as the believer's salvation and his service confounded, but other momentous subjects like the trustworthiness of predictive prophecy are cast in doubt.

In dealing with revealed truth, however, it is important to note that the Scriptures do not outline God's complete program in any one context. Here and there various segments of it, varying in comprehensiveness, are revealed. These sections will be found to dovetail with other revealed sections. The entire witness of Scripture must be painstakingly studied in relation to the separate portions. What, upon careful analysis, at first seems to be a disconnected mass of fragments, like a jig saw puzzle, will be found upon prayerful synthesis, to fit together perfectly and to produce a clear picture of the divine redemptive program.

2. THE EXPOSITOR MUST BELIEVE THE BIBLE IS A PRODUCT OF DIVINE INSPIRATION

It is not sufficient that one who aspires to expound the Bible believes that it is a divine revelation. He must also believe that God so wrought upon the human recipients of that revelation as to keep it free from error. This "supernatural influence exerted on the sacred writers by the Spirit of God, by virtue of which their writings are given divine trustworthiness."[5] is called inspiration.

Inspiration, which is so essential to God's self-disclosure

---

[5] Benjamin B. Warfield, "Inspiration," in the *International Standard Bible Encyclopedia* (Grand Rapids, Wm. B. Eerdmans Publishing Co., 1939), p. 1473.

to man because of the fallible human recipient, is inseparable from revelation. In fact, the doctrine of Scriptural inspiration, as Rollin Chafer correctly says, "is one of the disclosures of God's revelation and not something extraneous to it."[6] That the Scriptural doctrine teaches the plenary-verbal view is apparent from a careful consideration of II Timothy 3:16, 17: "All scripture is inspired by God and profitable for teaching, for reproof, for correction and for training in righteousness, that the man of God may be complete, equipped for every good work" (RSV).

This pivotal passage in explicit terms teaches five great truths concerning Scripture which are of basic importance to the expositor. First, the Bible is plenarily inspired — "all"; secondly, the plenary inspiration specifically concerns the Old Testament (and later when the Sacred Canon was completed, the New Testament also) — "all scripture"; thirdly, the divine authorship of Scripture — "is inspired by God" ("God-breathed"); fourthly, the supreme value of all Scripture to the spiritual life because of its inspiration — "profitable for teaching, for reproof, for correction, for training in righteousness"; fifthly, the holy purpose of Scripture, "that the man of God may be complete, equipped for every good work."[7]

Unless one who would expound the Bible is willing to subscribe to the testimony of the Scripture itself concerning its inspiration — that all of it is inspired by God not only the concepts or thoughts, but the very words themselves (I Cor. 2:13) — he will be seriously crippled in the work of an expositor. His view of inspiration is, in reality, fundamental. It is the rock-ribbed foundation upon which he must build the structure of his preaching.[8] It is the fountainhead whence must flow the stream of truth he is to propound. If the foundation is faulty, the structure built upon it will be shaky. If the spring is poisoned at its source, it will contaminate all the streams which flow from it.

[6] *Op. cit.*, p. 38.
[7] Cf. Merrill F. Unger, *Introductory Guide to the Old Testament* (Grand Rapids, Zondervan Publishing House, 1951), p. 25.
[8] Cf. Ramm, *op. cit.*, p. 48.

It is precisely for this reason that present-day professed movements toward conservatism, such as neo-orthodoxy, can never produce a basis for sound exegesis or foster reliable Bible expositors. In rejecting an infallible, plenarily inspired Bible this theological trend must at the same time reject any sound method of interpretation based on an infallible Bible, such as the grammatical-historical method. Instead it offers a mythological system.

By a mythological interpretation, however, the neo-orthodox theologian does not mean the fanciful or the imaginative. He simply holds that the persons or things that are claimed to exist in the tale or legend in order to symbolize some theological truth or concept, actually have no demonstrable existence. They are purely conveyors of theological truth in historical dress. But the theological truth, we are told, is quite independent of the actual unhistoricity of the garb.[9] Under this treatment such great events as the creation of Genesis 1 and 2, the fall of Genesis 3 and the flood of Genesis 6-9 are denied literality and actual historicity but nevertheless are claimed to be the valid conveyors of certain theological truths.

Under such handling of the Word a measure of theological doctrine may, it is true, be salvaged. However, a system of interpretation like this, based on such a view of the Bible, may square itself with the alleged findings of rationalistic higher criticism and the assumed conflicts of science with Scripture, but it can never produce sound and thorough Bible expositors. Although it may not incur the doctrinal sterility of liberalism, it will nevertheless not wholly escape its theological and interpretational superficiality.

The failure of neo-orthodoxy from the point of view of the Bible expositor is manifested not only in its *mythological* or symbolic approach, but also by its *existential* method of interpretation. In both of these ways neo-orthodox theologians reject the full authoritativeness of the Bible. The Scripture, which they allow to be historically and scientifically errant, is not so much the Word of God as it *becomes* the Word of

[9] *Ibid.*, p. 43.

God to one as it is made real to him in the existential or actual "life" situation.[10]

However, to the true expositor it is quite obvious that without the acceptance of full Scriptural authority, which is so inseparably connected with a sound view of Scriptural inspiration, there can be no correct and comprehensive exposition of the contents of the Bible. If the Bible is not objectively, and quite apart from its acceptance or non-acceptance, fully the Word of God, in all its parts as well as in its whole, its authoritativeness is made a matter of subjective human judgment, and hence becomes a variable element and practically valueless to the genuine expositor.

3. THE EXPOSITOR MUST BELIEVE THE BIBLE IS DIVINELY ILLUMINATED

Quite as essential to the work of an expositor as the belief that the Bible is a divine revelation and a product of divine inspiration is the conviction that it is a spiritually discerned Book and can only be comprehended as it is illuminated by the Holy Spirit. The necessity of the enlightening ministry of the Spirit appears from a simple comparison between revelation, inspiration and illumination. Revelation involves God giving truth. Inspiration concerns man accurately receiving and recording that truth under divine control. Illumination comprehends man correctly understanding the inspired record of the truth.

But it is quite obvious that, although God gave the truth and man under divine guidance accurately received and recorded the truth given, yet man would still be left incapacitated unless further divine aid were vouchsafed to him to understand it.

There is no fact that the successful expositor needs to realize more clearly than this — that he is shut up to the ministry of God's Spirit in order to understand the Word of God himself in order to expound it to others. Without a deep conviction of this truth manifested in a continual humble dependence upon the Spirit's teaching ministry there can

[10] *Ibid.*, pp. 44-47.

positively be no true advancement in the art of expository preaching. This attitude of complete reliance upon the Holy Spirit is absolutely indispensable to real expository work.

Our Lord stressed the importance of the illuminating ministry of the Holy Spirit in his significant prophecy of the advent of the Spirit. "When the Spirit of truth comes, he will guide you into all truth . . ." (John 16:13, RSV). "He will *conduct* you (lead you in the way, *hodegesei*) into all truth."

The Apostle Paul also lays great emphasis upon this vital point. The words which the true expositor speaks are "not in the words which man's wisdom teacheth, but which the Holy Ghost teacheth" (I Cor. 2:13). These Spirit-taught words, moreover, are said to be completely incomprehensible to the unsaved or "natural" man. The reason given is that they are "spiritually discerned" — *anakrinetai*, (spiritually judged or determined) (I Cor. 2:14). In other words, their meaning is elucidated by means of the Holy Spirit.

4. The Expositor Must Believe the Bible Can Be Accurately Interpreted

The development of expository preaching has been greatly retarded by a widespread spirit of doubt among ministers that the Bible is subject to detailed and systematic exposition, or that it was ever meant to be interpreted as a coherent whole in logical relation to its parts. However, until a student is prepared to adopt this view of the unity of the Bible, he will be seriously crippled in any successful expository efforts.

If, however, one is persuaded that Scripture is a divine revelation, inspired by God, and subject to divine illumination, he will have little difficulty believing the Bible may be accurately and exhaustively interpreted. It is only as an interpreter rejects the basic facts of Scriptural revelation, inspiration and illumination, that he robs himself of the opportunity of proving the Bible on this point. The student who is untrammeled by unsound presuppositions concerning Biblical revelation, inspiration and illumination will have little difficulty in being persuaded that the Bible has marvelous plan and purpose, and that it may be systematically and exhaustively expounded in a coherent and logical way. Honest and devout study along these lines will soon yield ample proofs of the wonderful unity and coherency of the divine plan of redemption.

LITERATURE ON THE DOCTRINAL PREREQUISITES OF AN EXPOSITOR

Burgon, J. W., *Inspiration and Interpretation* (London, J. H. and James Parker, 1861).

Young, William H., *How to Preach with Power* (Athens, Ga., How Publishing Co., 1897).

Tigert, John J., *The Preacher Himself* (Nashville, M. E. Church, South, 1899).

Garvie, Alfred E., *A Guide to Preachers* (New York, George H. Doran, 1906), pp. 273-339.

Forsythe, P. T., *Positive Preaching and the Modern Mind* (New York, A. C. Armstrong, 1908).

Angus, J. and S. G. Green, *The Bible Handbook* (New York, Fleming Revell, 1908; reprint, Grand Rapids, Zondervan Publishing House), Chaps. VI, X.

Jeffs, H., *The Art of Exposition* (Boston, The Pilgrim Press, 1910), Chap. IV.

Morgan, G. Campbell, *The Ministry of the Word* (New York, Fleming Revell, 1919).

Smith, Arthur H., *Preachers and Preaching* (Philadelphia, United Lutheran Publication House, 1925).

Hovey, A., *The Bible and How to Teach It* (Philadelphia, American Baptist Publication Society, n.d.), pp. 121-173.

Montgomery, R. Ames, *Preparing Preachers to Preach* (Grand Rapids, 1939).

Ramm, Bernard, *Protestant Biblical Interpretation* (Boston, W. A. Wilde Co., 1950), Chaps. III, VI.

Berkhof, L., *Principles of Biblical Interpretation* (Grand Rapids, Baker Book House, 1950), Chap. IV.

CHAPTER X

THE EXPOSITOR AND THE LAWS OF LOGIC

Although the Bible is a divine revelation, spiritually discerned, and can only be comprehended in its essential message through the ministry of the Holy Spirit as the interpreter is adjusted to the laws which govern the Spirit's operation,[1] it is nevertheless also a human book. As such it is a body of literature to be interpreted logically like any other piece of literature. Milton S. Terry is correct in stressing that the writers of the several parts of the Bible and those who assume to explain what is written in the Scriptures "are alike supposed to be in accord with the logical operations of the human mind."[2]

But little reflection is required to demonstrate the importance of sound logic in the work of an expositor. Despite the fact that the believer is Spirit-indwelt and Spirit-taught and, as a result, is divinely enabled to perceive the truth of the inspired revelation, an ability not possessed by the unregenerate, it remains also true that the attainment of a comprehensive and correlated knowledge of revelation is dependent upon strict observance of the laws regulating logical thought. Intelligent Bible study, therefore, predicates a logical procedure on the part of the student inasmuch as the Scriptures themselves are written in conformity with the laws governing the logical processes of the human mind.

The expository preacher, accordingly, needs training in the principles of logic, which may be defined in general terms as "the science of the principles which govern correct think-

[1] See Chapter VII, "The Spiritual Qualifications of an Expositor."
[2] Milton S. Terry, *Biblical Hermeneutics* (New York, Methodist Book Concern, 1911), p. 71.

ing and sound reasoning."[3] Only as the student learns to think correctly and reason soundly can he study to show himself "approved unto God, a workman that needeth not to be ashamed, rightly dividing the word of truth" (II Tim. 2:15).

But two basic presuppositions are necessary to the study of the principles of logical thinking. The first is that "there is such a thing as truth, which can be ascertained, and on which all minds, acting in accordance with the laws of thought must agree."[4] This postulate is true of all knowledge on the human plane which comes into the purview of the natural mind. It is true also of the human aspect of the Bible. But since Scripture has also a divine aspect, this principle must be expanded to include this unique factor in understanding the divine revelation. Accordingly, as postulated for Biblical study this presupposition may thus be stated. "There is such a thing as truth, which can be ascertained, and on which all minds, acting in accordance with the laws of thought and *under the Holy Spirit's tuition,* must agree."

The second presupposition underlying the science of logic, and important to the study of the Bible, is that it is possible "to state explicitly in language all that is implicitly contained in thought."[5] Logic deals ultimately with thought and concerns language only insofar as it expresses thought. Since the province of Bible exposition is to arrive at the meaning the inspiration of the Holy Spirit, the close connection be- of God's thought as recorded in human language through tween logic and the interpretation of Scripture is evident. Moreover, if it were impossible to convey thought to the human mind through the medium of language, both the science of logic and the interpretation of Scripture would be impossible.

The laws of logic important to exposition of the Bible are four in number. Clear understanding of them and careful

---

[3] Rollin Thomas Chafer, *The Science of Biblical Hermeneutics* (Dallas, *Bibliotheca Sacra,* 1939), p. 39.
[4] *Ibid.,* p. 45.
[5] *Ibid.,* p. 46.

observance of them are necessary to accurate interpretation of Scripture. Many sincere Christians are confused in their comprehension of large portions of revealed truth because they have taken up with illogical interpretations instead of the logical conclusions of the testimony of the Word itself.

1. THE LAW OF IDENTITY OR AFFIRMATION

This principle, which is the foundation of all consistent affirmative thinking, may be stated thus: "Everything is identical with itself, or what it is, and we may affirm this of it."[6] According to this law Scripture declares God is (Gen. 1:1; John 1:1) and that He is what He is, God, the Creator (Gen. 1:1) the Redeemer (John 1:14; 3:16). In addition, it asserts that He who is consistently identified with Himself as immanent and yet transcendant over all His creation, must be approached on the basis of faith. "For he that cometh to God must believe that he is . . ." (Heb. 11:6). This faith, moreover, is what it is, belief in the existence of God, as that existence is presented in the pages of revealed truth.

Moreover, regarding man the Bible declaration is that he came to exist as a direct creation of God (Gen. 1:27), that he was created innocent of evil and not subject to death (Gen. 2:17), but that he fell from his innocency (Gen. 3:1-13), into sin, thus incurring physical and spiritual death (Gen. 3:19; Rom. 5:15-21). Thus man is what he is declared to be, man, a direct creation of God, a creature who fell from his pristine state of innocence and is lost. To deny these facts of revelation is to be cast upon the limitless sea of human speculation. It is to assert that man was evolved, not created, that he did not fall and does not need salvation, that he did not spiritually die and does not need spiritual life.

In reference to sin the Bible affirms that it is what it is — sin — that it is a terrible reality, that it is rebellion against God (Is. 14:12-14), that it is lawlessness (I John 3:4), that it involves a far-reaching curse (Gen. 3:17-19) and, if unatoned, entails eternal separation from God in "the lake of fire" (Rev. 20:10). To deny that sin is what it is revealed to be results, for example, in the spiritual bankruptcy of

[6] *Ibid.,* p. 40.

modernism or the theological vagaries of such a cult as Christian Science.

The expositor cannot dodge this inexorable law of logic if he would expound the Sacred Scriptures. The reason is simple. Revealed truth is expressed according to the laws of logical thought. By the law of identity or affirmation the expositor must affirm that which is identical with itself, or what it is, and deny that which is not identical with itself, or what it is.

2. THE LAW OF CONTRADICTION OR NEGATION

This second important principle of thought is closely connected with the first. By the law of identity whatever is *is*. By the law of contradiction whatever is not *is not*.[7] Stated in other words: "Everything is not what it is not, and we may affirm this of it."[8] Often called the law of non-contradiction,[9] this principle states that "nothing can both be and not be,"[10] or that nothing can both be the same and different.

This elementary rule of logic is of immense importance to the expositor. Stated baldly it is so simple in its meaning as to be almost a truism. Yet no principle of logic is more widely violated than this. Whereas Scripture never identifies things that differ,[11] men in handling the Word of God ar' frequently guilty of this serious blunder. Popular theological systems of interpretations like amillennialism and postmillennialism flourish because of a failure to distinguish between things that differ. Many new sects are built on the same logical fallacy.

But the Scriptures never confound opposites. For example, the baptism of the Spirit and the filling of the Spirit, so commonly confused in popular theology of our day, are saliently differentiated in the Bible.[12] Moreover, when this

[7] F. Ryland, *Logic: An Introductory Manual* (London, G. Bell & Sons, 1900), p. 74.

[8] Chafer, *op. cit.,* p. 40.

[9] Ryland, *op. cit.*, pp. 74-77.

[10] *Ibid.,* p. 74.

[11] For a useful brief study of this see W. H. Rogers, *Things That Differ* (*Essential Principles and Discriminations for Biblical Interpretation*) (New York, Loizeaux Brothers, 1940), pp. 1-70.

[12] See the present author's, *The Baptizing Work of the Holy Spirit* (Wheaton, Ill., Van Kampen Press, 1953), pp. 15-20.

distinction is observed by the competent expositor, the theological basis of a number of modern sects is removed. Again, law and grace are plainly contrasted in Scripture. Observance of this one distinction alone would purge out the leaven of legalism that has so seriously corrupted the Gospel of Christ throughout the history of the Christian Church.

A thing cannot be what it is not. Paul states this principle in theological application to the much abused law-grace theme when he writes: "And if by grace, then is it no more of works: otherwise grace is no more grace. But if it be of works, then is it no more grace: otherwise work is no more work" (Rom. 11:6).

The Bible is literally filled with such truths that are to be connected, yet carefully differentiated. Failure to distinguish themes that differ is one of the most prolific sources of the doctrinal jumble that parades under the aegis of the Church of Christ. While not a few heresies are the result of denying or distorting the great declarations of truth recorded in Scripture concerning God, man, sin, salvation and kindred truths, in violation of the first law of logic, the preponderance of doctrinal confusion prevalent among Bible-believing conservatives is due to infraction of the second law. Whether in the interests of a sectarian dogma, some denominational hobby, or some unsound theory of interpretation, men in approaching the Bible do what they would not think of doing with any other piece of literature. They fail to distinguish things that differ and infringe upon the law of contradiction, which lies at the basis of all distinctions in thought.

Illustrations of infringement of this principle of logic may be cited almost ad infinitum. Some of the more important examples are salvation and rewards, position and present condition, Israel, the Gentiles and the Church of God, the Church and the kingdom, the Gospel of grace and the Gospel of the kingdom.

Salvation in the Bible is presented solely on the basis of faith in Christ. No part of it may be earned or merited; it is purely a free gift (John 3:16) accepted on the basis of the redemptive work of Christ (Eph. 2:8-10). By contrast, rewards are not gifts at all, but are the results of faithful service after one is saved (I Cor. 3:11-15). To confuse these two themes is to court confusion.

Likewise the believer is presented as possessing a standing "in Christ," which is perfect as Christ Himself is perfect, and unchangeable as God Himself is unchangeable (Heb. 13: 8). The believer's actual state, however, is a matter of knowledge of his unchangeable position, and of the exercise of faith to convert the position he has into a state he may enjoy (Rom. 6:11). The Scriptures distinguish these two vital aspects of the believer's salvation — his unchanging position in Christ and his changing experience of Christ. To ignore these distinctions, as many do, is to plunge the whole doctrine of deliverance from sin into utter confusion.

Another important contrast commonly ignored by Bible students is the ethnic distinction between Jew, Gentile, and the Church of God (I Cor. 10:32). Yet each of these three ethnic groups are carefully differentiated in this present age. The Bible clearly teaches that unsaved people today are either Jews or Gentiles. Saved people, however, lose their identity as "Jews or Gentiles" and are presented as baptized by the Holy Spirit into Christ (Rom. 6:3, 4) and into His Body (I Cor. 12:13), thus forming a unique entity "The Church of God."

The Church of God and the kingdom as promised to Israel (Acts 1:6) are two other Scriptural concepts that are trenchantly differentiated in the Bible, but completely confounded by many Bible teachers. The Church of Christ, formed by the baptism of the Spirit (Acts 1:5; 2:1-5), came into existence at Pentecost (Acts 5:14; 11:16), and is formed of all the saved from that time till the return of Christ for His Body (I Cor. 12:13; Tit. 2:13).

On the other hand, the kingdom promised so glowingly to Israel by Isaiah (11:1-16; 35:1-10) and other Old Testament prophets (Mic. 4:1-5; Zech. 14:1-10), preached by John the Baptist and Jesus (Matt. 3:1; 4:17), but which was rejected and the King put to death at His first advent, shall yet be established at the second advent (Rev. 19:11-16; Rev. 20:4).

The matter of the Gospel of the grace of God and the Gospel of the kingdom furnishes another example of the failure of many to distinguish what the Bible saliently distinguishes. The Gospel of the grace of God is the message of full and free salvation to the whosoever will believe (John 3:16) in the vicarious death and glorious resurrection of Christ (I Cor. 15:1-4). It is preached for the out-calling of the Church, the Body of Christ (Rom. 1:16, 17).

The Gospel of the kingdom by contrast is still good news and good news, of course, based upon Christ's finished work and resurrection. But its distinctive message is that the King is coming to set up His earthly reign over Israel and the nations (Matt. 24:14). Moreover, it will be preached during the Great Tribulation after the Church of God has been completed and taken to heaven (II Thess. 2:1-4) by the believing Jewish remnant of those days (Rev. 7:1-8).

To refuse to subscribe to this distinction of the Word of God results in contradiction and confusion. If "the gospel of the kingdom" is identical with the "gospel of God's grace" now preached, how can "he that shall endure to the end, the same shall be saved" (Matt. 24:13) be reconciled with full and free salvation as a gift to him that believeth (Eph. 2:8-10)?

In addition to these and other themes that obviously are not to be confused by identifying that which the Scriptures differentiate, the Bible presents eight different covenants, which must be carefully distinguished. These are the Edenic (Gen. 1:26-28; 2:15-17), the Adamic (Gen. 3:14-19), the Noahic (Gen. 9:1-17), the Abrahamic (Gen. 12:1-4), the Mosaic (Ex. 20:1-20), the Palestinian (Deut. 28-30), the Davidic (II Sam. 7:4-17), and the New (Heb. 8:6).

The average system of Biblical interpretation practically ignores these various covenants and substitutes either just the Old Testament (Covenant) and the New Testament (Covenant) or theorizes on the basis of an artificial "covenant of works" to designate blessings God has offered men on the basis of human merit and by which Adam before the fall was related to God and a "covenant of grace" (the term does not occur in Scripture) which supposedly describes all aspects of divine favor toward men in all ages. But this open violation of the law of contradiction can only mean confusion of interpretation.

Similarly, revealed truth plainly distinguishes seven different periods in God's dealing with the creatures of His creation (Eph. 3:2, Col. 1:25). These clearly defined time-periods are for the most part illogically ignored in the popular systems of interpretation of our day. In addition, in many instances an attitude of hostility is adopted against expositors who take into account these time distinctions, as if they were highly injurious to the truth. In reality, however, these teachers "rightly divide the Word" by not only accepting unquestioningly the great affirmations of the Bible, according to the first law of logic, but also by observing the distinctions on this particular subject which the Word plainly demands, according to the second law of logic.

Each of these periods, sometimes called dispensations, involves a distinctive divine dealing with man in respect to some revelation of the divine will. Each involves man's failure, with consequent divine judgment. The period of innocence involved the test of not eating the fruit of the knowledge of good and evil. Man's failure resulted in expulsion from the garden and the curse of sin upon the human race (Gen. 3:14-17).

The period of conscience involved man's knowing good and evil, living according to the dictates of his conscience and being responsible to do good and offer sacrifice (Gen. 4:4-7). The result was corruption of all flesh and the judgment of the flood (Gen. 7:11-24). Similarly, in the period of human government man had a fresh start in a righteous remnant preserved through the flood, with responsibility to rule the earth for God (Gen. 9:7-17). His failure culminated in the judgment of the tongues at Babel (Gen. 11:8, 9).

The period of promise, began with the call of Abraham, gave way to law when Israel accepted the responsibility of obeying

the Sinaitic legislation (Ex. 3:3 - 31:18). This era came to an
end in the crucifixion of Christ (Matt. 27:51), and was superseded by the dispensation of grace beginning with the resurrection and ascension of Christ and the advent of the Spirit
(Acts 2:1-5) to form the Church. This era will end with the
translation of the Church (I Thess. 4:13-18) and the judgment
of apostate Christendom (Rev. 4:1-19:21).

The period of peace, the last of the ordered ages before
the dawn of eternity, will be inaugurated at the glorious
coming of Christ. The test, to worship and serve the King
(Zech. 14:16-20), will result in man's eventual rebellion
(Rev. 20:8) and God's judgment (Rev. 20:10-15), which
will usher in the eternal state.

A correct knowledge of these ordered ages is necessary
to the logical handling of the Word of God. Disregard of
them will result in confusion, untenable systems of interpretation, unsolvable difficulties and inevitable contradictions.

3. THE LAW OF THE EXCLUDED MIDDLE

This principle of thought is much less self-evident than
either the law of identity or law of contradiction, but "it is
equally important and necessary with them."[13] The law
may be stated simply in these words: "Of two contradictories
one must be true and the other false. If one is affirmed,
the other is denied."[14] The designation of the law expresses
the fact that "there is no third or middle course; the answer
must be Yes or No."[15]

To illustrate, the Bible is either plenarily and verbally inspired or it is not. If by the law of identity it is a fact that
the Scripture declares that it is plenarily and verbally inspired, it is logical for the expositor whose business it is to
expound — not deny — what the Bible says, to affirm this
fact. Nor can he, by the law of the excluded middle, logically
affirm any other kind or degree of inspiration but plenary
and verbal, which embraces all the Bible and every word in

13 Jevons, W. S. and David J. Hill, *Elements of Logic* (New York, American
Book Co., 1911), p. 106.
14 Chafer, *op. cit.*, p. 44.
15 Jevons and Hill, *op. cit.*, p. 106.

the Bible. To posit inspiration of only part of the Bible or of anything less than the actual words, such as concepts or ideas, is to violate the law of the excluded middle and illogically to substitute for "Biblical inspiration" some opposite or contradictory term.

Again, predictive prophecy is either a component of the divine revelation or it is not. If, by the law of identity, it is a fact that the Scriptures contain predictive prophecy, then, by the law of the excluded middle, that they do not contain it is false.

Again, the Word of God can or cannot be comprehended by the unaided human intellect. If by the law of identity it is true that the Bible affirms the utter inability of the natural or unregenerate man to receive or to know "the things of the Spirit of God," because they are "spiritually discerned" (*i.e.*, "understood only by means of the Holy Spirit") (I Cor. 2:14), it is logical for the expositor of the Bible to assert this truth. Nor can he, by the law of the excluded middle, logically take any other position than that of man's complete dependence upon the Spirit of God to understand the Word of God.

4. THE LAW OF SUFFICIENT REASON

This important rule of thought, first formulated by the philosopher Gottfried von Leibnitz (1646), and by him placed side by side with the law of contradiction, is that "every judgment must be based upon some satisfactory ground which fully justifies it."[16] This principle is essentially the statement of the basic logical foundation upon which all inference rests — "that our knowledge forms a system of interrelated and coordinated parts, and that any single element can be determined only when its relation is known to some other element or elements upon which it depends."[17]

This law is of special importance to the expositor of the Bible because "it recognizes a reciprocal dependence of part

[16] J. G. Hibben, *Logic Deductive and Inductive* (New York, Charles Scribner's Sons, 1905), p. 102.
[17] *Ibid.*

to part throughout the entire body of knowledge."[18] In true Bible exposition nothing is more essential than this recognition of the mutual dependence of each part to the whole body of revealed truth. Failure rigidly to test isolated conclusions as well as over-all systems of interpretation in the light of the complete testimony of Scripture is one of the cardinal transgressions in the field of Bible exposition.

The law of sufficient reason is evident throughout Scripture. Paul's numerous "thens," "therefores," and "wherefores" in his epistles furnish an excellent example. Each argument is closely connected by way of inference or conclusion with his preceding argument. In Ephesians 4:1 he exhorts believers to an *experience* or walk (4:1 - 6:24) consonant with their glorious position in union with Christ (1:1 - 3:21). In I Corinthians 15:58 he exhorts his "beloved brethren" to be "stedfast, immoveable, always abounding in the work of the Lord" in the light of the great truths unfolded concerning the resurrection (I Cor. 15:1-57). In Colossians 3:1 he urges a heavenly walk and in Romans 6:12 a holy walk; in each case in the light of the preceding context.

In the four fundamental laws of reasoning it is evident that certain logical requirements are made to which all processes of thought, including, of course, Biblical thought, must adhere. The law of identity demands a basis of constant reference, which the inspired and authoritative Word of God supplies. The law of contradiction demands thorough and consistent treatment of the Sacred Text. The law of the excluded middle demands an exhaustive survey of possibilities of interpretation. The law of sufficient reason demands adequate bases and complete explanation for conclusions.

While there are many rules which exist for guidance in the various processes of inference, these are merely adaptations of some one or other of the several phases of the four fundamental principles of correct thinking. Strict observance of these basic laws of thought is of the utmost importance to the expositor of the Bible and will keep him from tolerat-

[18] *Ibid.*

ing untenable systems of interpretation or from being led astray by unsound conclusions.

Literature on Logic

Harvey, G. W., *A System of Christian Rhetoric* (New York, Harper & Brothers, 1873), pp. 219-240.

Davis, Noah K., *Elements of Deductive Logic* (New York, Harper & Brothers, 1896).

Hibben, J. G., *Logic Deductive and Inductive* (New York, Charles Scribner's Sons, 1905).

Ryland, F., *Logic: An Introductory Manual* (London, G. Bell & Sons, 1900).

Taylor, W. J., *Elementary Logic* (New York, Charles Scribner's Sons, 1909).

Jevons, W. S. and David J. Hill, *Elements of Logic* (New York, American Book Co., 1911).

Jevons, W. S., *Elementary Lessons in Logic* (New York, Macmillan & Co., 1916).

Chafer, Rollin Thomas, *The Science of Biblical Hermeneutics* (Dallas, *Bibliotheca Sacra*, 1939).

Thouless, Robert H., *How to Think Straight* (New York, Simon & Schuster, 1939).

Chapter XI

THE EXPOSITOR AND INDUCTIVE REASONING

Since the writers of the Bible and those who undertake to explain what is written therein are alike supposed to be in accord with the logical operations of the human mind, it is of the utmost importance that the expositor approach his task employing sound logical method. Unless his logic is sound, his conclusions and doctrinal generalizations are bound to be faulty.

The nature of the composition of the Bible further indicates the necessity of sound logic in dealing with its contents. As a collection of writings, certified by the Holy Spirit to be God's Word, it rarely, if ever, presents a complete statement of thematic teachings in a single passage. Here and there, it is true, brief summaries of important doctrines occur. But the general principle of the revelatory method is progressive. Partial statements of Biblical themes are scattered through several, or in some cases, through many of the writings.

This being true, the important question arises whether the logical approach is to be analytical or synthetic. Is the expositor to seek to establish broad principles and doctrinal generalizations by minute and exhaustive examination of particular cases? Or, on the other hand, is he to proceed from general principles or doctrines to the particular cases? In other words shall his method be inductive or deductive?

Protestant theology, as it has emerged in its variant forms from the Reformation period, has given a mixed, and to some extent, an inconsistent answer to this question. Many of its doctrines have been formulated through careful inductive study of the Scriptures, and the doctrinal conclusions have been generally accepted by all believers. On the other hand, especially in the realm of eschatology, many of its teachings have been arrived at deductively from premises arbitrarily set up without reference to the Scripture particulars of the respective themes. Consequently, in regard to these teachings there have always been disagreement and controversy.

This controversy hinges on the basic issue: Shall *every* doctrine of Biblical theology be formulated only as a result of painstaking inductive study of all its Scriptural particulars, or shall exceptions be made to this rule? Shall doctrines remain in our creed which have been deductively formulated from premises which cannot stand up under the test of the full Scriptural testimony?

Whatever answer is given to this question, the fact is nevertheless true that in the province of logical procedure, Biblical interpretation is principally dependent upon the inductive method. Moreover, the true expositor must not only be thoroughly acquainted with this logical approach to the Scriptures, but must rigidly and consistently test all of his conclusions by it. It is, therefore, necessary to consider this method of interpretation in some detail.

1. DEFINITION OF THE INDUCTIVE METHOD

Whereas deduction "is reasoning from the general to the particular,"[1] induction is "the process of inference by which we get at general truth from particular facts or cases."[2] According to Beardsley, "an inductive argument has two parts ... The reason is a set of one or more statements that are called the 'evidence' for the conclusion. The inductive argument makes a claim that the evidence is sufficient to make the conclusion, at the very least, more likely to be true than false."[3]

[1] *Webster's Collegiate Dictionary* (Springfield, Mass., G. & C. Merriam Co., 1941), p. 262.
[2] F. Ryland, *Logic* (London, G. Bell & Sons, 1900), p. 148.
[3] Monroe C. Beardsley, *Practical Logic* (New York, Prentice-Hall, Inc., 1950), p. 201.

In this process of reasoning from all the parts to the whole or from particular facts or cases to the general truth, the product of the induction is a generalization. In order that a true basis for the generalization may be laid two requirements are essential. First, there must be careful observation, analysis and classification of the facts to be generalized and explained to determine their validity and various relationships. Secondly, there must be accurate interpretation of the facts.

A complete induction is made when a full enumeration of the particular facts or cases is made and the whole sphere of the universal proposition or generalization is exhausted. An incomplete induction takes place when the generalization is made without the complete enumeration of all the particular facts or cases.

Two fallacies face all users of the inductive method and particularly plague expositors of the Bible. The first is "the fallacy of insufficient observation."[4] This is the result of careless and inexhaustive observation of facts. The second involves a hasty and inaccurate interpretation of the facts, resulting in an invalid generalization.[5] These fallacies underlie the various doctrinal vagaries of the heretical offshoots of Biblical Christianity for which Scriptural support is zealously claimed.

Many students likewise fall a prey to one or both of these fallacies. However, some arrive at a correct generalization without a complete induction simply because faith tides them over the neglected particulars necessary to sustain a logical conclusion. But such inability to think maturely is to be deprecated. Logical inefficiency of this kind has a twofold peril. It tends to cause the student to rely on the conclusions of others, and even though he himself may hold valid conclusions, he is nevertheless unable to support his position adequately with Scriptural proof. In addition, such a de-

---

[4] Cf. Rollin Thomas Chafer, *The Science of Biblical Hermeneutics* (Dallas, *Bibliotheca Sacra*, 1939), p. 47.
[5] *Ibid.*

ficiency exposes him to the danger of the subtle fallacies of
the cultists and the hazard of being ensnared by some sect.

Too much stress cannot be laid upon the necessity of a
sound inductive method for the work of an expositor. No
matter what other qualification a preacher of the Bible may
have — spiritual, technical, educational or cultural — if he is
deficient in his logical approach to the Scripture, he will be
seriously crippled as a reliable interpreter of the Sacred Scriptures.

A competent expounder of divine truth must rigidly discipline himself to study every theme of Scripture in a thoroughly inductive fashion. Only by complete induction, in
which all the particular facts or cases in question are exhaustively considered, can Scripturally dependable thematic
generalizations be made.

The relevancy of such logical handling of the Word of God
becomes apparent when the task of the expositor is defined.
His job, it must be remembered, is not to expound what
saith science, philosophy, or religion; nor what saith men's
creeds and criticisms. His mission is clear and inescapable.
What saith the Word of God? is the question of vital import
to him.

This being the case, he must study every theme of the
Bible inductively, collating, observing, analyzing, classifying
all the passages pertinent to the subject being treated. This
is the only valid procedure to take in order to find out what
God has revealed on any particular subject.

Since the expositor is interested above all else in what
God says about any matter, and this inductive method is
the valid way of finding out, he need not be disturbed by
frequent aspersions cast upon this mode of treating the
Scriptures. This serious manner of handling sacred truth has
been thoughtlessly called a "hop, skip and jump" method
and "seining through the Bible for proof texts."[6]

Only a moment's unbiased reflection, however, is necessary
to demonstrate the superficiality of such censures. If serious
theologians, for example, had not "hopped" from passage to

[6] *Ibid.,* p. 74.

passage of those which deal with such great doctrines of our faith as blood atonement, justification, sanctification, glorification, etc., and "skipped" irrelevant passages, how could we have ever had completely formulated and systematized statements of these momentous themes?

Moreover, if faithful expositors had not gone "seining" through the Scriptures to catch all the detached and fragmentary details of the subject of God's grace in relationship to man's salvation, this great doctrine would never have been put into complete form from all available Scriptural particulars so that sinners saved by grace might grasp the meaning and assurance of their security in Christ.

The student who would sedulously pursue inductive study of the Scriptures must be imbued with a deep desire to become acquainted with "the whole counsel of God." He must also be willing to divest himself of sectarian prejudices, unsound theological clichés, and man-made theories. As a seeker after truth, his one aim must be to amass *all* the evidence and after careful observation, classification and analysis, make generalizations that are soundly supported by the total testimony of the Bible on the subject.

2. ILLUSTRATION OF THE INDUCTIVE METHOD

It is widely taught in theological circles that there will be a "general and final judgment of angels and men," of "the righteous" and "the wicked" at the second advent of Christ.[7] This doctrine has evidently been deductively formulated from the Scriptures. The question, however, arises, Can this teaching be sustained inductively by a careful collation, observation, analysis and classification of all pertinent passages? If it cannot be supported in this manner by the testimony of the Word, it must be rejected in favor of a deductive generalization based upon all the available particulars.

When the testimony of Scripture is minutely examined, the fact appears that there are five separate judgments indicated in Scripture instead of one. This generalization must

---

[7] *The Constitution of the Presbyterian Church in the United States of America* (Philadelphia, Publication Board of Christian Education, 1936), pp. 182f.

be made when this subject is handled inductively and all
the facts and cases in question are considered. Five particulars of time, place, subjects, basis of judgment, and result
plainly differentiate various judgments.

The first judgment is that of believers for sin (John 5:24,
Rom. 8:1, 2). The time indicated is the crucifixion of Christ.
The subjects are believers. The place is Calvary. The basis
of the judgment is the finished work of Christ. The result
of the judgment is the death of Christ and the justification
of the believers (Rom. 10:4).

The second judgment is that of the believer for his works
(II Cor. 5:10). The time is after the translation of the Church
to heaven immediately following the Lord's coming (I Cor.
4:5). The place is "in the air" (I Thess. 4:17), before the
judgment seat of Christ (II Cor. 5:10). The subjects will
be believers only, "we . . . all" (II Cor. 5:10). The basis
of the judgment will not be the question of sin, but the
believer's "works," "the things done in the body" (II Cor.
5:10). The result will be rewards or forfeiture of rewards
(I Cor. 3:11-15).

The third judgment is that of the Jews (Ezek. 20:34-38).
The time will be that of "Jacob's trouble" (Jer. 30:4-7; Dan.
12:1), "the great tribulation" (Matt. 24:21-31). The place
will be Jerusalem and vicinity (Zech. 14:1-11). The subjects
of the judgment will be the Jews gathered back to Palestine
unconverted (Ezek. 20:34-38). The basis of the judgment
will be the Jewish rejection of the Godhead, Father (I Sam.
8:7), Son (Luke 23:18) and Holy Spirit (Acts 7:51-60). The
result will be the destruction of the wicked and the conversion of a remnant (Zech. 12:10), with the Jewish nation
"born [converted] in a day" (Is. 66:18; Rom. 11:26).

The fourth judgment is that of the Gentile nations (Matt.
25:31-46), and the fifth is that of the great white throne
(Rev. 20:11-15). These two judgments are combined and
made identical by those who teach a general judgment. But
when the two are treated inductively, they are found to
differ so widely that it is quite evident that they are not
identical.

As to time, the judgment of the Gentile nations is before the millennium (Matt. 25:34). The white throne judgment, on the other hand, is after the millennium (Rev. 20:7, 11). As to place, the former is on the earth, in the Valley of Jehoshaphat (Joel 3:2). The latter is in space, with heaven and earth fled away (Rev. 20:11). The subjects of the one are the living Gentile nations (Matt. 25:32), while the subjects of the other are the wicked dead (Rev. 20:12). In the former there is no resurrection; in the latter there is a resurrection (Rev. 20:12). In the one case the basis of judgment is the nations' treatment of Christ's brethren, the Jews (Matt. 25:40). In the other case it is the works (deeds) of the ungodly to determine the degree of their punishment (Rev. 20:12, 13). The result of the judgment of the nations, moreover, is that some nations are spared as nations to exist as such in the millennium (Matt. 25:41), while in the great white throne judgment the wicked dead are consigned as individuals to the lake of fire (Rev. 20:15).

The fallen angels who are "reserved in everlasting chains under darkness" will likewise be judged at the great white throne, which Jude calls "the judgment of the great day" (Jude 6).

It is quite impossible, therefore, on the basis of sound inductive logic to make a case for a "general and final judgment of angels and men," including both the righteous and the wicked, at the second advent of Christ. Under similar inductive treatment the doctrine of a general resurrection of the bodies of the saved and unsaved immediately preceding the eternal state is found to be untenable in the light of all the Scriptural particulars.[8] The only valid doctrinal generalization that can be made from all the Scriptural evidence is that there are two resurrections, separated by at least a thousand years. One consists of "the bodies of believers only at the coming of Christ" and the other comprises "the bodies of unbelievers only after an intervening period of time speci-

8 For an exhaustive inductive refutation of this doctrine, see Chafer, *op. cit.*, pp. 49-64.

fied in the final revelation on the subject to be a thousand years."[9]

The doctrines of a general resurrection and a general judgment are merely samples of numerous other teachings that are current in many present-day theological systems, but which are built upon faulty logical processes. Inaccurate doctrines concerning the person of Christ, the work of the Holy Spirit, the mission of the Church, the meaning of the kingdom of God, and similar Bible themes furnish other examples of logical fallacy. There is either a well-intended but superficial and inadequate observation of particulars or a deliberate ignoring of essential particulars which would tend to detract from the tenability of the theory propounded.

The careful expositor, however, must lay aside all preconceived theories and creedal cliches and be like the noble Bereans of old, who "received the word with all readiness of mind, and searched the scriptures daily, whether those things were so" (Acts 17:11). The diligent student of the Word can only know whether the things he hears and reads are so by subjecting them with inexorable logic to the all-determinative criterion, "What saith the Word of God?"

Careful searching of the Holy Scriptures under a sound inductive method of dealing with what is discovered there, coupled with the Holy Spirit's guidance, will guarantee the sincere seeker after truth that his goal will be reached. The Spirit of truth will delight to guide into all truth the student who has disciplined himself on the human plane to think accurately.

LITERATURE ON INDUCTIVE LOGIC

Hamilton, Sir William, *Lectures on Logic* (London, 1859).
Fowler, Thomas, *The Elements of Inductive Logic* (10th ed., Oxford, 1892).
Hyslop, J. H., *Elements of Logic* (New York, 1892).
Bosanquet, Bernard, *The Essentials of Logic* (New York, 1895).
Bain, Alexander, *Logic, Inductive and Deductive* (2 vols., London, 1895).
Mill, John Stuart, *A System of Logic, Ratiocinative and Inductive* (8th ed., New York, 1900).

[9] *Ibid.,* p. 63f.

Welton, James, *Manual of Logic* (2 vols., London, University Tutorial Press, 1904).

Creighton, J. E., *Introductory Logic* (3d ed., New York, 1909).

Taylor, W. J., *Elementary Logic* (New York, Charles Scribner's Sons, 1909).

Jones, A. L., *Logic Inductive and Deductive* (New York, 1909).

Bradley, F. H., *Principles of Logic* (1922).

Keynes, J. N., *Studies and Exercises in Formal Logic* (4th ed., 1929).

Crumley, T., *Logic, Inductive and Deductive* (rev. ed., 1934).

Cotter, A. C., *Logic and Epistemology* (rev. ed., 1936).

Robinson, D. S., *Principles of Reasoning* (rev. ed., 1936).

CHAPTER XII

THE EXPOSITOR AND DEDUCTIVE REASONING

From the study of the preceding chapter it is quite apparent that the inductive approach is admirably fitted to the nature of the Scriptures. This is true, as noted, because of the progressive character of Biblical revelation. Since doctrines are seldom presented in a complete statement in any one passage, but partial statements of Biblical themes are interspersed through several, and in some cases, through many books, it is quite obvious that Biblical interpretation will always of necessity be chiefly dependent upon the inductive method of approach. In fact, the question is not whether the inductive method should be cultivated less, but how, under these circumstances, the deductive method can be employed to supplement the inductive approach.

Despite the fact that deductive reasoning as applied to the Scriptures has resulted in many erroneous conclusions, such as the teaching of one general resurrection and one general judgment, it certainly does not follow that this type of logical procedure ought to be ruled out of Biblical interpretation altogether. Legitimately employed, both induction and deduction have their proper place and should supplement each other.

For example, if sufficient knowledge is not possessed to posit the appropriate universal proposition from which to reason deductively, it is possible to proceed in an inductive manner to search for this proposition. In fact, in dealing with Scripture no premise ought ever to be used in deductive reasoning that cannot be sustained by sound induction. Likewise if theories and systems of interpretation in common use cannot be defended by rigid inductive reasoning based on what the Scriptures really say, they ought to be abandoned.

As far as the expositor is concerned, the only thing that really matters is, What does the Bible teach on the subject? He dare not allow preconceived notions, blind loyalty to a system of interpretation, some sectarian hobby, or theological prejudice to stand in the way of his accepting without reservation what the Scriptures teach. Nor dare he presume to attach value to any theological conclusion based upon an extra-Biblical generalization. If he uses deductive reasoning, he must rigidly test the premises upon which he bases his conclusion by inductive logic, for no conclusion can be sound if its premises are unsound.

1. DEFINITION OF THE DEDUCTIVE METHOD

Whereas induction is reasoning from the particular to the general, deduction "is reasoning from the general to the particular."[1] It involves deriving or inferring a specific fact or truth from a general fact or principle. Deduction is based upon an argument expressed in strict logical form called the syllogism. This schematic arrangement consists of two propositions, called premises, from which the inference or conclusion is drawn. The subject of the conclusion is called the minor term, and its predicate the major term. The third term with which the minor and major terms of the conclusion are compared in the premises, is called the middle term.

The premise which brings into relation the major and the middle terms is called the major premise. That which brings the minor and middle terms into a similar relation is called the minor premise. Thus in the syllogism — All A is B (major premise), all C is A (minor premise), therefore, all C is B (conclusion) — B is the major term, C the minor term, and A is the middle term. If words are substituted for letters, the syllogism runs: All ruminants are quadrupeds (major premise); all deer are ruminants (minor premise); therefore, all deer are quadrupeds (conclusion).

---

[1] *Webster's Collegiate Dictionary* (Springfield, Mass., G. & C. Merriam Co., 1941), p. 262.

The syllogism is valid because the conclusion logically follows from the premises. If the conclusion does not so follow, the syllogism is invalid and constitutes a fallacy. Moreover, the conclusion is also true because the premises from which it is logically deduced are true. If either of the premises is untrue, the conclusion cannot be true.

2. ILLUSTRATION OF THE DEDUCTIVE METHOD

Syllogisms are commonly classified categorical and conditional.[2] In the categorical form the major and minor premises and the conclusion are stated positively or absolutely. Example, murder and adultery are violations of the sixth and seventh commandments of the law. David committed murder and adultery in the matter of Uriah the Hittite and Bathsheba; therefore, David violated the sixth and seventh commandments of the law.

The conditional syllogism may be either hypothetical or disjunctive. The hypothetical judgment states a supposition, and is commonly introduced by the words *if, in case, provided that,* and the like. The disjunctive judgment states alternatives, and is most frequently expressed by the disjunctive words *either . . . or.*

In the syllogism the conditional proposition occurs only as major premise. The minor premise is categorical. In the hypothetical form the clause introduced by *if* or its equivalent is called the *antecedent,* while the clause indicating the result upon the condition is known as the *consequent.* The minor premise, being categorical, either affirms the antecedent or denies the consequent.

If the minor premise affirms the antecedent, it leads to an affirmative conclusion, which declares the consequent to be true. If the minor premise denies the consequent, it results in a negative conclusion, which negates the truth of the antecedent. The former is called a constructive hypothetical syllogism, the latter a destructive hypothetical syllogism. Example of the constructive variety: If believers are indwelt by the Holy Spirit, they are Christians. But believers are indwelt

[2] Cf. W. J. Taylor, *Elementary Logic* (New York, Charles Scribner's Sons, 1909), p. 147.

by the Holy Spirit. Therefore, they are Christians. Example of the destructive variety: If Mohammedans trust Christ as Redeemer they are saved. But Mohammedans do not trust Christ as Redeemer. Therefore they are not saved.

The disjunctive syllogism is another common form of the conditional variety.[3] It contains a disjunctive proposition consisting of a subject term of which alternate predicates are asserted. Commonly the predicates are two, and the disjunction is expressed by the words *either . . . or*. However, the predicates may be three or more. In this case *or* is usually placed between them. Such a proposition comprises the major premise. The minor premise is categorical, either affirmative or negative.

In contrast to the ordinary syllogism an affirmative minor premise gives a negative conclusion and a negative minor premise an affirmative conclusion. This produces two moods, that which by affirming denies and that which by denying affirms. Example of the first: There is a general simultaneous judgment of the righteous and the wicked or the judgment of the righteous and that of the wicked are entirely distinct and separate. But the judgment of the righteous and the wicked are separated by at least a thousand years. Therefore, there is not one general judgment of saved and unsaved. Example of the second: There is a general simultaneous judgment of the righteous and the wicked or the judgment of the righteous and that of the wicked are distinct and separate. But there is not one general simultaneous judgment of the righteous and the wicked. Therefore the judgment of the righteous and that of the wicked are entirely distinct and separate.

A curious combination of the two kinds of conditional propositions, the hypothetical and the disjunctive, is the so-called dilemma.[4] This form consists of a conditional major premise having more than one antecedent, and a minor premise which is disjunctive. The two pairs of antecedents and their consequent or consequents make the *horns* of the

3 F. Ryland, *Logic* (London, G. Bell & Sons, 1900), pp. 126-129.
4 Taylor, *op. cit.*, pp. 152-154.

dilemma.[5] A number of forms of this syllogistic form occur. The simple constructive type is sufficient for illustration. If A is B, C is D, and if E is F, C is D; but either A is B, or E is F. Therefore, C is D.

If this type is put into words, it runs thus: If we face difficulties in the Christian life which we can overcome, we ought not to worry about them. If we are confronted with difficulties in the Christian life which we cannot overcome, we ought not to worry about them. But all difficulties in the Christian life can or cannot be overcome. Therefore, we ought not to worry about the difficulties in the Christian life.[6]

If, in the dilemma, the major premise is absolutely true, and the minor absolutely exhaustive, the argument is formally valid. However, this form is often fallacious because the alternatives of the minor premise are rarely absolutely exclusive. Some third factor is usually possible, which enables escape from both horns.[7]

Various other forms and variations of the syllogism occur, such as the enthymeme in which one of the propositions is omitted, to be supplied by the mind,[8] or the sorite, consisting of a series of premises whose conclusions excepting the last are not expressed.[9] Discussions of these and other forms may be found in books on logic.[10]

3. FALLACIES OF THE DEDUCTIVE METHOD

The syllogistic form of reasoning is valuable as a means of analysis, but it is peculiarly susceptible to fallacy. Deductive fallacies fall into two categories. First are those which are due to incorrectness of syllogistic form. These are called logical or formal fallacies.[11] Those resulting from a mis-

[5] Ryland, op. cit., pp. 131-134.
[6] Rollin Thomas Chafer, The Science of Biblical Hermeneutics (Dallas, Bibliotheca Sacra, 1939), p. 66.
[7] Ryland, op. cit., p. 132.
[8] Taylor, op. cit., pp. 157-164.
[9] Noah K. Davis, Elements of Deductive Logic (New York, Harper & Brothers, 1896), pp. 134-136.
[10] Monroe C. Beardsley, Practical Logic (New York, Prentice-Hall, Inc., 1950), pp. 315-399.
[11] Taylor, op. cit., p. 166; pp. 120-164.

understanding of the content or subject matter of the argument are called material fallacies.

Especially in the study of the Bible the deductive method has been peculiarly productive of unsound views. This has no doubt been due occasionally to incorrectness of syllogistic form. But far more common are the fallacies which are due to a misunderstanding of material content.

Assuming the syllogism to be correct and expressed in strict logical form, it follows that "its conclusiveness is manifest from the structure of the expression alone, without any regard to the meaning of the terms."[12] Thus the necessity of rigidly testing the premises of the syllogistic statement is apparent when this type of reasoning is employed.

Fallacies of material content in deductive reasoning may be classified in two categories. Those which originate in the exceedingly common practice of unconsciously assuming the issue to be determined by the argument and those which originate from some ambiguity. Of these two the former, embracing the fallacies of unwarranted assumption, is by far the most serious that arises in connection with Biblical interpretation.

Of the fallacies of unwarranted assumption perhaps the most detrimental to expository work is the fallacy of *accident and its converse*, especially the latter. Both of these fallacies are due to confusion between the general and the particular. The fallacy of accident consists "in arguing erroneously *from a general rule to a special case*, where a certain accidental circumstance renders the rule inapplicable."[13] The converse fallacy consists in arguing *from a special case to a general one*.[14]

An example of the fallacy of accident is contained in the following: Whoever murders another ought to be put to death. An executioner in executing a criminal commits murder, therefore he ought to be put to death. It is obvious that

[12] Webster's *New Twentieth Century Dictionary* (New York, Publishers Guild, Inc., 1942), p. 1729.
[13] W. S. Jevons and David J. Hill, *Elements of Logic* (New York, American Book Co., 1911), p. 169.
[14] *Ibid.*

the error stems from confusing a statement under a condition with a statement without that condition.

The converse fallacy of accident is multifariously illustrated whenever a text is torn from its context and is stated as a general truth without reference to the particular circumstance under which it appears in Scripture. When the New England Puritans passed their three famous resolutions, they committed this fallacy at least twice: "Resolved, *first*, that the earth is the Lord's and the fulness thereof; *secondly*, that He hath given it to His saints; *thirdly*, that we are His saints."[15]

Another common type of fallacy is that of irrelevant conclusion in which the feelings, passions and prejudices of those to whom the argument is addressed are appealed to in order to deflect attention from the real point at issue. It has many variations. In the *argumentum ad hominem* the general character of the person opposed in argument is assailed instead of proving the actual charges made against him. This device is often employed in religious controversy when Scripturally untenable doctrines are defended. Such teachings are also defended by a sophistic device called *argumentum ad vericundiam* in which a great and reputable or prominent book is enlisted in support of a position instead of proving it on rational grounds. This particular form of irrelevant argument is all too prevalent in theological circles.

In the *argumentum ad populum* the argument is addressed to "a body of people calculated to excite their feelings and prevent them from forming a dispassionate judgment upon the matter in hand."[16] In the *argumentum ad ignorantiam* the burden of proof is thrown upon the other party when in the nature of the case disproof is as impossible as proof. It is the old practice of holding a thing is true because you cannot prove it untrue.

Another fallacy of unwarranted assumption is *begging the question*. "It consists in taking the conclusion itself as one of the premises of an argument."[17] Attempting to prove a

[15] Ryland, *op. cit.*, p. 260.
[16] W. S. Jevons, *Elementary Lessons in Logic* (New York, Macmillan & Co., 1916), p. 179.
[17] Jevons, Hill, *op. cit.*, p. 173.

proposition by itself is as reasonable as attempting to support a body upon itself. An illustration would be furnished if a church council were assembled to decide whether a certain doctrine ought to be condemned. To argue that the particular doctrine is *heresy*, and therefore ought to be condemned would be begging the question, because every one understands by heresy a doctrine which is to be condemned.

Very common is the fallacy of *false cause* in which one thing is assumed to be the cause of another without any sufficient grounds. The Latin phrase *post hoc ergo propter hoc* ("after this and therefore in consequence of this") exactly describes the character of these false conclusions that confound the real cause or causes of an effect with what may be a mere sign or symptom. Illustrations of this fallacy of false generalization abound. Illustration: The baptism of the Holy Spirit occurred at Pentecost (Acts 1:5; 11:16). The people spoke in supernatural languages at Pentecost. Therefore, speaking in tongues is the result of the baptism of the Spirit. This reasoning completely ignores that in addition to baptizing — the Spirit regenerated, indwelt, sealed and filled (Acts 2:4). How precarious, then, to select the so-called "baptism" and arbitrarily equate it with the filling, ignoring also other possible factors explaining the "tongues."

The fallacy of *non sequitur* includes all loose reasoning where the conclusion has no bona fide relation to the premises. Under this category "might be brought all fallacies of inference, that is, all fallacies whatever."[18]

It is quite obvious in the study of the various fallacies of deductive reasoning that the conclusion can never be any more certain than the premises. Errors abound in both science and philosophy because of a failure to remember this. When one comes to the realm of theology, the situation is truly appalling. Generalizations that cannot be sustained inductively from the Scriptures are frequently used as premises in deductive reasoning. Since in a properly constructed syllogism the conclusion comes out of the premises mechanically, the real problem is to prove that the premises are sound.

[18] Ryland, *op. cit.*, p. 264.

The Bible expositor must constantly bear in mind that, since logical deduction involves the drawing out of a particular doctrine or teaching from a universal premise, the sole question of moment is, Is the premise from which this conclusion is drawn Scripturally true? Is it consonant with the complete testimony of the Bible or is it only apparently in agreement?

A large segment of Protestant theology as it has come down to our day, especially in the sphere of prophecy and eschatology, is based upon premises that only apparently conform to the total witness of the Word on the subject under discussion. Examples of this are very numerous. But before the expositor can accept such plausible conclusions — for example, one general resurrection and judgment, the identity of the church and the kingdom, the rejection of a future earthly career for Israel in the millennium and other alleged deductive truth — he must make an honest attempt to find the Scripture material for the assumed universal premises involved.[19]

If as the result of complete induction, taking *all* Scripture evidence into account, the premises underlying any deduction are found not to be fully supported, the expositor must reject the conclusions that have been drawn, no matter how plausible they may be or how canonical as a result of ecclesiastical reception and creedal authority.

Besides the fallacies of unwarranted assumption against which the deductive reasoner must beware, there are fallacies of ambiguity.[20] First, there is the common fallacy of equivocation. It occurs when a word in the major, minor or middle term of a syllogism is used in more than one meaning. Example: The apostles were *saved* before Pentecost; the baptism of the Holy Spirit at Pentecost was subsequent to their being saved. Therefore, the baptism of the Holy Spirit is a second experience after one is *saved*.

Here the fallacy hinges on the ambiguous use of the term "saved." At Pentecost every one converted was regenerated,

[19] Chafer, *op. cit.*, p. 68.
[20] Taylor, *op. cit.*, pp. 167-174.

baptized by the Spirit into Christ, indwelt by the Spirit, sealed by the Spirit and granted the privilege of being filled with the Spirit, as is the case of *every* believer since that day. But although the apostles were "saved" before Pentecost, they were not baptized into Christ, indwelt, sealed and granted the privilege of filling. Could they then be said to have been saved in the sense that every believer is since Pentecost?

Another form of ambiguity is an error of grammatical construction that admits of a double interpretation. A classical example is the line from Shakespeare's Henry VI: "The duke yet lives that Henry shall depose." This may mean that Henry will depose the duke or the duke will depose Henry.

In the Scriptures there are corresponding translation ambiguities. Compare James 3:2: "For in many things we offend all" (AV). The original is ". . . we all offend." In Matthew 26:27, "Drink ye all of it" (AV) correctly rendered is "Drink of it, all of you" (RSV). In Acts 19:2, "Have you received the Holy Ghost since ye believed?" (AV) is given correctly: "Did you receive the Holy Spirit when you believed?" (RSV).

The latter ambiguity has furnished the basis for the following inductive fallacy: The Ephesian disciples in Paul's time believed, but did not receive the Holy Spirit. Therefore, it is possible to believe now and not receive the Holy Spirit. In addition to the misleading idea that the Holy Spirit may be received subsequent to believing faith, based on a mistranslation, the term "believe" is used ambiguously. What did these disciples believe? Not the Christian message certainly (Acts 18:24-27), but only John's preparatory and now superseded message, which knew nothing of the gift of the Spirit as an accomplished fact.

Various types of ambiguity exist such as using terms in a different sense than the Scriptures use them, confusing reality with ritual, placing misleading emphasis or special accent on that which ought not to be stressed, and construing a manifest figure of speech literally.

A good example of using terms in a different sense than Scripture employs them is furnished by the common fallacy of construing the reference to baptism in Romans 6:3, 4; Galatians 3:27; Ephesians 4:5, and Colossians 2:12 to mean the water ceremony instead of the spiritual reality (Spirit baptism).[21]

Examples of the fallacy of placing misleading stress on some point or doctrine that Scripture does not emphasize are very common. For instance, the early rabbis laid undue emphasis on the word "neighbor" in "Thou shalt love thy *neighbor*" (Lev. 19:18), with the implication "and hate thine enemy." Such a fallacy is corrected by our Lord in Matthew 5:43-48.[22] Indeed, in close exegetical work one has to be well trained in the original languages to be able to stress what the Word itself stresses, in order to avoid lopsided teachings.

Also in public reading merely the tone of voice "may make all the difference between truth and falsehood."[23] To cite an example, sarcasm is commonly indicated by the circumflex accent. Unless this stress or appropriate tones are employed, the meaning is perverted. This is true of Paul's words to the Corinthians. "For what is it wherein ye were *inferior* to other churches, except it be that I myself was not burdensome to you? forgive me this wrong" (II Cor. 12:13). Compare also I Kings 13:27, Job 12:2, and Psalm 2:10.

Although serious transgression is committed against Biblical interpretation by anti-literal, spiritualizing methods, it is possible, on the other hand, to sin against manifest figures of speech by reducing them to a bald literalism. This fallacy is subtle and quite common. An instance is seen in pressing anthropomorphic and anthropopathic expressions in the Bible as applied to God to a grossly material conception of Deity as actually having hands and feet and hearing, seeing, smelling and repenting as human beings do (cf. Gen. 6:5, 6; 8:21; 11:5; Is. 53:1, etc.).

[21] Cf. the present author's, *The Baptizing Work of the Holy Spirit* (Wheaton, Ill., Van Kampen Press, 1953), pp. 83-99.

[22] Davis, *op. cit.*, p. 188.

[23] *Ibid.*, p. 189.

Literature on Deductive Logic

Davis, Noah K., *Elements of Deductive Logic* (New York, Harper & Brothers, 1896).

Fowler, Thomas, *The Elements of Deductive Logic* (10th ed., Oxford, 1892).

Jevons, W. S., *Studies in Deductive Logic* (3d ed., New York, 1896).

Dewey, John, *Studies in Logical Theory* (Chicago, 1903).

Hibben, J. G., *Logic Inductive and Deductive* (New York, 1905).

Jevons, W. S., *Elementary Lessons in Logic* (New York, Macmillan & Co., 1916).

Dinwiddie, William, *Essentials of Logic* (New York, 1914).

Atkinson, W. W., *Reasoning Power* (1922).

Sellars, R. W., *Essentials of Logic* (rev. ed., 1925).

Latta, R., and A. MacBeath, *Elements of Logic* (1929).

Stebbing, L. S., *Modern Introduction to Logic* (1931).

Jorgensen, J., *Treatise of Formal Logic* (1931).

Eaton, R. M., *General Logic* (1931).

Thouless, Robert H., *How to Think Straight* (New York, Simon & Schuster, 1939).

CHAPTER XIII

THE EXPOSITOR AND GRAMMATICAL INTERPRETATION

The history of Biblical exposition, as demonstrated in the works of the great exegetes and critics, reveals a large number of different methods of interpretation that have at various periods prevailed. Many of these methods are erroneous, some even absurd, and in many ways, and considered as a whole, the progress of Biblical interpretation presents a disappointing spectacle from the point of view of true exposition. However, "from the first moment that one human being addressed another by the use of language down to the present hour, the essential laws of interpretation became, and have continued to be, a practical matter."[1] Only as false notions of the Bible itself have prevailed have men abandoned a sound and practical approach toward understanding the message of the Sacred Scriptures.

On the one hand, a superstitious reverence for the letter of Scripture has given rise to such methods as the mysterious and speculative interpretations of the ancient Jews, the allegorical and mystical exegesis of early Christians, and the fantastic interpretations of Emmanuel Swedenborg. Undue stress upon guidance by an "inward light," received as "an unction from the Holy One" (I John 2:20), to the point of discarding the plain meaning of words and the obvious implications of grammar, led to the pietistic interpretations of

[1] M. Stuart in the *American Biblical Repository* for January, 1832, p. 125. For a discussion of various erroneous kinds of interpretation see Robert A. Traina, *Methodical Bible Study* (New York, Ganis and Harris, 1952), pp. 167-181. Cf. also L. Berkhof, *Principles of Biblical Interpretation* (Grand Rapids, Baker Book House, 1950), pp. 11-39.

some of the Pietists of Germany and many of the Quakers of England and America.

On the other hand, prejudices and assumptions contrary to the spirit of the holy writings have produced methods of interpretation which pervert and frequently flatly contradict the plainest statements of Scripture. Of such a nature is the theory of accommodation of J. S. Semler, called "the father of the destructive school of German rationalism,"[2] which rejects the miraculous in Scripture as a mere adaptation to the ignorance of the times.

Other rationalistic approaches to Scripture, such as the moral interpretation of Kant, likewise set aside the plain grammatical and historical teaching, when a passage was adjudged to be without a moral lesson. David Friedrich Strauss' mythical theory was another influential attempt of the rationalism of the nineteenth century to interpret the Scriptures on a naturalistic plane. The development of speculative philosophy, notably that of Kant and Hegel, produced the critical method of Reuss, Kuenen and Wellhausen, which when applied to the Old Testament Scriptures was not a candid examination of the contents of these books in the light of grammar and the testimony of history but rather the superimposing upon them of a particular philosophy of history.

Skeptical and rational assaults upon the Scriptures in the nineteenth and twentieth centuries down to the present hour have called forth a method of interpretation that may be called apologetic and dogmatic. While such an approach to the Bible has a legitimate place, it is not the expository method, and the dogmatism it calls forth is often that engendered by controversy and is frequently the product of traditionalism or sectarianism rather than the established teaching of the Scriptures.

In distinction to these various methods of interpretation of Scripture — the mysterious, the speculative, the mystical, the allegorical, the pietistic, the accommodational, the rational, the moral, the critical, the apologetic and the dogmatic, is

2 Milton S. Terry, *Biblical Hermeneutics* (New York, Methodist Book Concern, 1911), p. 62.

the method which seeks to arrive at the precise meaning of the language of each of the Biblical writers as is required by the laws of grammar and the facts of history. This is the grammatical-historical method. This approach is that which the expositor must pursue with diligence and uncompromising loyalty, if he would arrive at the actual meaning of the Scriptures themselves and be in a position to expound their meaning to others.

Of primary importance in the grammatical-historical method is the study of the vocabulary and grammatical usages of an author. This is grammatical interpretation in which the successful expositor must excel.

1. The Expositor As a Philologian

The first work of an expositor is philological. He must know the meaning of words, not only in the original languages of Scripture but also in his native tongue in which he preaches. He who has no genuine interest in words and their meaning will never make a good expositor, for it is impossible to know the thoughts of a writer without an accurate comprehension of his vocabulary.

Etymology. In his study of words the expositor needs to keep in mind their original meaning as well as their actual connotation as developed in common usage. The primitive or root signification of a word, called etymology (from Greek *etymon*, "true or real" and *logos*, "word"), is often of immense value to the student of the Scriptures in suggesting word pictures and illustrations and in furnishing background for a clear understanding of the derived and developed meaning as it may occur in the passage in hand.

Sometimes the etymological meaning of a word is indispensable to the meaning of a passage, especially if there is reason to believe the author considered this meaning when he wrote. Such is the case with the Messianic promise of a virgin-born Saviour in Isaiah 7:14, who is called Immanuel (*El,* "God," *immanu,* "with us"), clearly suggesting the deity and humanity of the promised Deliverer.

Usus Loquendi. In other instances the etymological meaning of a word must give way to the current established usage, called *usus loquendi* ("employment by the one speaking" or writing). The word "spirit," *pneuma*, is a case in point. Derived from the verb *pneo* "to breathe," the expression originally meant "breath," then came to mean "wind," and finally "spirit," in which sense with rare exception it is used throughout the New Testament, where it apparently does not appear in its primitive sense of "breath."

In order to determine the current usage of a word as employed by a particular writer, that is its *usus loquendi*, in distinction to its original or etymological significance, its precise occurrence in contemporary literature must be studied if it happens to be used extra-Biblically.

In regard to the Biblical use of the term in question, its meaning must be noted particularly in those passages nearest as far as context is concerned and most akin in point of authorship, date and character of composition.

The word *logos* of I John 1:1 furnishes an example. This *logos* is said to be "that which was from the beginning . . . which we have heard . . . which we have seen with our eyes . . . and our hands have handled." Although the word *logos* occurs hundreds of times in the New Testament, nowhere else except in John 1:1-18 do we find a similar use of the expression, where it is said the "Logos was with God and was God" (1:1 and "became flesh" (1:14). Clearly, then, this is the Logos, Christ, the Son of God, of whom John is speaking in his first epistle. It is quite evident also from this illustration that the most valuable occurrences of a word are those on the same subject, by the same author, written in similar style.

Often, however, it is necessary for a full understanding of the Scriptural use of a word to consider its occurrence in contemporary literature. For example, the term *paraclete*, translated "Comforter" (John 14:16; 15:26; 16:7) when referring to the Holy Spirit, is rendered "Advocate" in I John 2:1, where it applies to Christ in heaven. In none of the passages, however, is the concept of "Comforter" obvious. Study of the word in the Septuagint, in Philo and in classical Greek suggests more the idea of "Helper" or "Advocate," than "Comforter."

Idioms. Every language has peculiar modes of expression and phraseology unique to it. These are called idioms (from Greek *idiousthai,* "to make one's own," from *idios,* "one's own, private peculiar"). These forms of speech peculiar to a language belong to its very structure and differ from *dialecticisms,* which are varieties of usage engrafted upon a language through ignorance of the correct use of it or as the result of developments in particular localities. Phoenician, Moabite and other neighboring tongues of peoples adjacent to ancient Israel were practically dialects of Hebrew. Moreover, for this reason it is easy to see that a knowledge of these tongues as derived from the inscriptions is useful to the Biblical scholar. But more important to the expositor is an understanding of basic Hebrew and Greek idioms. This knowledge is invaluable and cannot be acquired cheaply. Only diligent application and study of the best grammars, lexicons and works on history and archeology can give the student the full facility he needs in this field.

Examples of idioms are innumerable. Reference to a few must suffice. A Hebrew idiom, to cite an instance, which has a prominent place in the interpretation of many important passages is the use of the infinitive absolute as an inner accusative to stress the root idea of the finite verb. "But of the tree of the knowledge of good and evil, thou shalt not eat of it: for in the day that thou eatest *a dying thou shalt die,*" that is, "thou shalt *surely* die" (Gen. 2:17). Another idiom involves two infinitives absolute combined in an adverbial sense. "And the waters returned from the earth continually" (Hebrew — *going and returning, halok washov*).

A much misunderstood idiom, clarified by archeology, is the use of *ben,* "son," with a following genitive. Followed by a genitive of place it denotes one born or brought up there. "Hadadezer ben Rehob" (II Sam. 8:3) is equivalent to "Hadadezer of Beth-Rehob." Particularly as applied to royalty, "son of" may mean nothing more than a royal successor of" (cf. Dan. 5:2). For Greek idioms compare the common phrase *kai egeneto,* "and it came to pass" and the double negative idea contained in I John 2:22.

Rare Words. Often a word occurs so rarely in Scripture (especially is this true of the Old Testament) that its meaning, as far as Biblical usage is concerned, is doubtful. In such cases, when the etymology and the testimony of the ancient versions help little, the aid of cognate languages must be sought. Ancient languages closely akin to Hebrew, such as Arabic, Akkadian, Aramaic, Ugaritic, Phoenician and Ethiopic, frequently enable the lexicographer to define more precisely Old Testament words that are otherwise obscure.

The word *re'em* furnishes an example. It occurs some eight times (Num. 23:22; 24:8; Deut. 33:17, Ps. 22:21; 29:6; 92:10; Job 39:9; Is. 34:7), and although the contexts demonstrate that it was a strong, wild, untamable animal with horns, they do not indicate exactly what species of beast it was. The root word *ra'am* means "to be high," but does not identify the animal. The ancient versions give no clue for they fell into the error copied by the Authorized Version of making the creature a fabulous one-horned legendary creation, "the unicorn" (Septuagint, *monokeros,* "one-horned," Latin, *unicorn*).

Turning to the cognate languages, however, real help is secured. In Arabic the *rimu* is a large antelope, which does not suit the strength and ferocity of the Biblical passages. In Akkadian *rimu,* on the other hand, means a wild ox, which meets all the requirements of the Biblical word, and is obviously the species intended in the Biblical passages. The Revised and Revised Standard Versions are, therefore, correct in thus rendering the expression. Admirable representations of the wild ox by Assyrian artists "show it to be the aurochs (Bos primigenius)."[3] Tiglath-pileser I (c. 1115-1102 B.C.) hunted the powerful large-horned beast in the land of the Hittites at the foot of Lebanon, but it later became extinct and the real meaning of the word was eventually lost.

Hapax legomena. Sometimes, to increase difficulties en-

---

[3] Henry Snyder Gehman, *The Westminster Dictionary of the Bible* (Philadelphia, The Westminster Press, 1944), p. 617.

countered in definition, a word occurs only once in Scripture. Such an expression is called a *hapax legomenon* ("that which is spoken, or written, only once"). Obviously it is then impossible to get any idea of the Biblical use of such a term outside its own immediate context. Its etymology may be very suggestive and also its translation in the ancient versions. Most helpful, however, will normally be the study of its use in the cognate languages.

The word *sullam* occurs only in Genesis 28:12. The etymology is suggestive. Apparently it is derived from *salal*, "to cast up" or "to raise." From the same root occurs the term *mesillah*, referring to an embanked or raised highway (Judg. 10:32, Is. 40:3; 42:10) and also to steps or stairways to the temple (II Chron. 9:11). When the cognate languages are examined, the Arabic *sullum*, Phoenician (plural *slmt*), and Akkadian *simmiltu*,[4] are found to confirm the meaning of a "rising flight of stones, stair (ladder),[5] which sense is clearly suggested by the context of the passage in Genesis.

Hapax legomena are quite numerous in the Old Testament, which embodies substantially all the remains of the ancient Hebrew language. Modern discoveries of languages and dialects closely allied to ancient Hebrew, like Ugaritic, whose extensive literature was uncovered at Ugarit (Ras Shamra) in North Syria from 1929-1937, however, have done much to alleviate the lack of comparative philological material.[6]

As far as the New Testament is concerned an extensive extant literature of the Greek language enables the New Testament expositor to determine without great difficulty the roots and usage of most of the words with which he has to deal. However, there are instances also in the New Testament of *hapax legomena*, such as *epousion* in the Lord's prayer (Matt. 6:11; Luke 11:3). Since this word occurs nowhere else in Greek literature, interpreters are thrown back upon its etymology, in which case it may mean either "give

[4] *Zeitschrift fuer Assyriologie*, 41, 230f.
[5] Koehler, Ludwig and Walter Baumgartner, *Lexicon in Veteris Testamenti Libros* (Leiden, E. J. Brill, 1952), p. 660.
[6] Cf. Claude F. A. Schaeffer, *The Cuneiform Texts of Ras Shamra-Ugarit* (London, Oxford Press, 1939), pp. 1-96.

us our *coming* bread" that is, bread for the coming day, or
tomorrow's bread (from *epi* "toward" and *ienai* "go, approach")
or "give us our *essential* bread" (from *epi* and *ousia,* "existence, subsistence"), that which is necessary for existence. Careful consideration of the context suggests that the latter meaning is correct.[7]

It is thus apparent that in deciding upon the meaning of
hapax legomena the student has to be guided by the context, by the analogy of kindred roots in the language, by
the translation of the word in ancient versions, and by whatever traces of the word may remain in cognate tongues.
Phenomenal advance in archeological research in Bible lands
gives promise of great strides in the last-named field, that of
the domain of comparative philology. The abundant light
shed on New Testament philology by the papyri finds in the
koine Greek is somewhat paralleled in the Old Testament
by the remarkable recovery of a vast Assyro-Babylonian (Akkadian) cuneiform literature and the Biblically significant
alphabetic cuneiform poems and epics at Ras Shamra Ugarit.

Synonyms. Every developed language, like Biblical Hebrew
and Greek, contains many words which have the same or
essentially the same general meaning. Such words, called
synonyms, are marks of a cultivated language, and abound
in both the Old and New Testament. The careful Biblical
expositor must be diligent in developing skill and discernment in determining the nice distinctions and various shades
of meaning implicit in Hebrew and Greek synonyms. This
is true because "often the exact point and pith of a passage
will be missed by failing to make the proper discrimination
between synonymous expressions."[8]

Hebrew, for example, has various names for God, which
the expositor must painstakingly distinguish to get a full
understanding of the Old Testament revelation of Deity. Of
the primary names there are three: God (*El, Elah, Elohim,*
Gen. 1:1, *et al.*), *Jehovah* or *Yahweh* (Gen. 2:4, *et al.*) and
Lord (*Adon* or *Adonai,* Gen. 15:2, *et al.*). There are also

[7] Terry, *op. cit.,* p. 77.
[8] *Ibid.,* p. 89.

numerous compounds with El (God): God Almighty (*El Shaddai*, Gen. 17:1, *et al.*), Most High God (*El Elyon*, Gen. 14:18, *et al.*) and Everlasting God (*El Olam*, Gen. 21:33, *et al.*). In addition there are names compounded with Jehovah: Lord God (*Jehovah Elohim*, Gen. 2:4, *et al.*), Lord God (*Adonai Jehovah*, Gen. 15:2) and Lord of Hosts (*Jehovah Sabaoth*, I Sam. 1:3, *et al.*).[9]

Likewise, in its revelation of man the Old Testament uses a number of words similar in thought to complete the picture. Adam (*'adam*, Gen. 1:26, occurring also in Ugaritic and Arabic) presents man of the earth, earthy. Ish (*'ish*, Gen. 2:23) presents him with immaterial and personal existence.[10] Enosh (*'nsh*, occurring also in Ugaritic) connects him with weakness and mortality. Gever (*gever*, Deut. 22:5) connects him with human strength and might.

In the matter of terminology for sin, for example, the Hebrew language is remarkably rich. No fewer than twelve words are used to express this clear-cut concept, which is so important theologically. The common word is *hatah*, which originally meant "to miss the mark" (Judg. 20:16). The term *shagah* signifies "to err," "to stray" (Lev. 4:13), *pasha'*, "to rebel" (Prov. 10:12); *'amal*, "to labor," describes sin in its aspect of a burden, that which turns work into toil and travail (Gen. 41:51). The idea of transgression, or crossing over the boundary of right and entering the forbidden land of wrong, is denoted by the word *'avar*, "to cross over" (Ps. 17:3; Hos. 6:7). The term *'aven* connotes sin in the sense of emptiness, or "vanity" (Amos 5:5). *'Asham* portrays it as guilt (Lev. 5:2, 3). *Ma'al* points to the treachery of sin, representing wrongdoing as a breach of trust (Josh. 7:1; 22:16). The term *'aval* denotes iniquity (Mal. 2:6). *Ra'* connects sin with harm and injury (Ps. 141:5). *Rasha'* connects it with confusion (Is. 57:20, 21).

The elaborate and clear-cut concept of sin in the Hebrew tongue is all the more remarkable against the general background of contemporary paganism with its blurred notions

[9] Cf. R. B. Girdlestone, *Synonyms of the Old Testament* (reprint, Grand Rapids, Wm. B. Eerdmans Publishing Co., 1948), pp. 18-44.
[10] *Ibid.*, p. 45.

of human depravity and guilt. To comprehend the Old Testament doctrine of sin the expositor must be able to differentiate clearly between the various terms employed in the Hebrew.

Synonyms in the New Testament play a similarly significant role. For instance, seven different Greek words are employed for prayer. Each one is distinctive and sets forth a distinguishable shade of thought. Taken together they give a full-orbed picture of the doctrine of prayer in the New Testament. Four of them occur together in I Timothy 2:1: "I exhort, therefore, that supplications, prayers, intercessions, thanksgivings, be made for all men" (ARV).

The term *proseuche* is regularly used of prayer to God (Matt. 16:13, 16).[11] *Euche* is prayer as a general desire (Jas. 5:15) or as a vow (Acts 18:18; 21:23). *Deesis* has the idea of fervent asking, entreaty or supplication addressed to God or man as the result of need or want.[12] *Proseuche* is limited to prayer to God. *Enteuxis* contains the thought of lighting upon or meeting with and implies "free, familiar prayer, such as boldly draws near to God."[13] *Eucharistia* emphasizes the note of thankful gratitude in prayer. Somewhat rare elsewhere, it is of frequent occurrence in New Testament Greek, stressing the attitude which ought always to characterize the Christian for great benefits received.[14] *Aitema* is prayer as petition (Luke 23:24; Phil. 4:6). *Hiketeria* (*hikesia*) is supplication, as when a suppliant carries an olive branch in fervent entreaty.[15]

In similar fashion such New Testament synonyms as *phileo* and *agapao* ("to love"); *oida* and *ginosko* ("to know") are richly suggestive in their different shades of meaning. Nouns like *bios* and *zoe* meaning "life" and adjectives like *kainos* and *neos* meaning "new" and numerous other synonyms are of paramount importance to correct exegesis. The expositor, we repeat, must be a student of words.

[11] G. Abbott-Smith, *A Manual Greek Lexicon of the New Testament* (3d ed.; Edinburgh, T. & T. Clark, 1937), p. 384.
[12] *Ibid.*, p. 99.
[13] R. C. Trench, *Synonyms of the New Testament* (reprint, Grand Rapids, Wm. B. Eerdmans Publishing Co., 1948), p. 190.
[14] *Ibid.*, p. 191.
[15] Cf. Abbott-Smith, *op. cit.*, p. 215.

2. The Expositor As a Grammarian

With the study of words must be coupled a knowledge of the grammatical structure of the languages of Scripture. Only as grammar is mastered can the exact meaning of the words be ascertained in relation to one another and the thoughts of the author discovered. The vocabulary and grammar of Biblical Hebrew and Greek, therefore, constitute the working tools of the expositor with which he is enabled to produce his exegesis of the sacred text.

Moreover, the student who would qualify as an authoritative interpreter of divine truth cannot possibly avoid the severe discipline necessary to acquiring a working knowledge of Hebrew and Greek. No seminary course that aims to train men to "preach the Word" can dispense with this requirement, or indeed, measurably reduce it without depriving its graduates of an essential tool for effective Bible preaching.

Grammar, as commonly taught in the seminary classroom, is usually divided into three parts — phonology, morphology and syntax. Phonology (from Greek *phone*, "sound" and *logos*, "study") involves pronunciation and oral reading of the letters and words of the language. It is essential, but less important to Biblical interpretation than morphology or syntax.

In inflected languages like Hebrew and Greek, morphology (from Greek *morphe*, "form" and *logos*, "study") is of paramount importance. As the particular form of a word indicates its case or its tense, gender, number, and person, according whether it is a noun, pronoun or a verb, to master these inflected elements in Biblical languages is indispensable to understanding the meaning of the sentence.

Coupled with morphology and also vitally important to an expositor's equipment is a comprehensive knowledge of the syntax of Hebrew and Greek. Syntax (from *suntaxis*, "a putting together in order," *sun*, "with," and *tassein*, "to put or place") "with reference to language . . . means the due arrangement of words in sentences and their agreement."[16]

[16] J. Wash Watts, *A Survey of Syntax in the Hebrew Old Testament* (Nashville, Broadman Press, 1951), p. 4.

The study of morphology lays the foundation for study in syntax. However, it is the latter that elucidates the meaning of the original languages of Scripture.

The benefits of adequate training in Hebrew and Greek syntax are varied and far-reaching for the expositor. Rays of light from many angles are shed upon the sacred passage being dealt with. A few examples selected at random are sufficient to demonstrate this fact.

Take, for instance, the syntax of the Hebrew sentence in general. Two kinds of sentences are found — the verbal and the nominal.[17] The verbal sentence contains a finite verb in the predicate, and this being the naturally stressed word, it is commonly placed first, the normal word order being verb, subject, object. If, however, the subject or object comes first, these elements naturally take the place of emphasis normally accorded the verb. Isaiah 1:3 furnishes an excellent example and the stressed words are italicized:

> "The ox knows its owner,
> and the ass its master's crib;
> but *Israel* does not know,
> *my people* does not understand" (RSV).

The Hebrew order in these verbal sentences is:

> Verb, subject, object
> (Verb) subject, object
> Subject, verb (object)
> Subject, verb, (object)

The Hebrew word order thus normally stresses the verb as in the first two clauses. The ox *knows* . . . the ass *knows*. However, in placing the subject before the verb in the last two sentences, the original transfers the emphasis to the subject and thereby presents a vivid contrast.

> "The ox knows . . . the ass [knows] . . .
> but *Israel* does not know,
> *my people* does not understand."

In Isaiah 1:14 the order is object, verb, subject, laying stress on the object:

[17] A. B. Davidson, *Hebrew Syntax* (3d ed.; Edinburgh, T. & T. Clark, 1942), pp. 144-148.

> *"Your new moons and your appointed feasts*
>   my soul hates."

In verse 15 (last clause) the order is subject, object, verb. Thus stress is laid upon the subject and especially upon the object:

> *"Your hands* are full of *blood."*

The nominal sentence in Hebrew does not contain a finite or regularly inflected verb, both the subject and predicate being a noun or its equivalent. In this type of sentence the subject is naturally emphatic and the normal order is subject and predicate: *"And the men of Sodom* were wicked" (Gen. 13:13). However, there is considerable freedom in the disposition of the parts of the nominal sentence "and emphasis on the predicate may give it first place."[18] Thus a simple adjective, when predicate, is often placed first in the emphatic position: *"Righteous* art thou, Jehovah" (Jer. 12:1). *"Holy, holy, holy* is the Lord of hosts" (Is. 6:3).

Turning to the New Testament the matter of word order in the sentence is also important to the expositor. There is, however, a notable freedom from rules in Greek and apparently a larger measure of spontaneity than in Hebrew, although the latter is by no means stereotyped. Often the predicate comes first, as in the Semitic verbal sentence, "simply because, as a rule, the predicate is the most important thing in the sentence."[19] *"Happy are* the poor in spirit" (Matt. 5:3). "And they all *went* to be enrolled, each to his own city" (Luke 2:3). The Greek order is "And *went* all to be enrolled" (*kai poreuonto pantes . . .*).

In Greek the matter of emphasis "is one of the ruling ideas in the order of words."[20] This stress may be at the end as well as at the beginning of a sentence. It may also occur at the middle in case of antithesis. In any event the emphasis consists in removing a word from its usual position to an unusual one. In I Corinthians 1:17 the negative idea is sharply emphasized by placing the *ou* ("not") first, and the

18 *Ibid.,* p. 145.
19 A. T. Robertson, *A Grammar of the Greek New Testament in the Light of Historical Research* (New York, Harper & Brothers, 5th ed., n.d.), p. 417.
20 *Ibid.*

object "me" is also given prominence by being placed before the subject, "Christ": *ou gar apesteilen me Christos baptizein alla euaggelizesthai.* "For Christ did *not* send *me* to baptize, but to evangelize." Likewise in I Corinthians 2:7, "God's wisdom" (*theou sophian*) instead of "the wisdom of God" (*ten sophian tou Theou*) throws proper emphasis upon "God's wisdom." The ARV is to the point: "But we speak God's wisdom in a mystery." The contrast is: "God's wisdom," not "the wisdom of this world nor of the rulers of this world" (I Cor. 2:6).

What is true of the word order in the Hebrew or Greek sentence is true of every other part of the sentence and every part of speech. Careful deductive study of the grammar and syntax of the Biblical languages is the only means of arriving at the accurate interpretation of the original languages of Scripture. It is the only solid basis for a systematic Biblical theology as well as the only sure foundation for authoritative Bible exposition.

The expositor who aspires to be fully qualified for his task must view his mastery of the grammar of the original languages of Scripture as the *sine qua non* of his preparation for his preaching and teaching ministry. Since the inspired originals constitute the fountainhead from which truth is drawn, he must learn how to tap this source of doctrine and precept. Since the Hebrew and Greek Scriptures are the mine from which the facts of revelation are dug, he must learn to use the tools of grammar for recovering these treasures buried in these ancient Biblical languages.

3. THE EXPOSITOR AS THE SELECTOR OF A BASIC EXEGETICAL LIBRARY

The interpreter of the Bible must build up an adequate library to aid him in his task. This is absolutely essential. These indispensable reference books are his tools, which he must not only learn to use skillfully, but constantly. Without such a collection of standard source volumes the best trained expositor is seriously handicapped. The following lists are minimal:

Editions of the Bible

For the Old Testament

 Kittel, R., *Biblia Hebraica* (Leipzig, 1906; 3d ed., giving Ben Asher's text edited by Paul Kahle and Otto Eissfeldt: Stuttgart, 1929-1937; 4th ed., 1945). These critical editions with copious notes and readings from the ancient versions are indispensable to careful study of the original text.

 Ginsburg, C. D., *The Old Testament diligently revised according to the Masorah and the Early Editions, with the Various Readings from Manuscripts and the Ancient Versions* (4 vols.; London, 1926).

For the New Testament

 Nestle, Eberhard, *Greek New Testament* (16th ed. rev. by Erwin Nestle).

For the Septuagint

 Rahlfs, Alfred, *Septuaginta* (2 vols.; Stuttgart, 1940).

Bible Lexicons

For the Old Testament

 Gesenius, W., *Hebrew and Chaldee Lexicon to the Old Testament Scriptures*, translated by S. P. Tregelles (reprint, Grand Rapids, Wm. B. Eerdmans Publishing Co., 1949).

 Buhl, F., *Hebraeisches und aramaeisches Handwoerter Buch ueber das Alte Testament* (1921).

 Brown, Driver, Briggs, *Hebrew and English Lexicon of the Old Testament* (1917).

 Koehler, Ludwig and Walter Baumgartner, *Lexicon in Veteris Testamenti Libros* (Leiden, E. J. Brill, 1951). This work includes Ugaritic words and many of the latest discoveries of archeology.

 Feyerabend, Karl, compiler, *Hebrew-English Pocket Dictionary* (4th ed.; Berlin, n.d.).

For the New Testament

 Thayer, J. H., *Greek-English Lexicon of the New Testament* (New York, 1889).

 Abbott-Smith, G., *A Manual Lexicon of the New Testament* (Edinburgh, T. & T. Clark, 1937).

 Moulton, J. H. and G. Milligan, *The Vocabulary of the Greek New Testament* (reprint, Grand Rapids, Wm. B. Eerdmans Publishing Co.).

 Cremer, H., *Biblical Theological Lexicon of the New Testament Greek* (ed. by Koegel, English translation of the 4th ed.).

 Souter, A., *The Pocket Lexicon to the Greek New Testament*. Contains material from the papyri.

 Green, Thomas S., *A Greek-English Lexicon* (22d ed., New York, Harper & Brothers, n.d.). Pocket lexicon.

BIBLICAL GRAMMARS

FOR THE OLD TESTAMENT

Gesenius-Kautsch, *Hebrew Grammar* (rev. by Cowley, Oxford, 1910).

Davidson, A. B., *Hebrew Grammar* (rev. by J. E. McFadyen, 24th ed.; New York, 1946).

———, *Hebrew Syntax* (3d ed.; Edinburgh, T. & T. Clark, 1942).

Driver, S. R., *A Treatise in the Uses of Tenses in Hebrew* (1892).

Bauer, H. and P. Leander, *Historische Grammatik der hebraeischen Sprache des Alten Testaments.*

Harper, W. R., *Elements of Hebrew* (New York, 1881).

———, *Elements of Hebrew Syntax* (New York, 1888).

Watts, J. Wash, *A Survey of Syntax in the Hebrew Old Testament* (Nashville, 1951).

FOR THE NEW TESTAMENT

Dana, H. E. and J. R. Mantey, *A Manual Grammar of the Greek New Testament* (New York, 1946).

Machen, J. G., *New Testament Greek for Beginners* (New York, 1947).

Robertson, A. T., *A Grammar of the Greek New Testament in the Light of Historical Research* (5th ed.; New York, 1931).

Chamberlain, *An Exegetical Grammar of the Greek New Testament.*

BIBLICAL CONCORDANCES

HEBREW

Davidson, A. B., *A Concordance of the Hebrew and Chaldee Scriptures* (London, Bagster, 1876).

Mandelkern, Solomon, *Veteris Testamenti Concordantiae* (Leipzig, 1896).

SEPTUAGINT

Hatch and Redpath, *A Concordance to the Septuagint.*

NEW TESTAMENT

Greenfield, W., *A Concordance to the Greek New Testament: Englishman's Greek Concordance.*

Moulton and Geden, *A Concordance of the Greek New Testament.*

Cruden's and Young's concordances are very useful.

COMMENTARIES

FOR THE OLD TESTAMENT (HIGHER CRITICAL)

The International Critical Commentary (Edinburgh, 1895——).

Westminster Commentaries, ed. by W. Locke and D. C. Simpson (London, 1904——).

The Expositor's Bible, ed., by W. Robertson Nicoll (London, 1887——; 6 vols.; reprint, Grand Rapids, Wm. B. Eerdmans Publishing Co.).

The Cambridge Bible for Schools and Colleges, ed. by A. F. Kirkpatrick (Cambridge, 1880——).

The New Century Bible, ed. by W. F. Adeney (Edinburgh, 1904——).

The Interpreter's Bible (New York, 1952——).

For the Old Testament (Conservative)

Grant, F. W., *The Numerical Bible.* Pentateuch, Joshua to II Samuel, The Psalms and Ezekiel (New York, 1889——).

Coates, C. A., *An Outline of Genesis, Exodus, Leviticus, Numbers and Deuteronomy* (Kingston on Thames, n.d.).

Gaebelein, A. C., *The Annotated Bible* (New York, 1913——).

Leupold, H. C., *Exposition of Genesis* (2 vols.; reprint, Grand Rapids, Baker Book House, 1950).

Ellicott, C. J., *A Bible Commentary for English Readers* (5 vols.; New York, n.d.; reprint, Grand Rapids, Zondervan Publishing House).

Keil, C. F. and F. Delitzsch, *Biblical Commentary on the Old Testament* (reprint, Grand Rapids, Wm. B. Eerdmans Publishing Co., 1949).

See also the works of Hengstenberg, Pusey, Jamieson, Fausset, Brown, Matthew Henry, F. C. Jennings, Candlish, Darby, Baron, Lange series, etc.

For the New Testament

Alford, Henry, *The Greek Testament* (4 vols.; Cambridge, 1868).

The Expositor's Greek Testament, ed. by W. Robertson Nicoll (5 vols.; reprint, Grand Rapids, Wm. B. Eerdmans Publishing Co., n.d.).

Ellicott, C. J., *A New Testament Commentary for English Readers* (3 vols., New York, 1883; reprint, Grand Rapids, Zondervan Publishing House).

Ryle, J. C., *Expository Thoughts on the Gospels* (4 vols.; reprint, Godet, Candlish, Newell (Romans and Revelation), Lange series, etc.

Conybeare and Howson, *The Life and Epistles of St. Paul* (New York, 1877; reprint, Grand Rapids, Wm. B. Eerdmans Publishing Co.).

See also works by Lenski, Moule, Seiss, Saphir, Westcott, Meyer, Godet, Candlish, Newell (Romans and Revelation), Lange series, etc.

With critical editions of the Biblical text, standard lexicons of the Greek and Hebrew Scriptures and concordances of the original languages, the student has the basic tools for effective grammatical interpretation of the Word of God. Commentaries and other helps he will consult. But the aim of the expositor ought to be to search out the meaning of the original inspired text for himself under the guidance of the Holy Spirit.

But independent and accurate exegetical work can only be done as the interpreter thoroughly prepares himself on the human side by securing a working knowledge of Biblical Hebrew and Greek. Securing this equipment the expounder of sacred truth overcomes the common disadvantage of so many preachers of being shut up to secondary sources. Instead of being confined to others' translations, comments and conclusions, he finds himself having access to the primary source of the original Scriptures themselves, where the Holy Spirit is free to lead him into independent and reliable discovery of truth for himself from the very source of truth — the Word of God in the original tongues.

LITERATURE ON GRAMMATICAL INTERPRETATION

Davidson, Samuel, Sacred Hermeneutics (Edinburgh, 1843).

Cellérier, J. E., Manuel D'Hermeneutique Biblique (Geneva, 1852).

Stowe, C. E., "The Right Interpretation of the Scriptures," Bibliotheca Sacra (1853), pp. 34-62.

Fairbairn, Patrick, Hermeneutical Manual (Edinburgh, T. & T. Clark, 1858), pp. 63-166.

Immer, A., Hermeneutics of the New Testament, translated by A. H. Newman (Andover, 1877).

Farrar, F. W., History of Interpretation (New York, Macmillan & Co., 1886).

Angus, J. and S. G. Green, The Bible Handbook (New York, Fleming Revell, 1908; reprint, Grand Rapids, Zondervan Publishing House).

Terry, Milton S., Biblical Hermeneutics (New York, Methodist Book Concern, 1911).

Lockhart, Clinton, Principles of Interpretation (Ft. Worth, S. H. Taylor, 1915).

Girdlestone, R. B., Synonyms of the Old Testament (reprint, Grand Rapids, Wm. B. Eerdmans Publishing Co., 1948).

Trench, R. C., Synonyms of the New Testament (reprint, Grand Rapids, Wm. B. Eerdmans Publishing Co., 1948).

Chapter XIV

THE EXPOSITOR AND HISTORICAL INTERPRETATION

Inseparably connected with the grammatical interpretation of the Bible is its historical study. While the definition of words and the grammatical construction of sentences are of primary importance in understanding the text of the Bible, the grammatical sense is not sufficient. There must also be the historical sense. There must be such an interpretation of the language of the inspired writers as is not only required by the laws of scientific grammar but demanded by the authentic facts of history as well.

Little reflection is necessary to demonstrate that the Word of God originated in a historical way, and accordingly can only be understood in the light of history. This most certainly is not to maintain that everything the Bible contains can be explained on a historical plane. As a supernatural divine revelation it, of course, presents much that transcends the limits of the historical, and the natural realm in general. But it does point out the fact "that the contents of the Bible are to a great degree historically determined and to that extent find their explanation in history."[1]

It is only natural that the Bible as a divine-human Book would, on the human side, be a product of the various authors and a reflection of the particular era in which they wrote, and be conditioned by the social, political and religious influences operating at the time.

1. The Expositor and the Biblical Author

In the historical interpretation of a book of the Bible it is often of great importance exegetically to know its human

[1] L. Berkhof, *Principles of Biblical Interpretation* (Grand Rapids, Baker Book House, 1950), p. 114.

author. However, the problems involved are not always simple, even when it is the mere critical question of a name. But in historical interpretation the question is far more than merely academic.

It is true that there are books in both the Old and New Testament that are anonymous insofar as human authorship is concerned, such as the books of Judges, Samuel, Kings, Ruth, Esther, etc. in the Old Testament and notably the Epistle to the Hebrews in the New Testament. But the authorship of most of the books of the Bible is known, and a knowledge of a writer is indispensable to the most effective exposition of what he wrote.

Only as an interpreter becomes familiar with the author of a book will he be in a position to understand properly his words. Certain phrases and sentences will in an unexpected way be illuminated. Allusions and figures otherwise unintelligible will become clear. Most important, the literary productions of the author, when he is known, will be lifted out of the purely abstract and begin to glow with energy and meaning as the embodiment of a living force.

The biographical data of Moses in the Pentateuch, of Isaiah, Jeremiah, Ezekiel, Amos and Hosea in their prophecies, of Paul in The Acts and in his Epistles, of John in his writings, of Peter in the Gospels, The Acts and in his own two epistles, aid immeasurably in elucidating these various portions of Scripture.

Of special importance are the geographical, social and political circumstances under which the author lived and wrote. Many passages, especially in the Old Testament, will be completely unintelligible unless the expositor takes pains to inform himself of the climate, the geography, the customs, and the economic conditions that prevailed in the particular era from which a writing stems.[2]

For example, Abraham's enthusiastic hospitality when he entertained three strangers, who proved to be angels (Gen.

[2] Cf. Edwin Cone Bissell, *Biblical Antiquities* (13th ed.; Philadelphia, American Sunday School Union, 1888); Albert E. Bailey, *Daily Life in Bible Times* (New York, Charles Scribner's Sons, 1943), Fred H. Wight, *Manners and Customs of Bible Lands* (Chicago, Moody Press, 1953).

18:2-7; cf. Heb. 13:2), can only be fully understood in the light of the Orientals' attitude toward entertaining a guest. Hospitality in the East is regarded as a sacred duty, and a person who becomes a guest is believed to be sent by God. It is not uncommon for an Oriental host to weep tears of joy at the privilege of entertaining, believing that "heaven had sent him guests."[3] Abraham's attitude was much the same as the modern bedouin of the desert. When he "ran to meet" the three men and "hastened into the tent unto Sarah" to get her to prepare a feast, and "ran unto the herd" to fetch a calf which he "hasted to dress," his unbounded joy would indicate his belief that those he was to entertain were sent him by the Lord.

Such instances of illumination of the sacred narrative by light from ancient manners and customs of Bible lands could be enumerated almost ad infinitum. One additional example is furnished in the practice of the midday siesta. During the summer season the time of the greatest heat is from noon to about three o'clock in the afternoon. During this period there is cessation of most activity and people rest at home or wherever they may be and can find a suitable place. Not uncommonly a place of business will be closed during these hours.

The midday rest period was common in Old Testament times. Abraham "sat in the tent door in the heat of the day" (Gen. 18:1). Ishbosheth, Saul's son, was murdered as he "lay on his bed at noon" (II Sam. 4:5). Saul entered the cave where David and his men were "to cover his feet" (I Sam. 24:3), that is, most certainly to take his middle-of-the-day nap.[4]

Often the political and religious conditions which furnished the background of a writer must be comprehended in order to understand the sacred narrative. Such a passage is Judges 21:25: "In those days there was no king in Israel: every man did that which was right in his own eyes." It must be borne in mind that Israel during the period of the Judges was a

<hr>

[3] Cf. Wight, *op. cit.*, p. 69; H. Clay Trumbull, *Studies in Oriental Social Life*, (Philadelphia, The Sunday School Times Co., 1894), p. 97.
[4] Wight, *op. cit.*, p. 86.

religious confederation organized loosely around the central sanctuary at Shiloh and that spiritual defection, manifested in a serious lapse into Canaanite Baal worship, dangerously nullified the unifying effect of their amphictyonic political organization. This furnishes the explanation of the anarchic conditions which prevailed during the period.[5]

The importance of understanding the historical and religious environment of Biblical writers finds salient illustration in the uncompromisingly severe attitude of the Old Testament toward the Canaanites and their religion. Archeological confirmation of the utterly corrupt nature of Canaanite cults and their debilitating effect upon Canaanite culture furnishes indispensable background material for accurate evaluation of such episodes as the total destruction of the people of Jericho and the conquest of the pre-Israelite inhabitants of Palestine, episodes which modern critical scholars show a tendency to misconstrue.[6]

2. THE EXPOSITOR AND THE SPEAKER

Besides a knowledge of the author and his circumstances and historical background, it is often of vital import in expounding a passage to know whether the writer himself or some other person is speaking. The Biblical writers frequently introduce others as speakers. The sense of the passage, accordingly, obviously depends upon accurately distinguishing the words of the author himself from those of the speaker or speakers introduced. In the historical books the identity of the writer is usually quite certain. However, even there exceptions occur. For instance, it is by no means obvious whether the words found in John 3:16-21 were spoken by Jesus to Nicodemus or whether they constitute a passage added by the Apostle John explanatory of the preceding context.

In the prophets a transition from the human to the divine

---

[5] Cf. W. F. Albright, *From the Stone Age to Christianity* (Baltimore, The Johns Hopkins Press, 1940), pp. 214-217.

[6] For example, H. H. Rowley, *The Relevance of the Bible* (New York, 1944), pp. 1-161. For historical and archeological light on the religion of the Canaanites see W. F. Albright, *Archeology and the Religion of Israel* (Baltimore, The Johns Hopkins Press, 1942), pp. 68-94.

is usually indicated by a change from the third person to the first in connection with the character of what is said (Hos. 9:9, 10; Zech. 12:8-10). In the poetical books the question of the speaker is often quite a thought-provoking problem as in Psalm 2. In the Song of Solomon it is often exceedingly difficult to determine who is speaking, whether the bride, the bridegroom, or the daughters of Jerusalem. Often, however, as in the Book of Job the identity of the speaker is quite obvious.

Sometimes a dialogue is presented between a speaker and an imaginary opponent as in Malachi 3:13-16 and Romans 3:1-9. Failure to differentiate between the two results in serious misinterpretation. Occasionally a speaker or writer expresses purely personal reactions, as the Apostle Paul does concerning widows in I Corinthians 7:40, or even expresses ideas contrary to truth, as Moses does concerning the serpent's lie in Genesis 3:4. Such sentiments must be clearly distinguished from the writer's thoughts or the mind of the Spirit, and perceived in their proper relationship to inspired truth.

3. THE EXPOSITOR AND THE SCOPE OR PLAN OF A BOOK

Of utmost importance to the accurate interpretation of the various books of the Bible is a clear understanding of the object the individual authors had in mind when they wrote. The end or purpose of their writing is called the *scope* and the order or arrangement of argument calculated to achieve this aim is called the *plan*. Since every writer has some end or purpose in view, the interpreter must make it his business to discover this purpose and to keep it constantly in mind with reference to the plan of the book.

It is necessary to believe that the mind of the writer under the control of the Holy Spirit was guided in the selection of his material and in the expression of his thoughts. Since this is true, it is quite evident that a knowledge of the end the author had in mind is not only indispensable to a grasp of the book as a whole, but is also necessary to understand the details. When once the expositor grasps the scope and plan of the author, light will shine upon obscurities, the true meaning will appear when several interpretations are possible, the literal will be distinguished from the figurative, the relative from the absolute, and main ideas will stand out from secondary thoughts.[7]

The scope or purpose of a book will be formally stated, implied or be apparent from the general course of the thought. There are cases where the scope or purpose is definitely announced, as in the Book of Proverbs:

> That men may know wisdom and instruction,
>   understand words of insight,
> receive instruction in wise dealing,
>   righteousness, justice, and equity;
> that prudence may be given to the simple,
>   knowledge and discretion to the youth —
> the wise man also may hear and increase in learning,
>   and the man of understanding acquire skill,
> to understand a proverb and a figure,
>   the words of the wise and their riddles.
>   (I:2-6, RSV)

The scope of the Book of Ecclesiastes is also specifically declared:

> Vanity of vanities, says the Preacher,
>   vanity of vanities! All is vanity.
> What does man gain by all the toil
>   at which he toils under the sun?
>   (I:2, 3, RSV)

The definite purpose of the Apostle John in writing the fourth gospel is also indicated: "Many other signs therefore did Jesus in the presence of his disciples, which are not written in this book: but these are written that ye may believe that Jesus is the Christ, the Son of God; and that believing ye may have life in his name" (John 20:30, 31, ARV).

Likewise in Jude's Epistle the clear object of the writer is set forth. However, it is modified by a pressing circumstance in the form of serious inroads by false teachers which forced the apostle to abandon his original purpose: "Beloved, while I was giving all diligence to write unto you of our common salvation, I was constrained to write unto you exhorting you to contend earnestly for the faith which was once

---

[7] Cf. Berkhof, op. cit., p. 126.

for all delivered unto the saints" (Jude 1:3, ASV). He then proceeds to expose the apostasy and duplicity of the false teachers who were threatening the message of common salvation.

Frequently, however, the scope of a writing is not definitely stated or clearly implied in any one passage, but can be determined only by a careful analysis of the contents of the book as a whole. In some instances a knowledge of the original readers and their particular circumstances that called forth the composition of the book is necessary to discover its purpose. The Corinthian and Thessalonian letters are of such a character as well as the Epistle to the Hebrews.

In other cases the clue to the purpose of a book is not found in a knowledge of the original readers and their particular needs, but is arrived at only by repeated careful reading of the text. The Book of Genesis furnishes an example. The tenfold "these are the generations of," *'elleh hattoledoth* (2:4; 5:1; 6:9; 10:1; 11:10; 11:27; 25:12; 25:19; 36:1; 37:2), furnish its skeletal plan and point to it as a book of births or beginnings.

The Book of Exodus in similar fashion displays its clear purpose to be to record the history of Egyptian bondage and deliverance (chaps. 1-18) and to give an account of the legislation from Sinai (chaps. 19-40). As a book of redemption, Exodus introduces the Book of Leviticus, which in turn recounts the cleansing, worship and service of the redeemed people. Leviticus in turn introduces Numbers as the book of the service and walk of God's redeemed people.

4. THE EXPOSITOR AND THE CONTEXT

Inseparably connected with the scope and plan of a writing is the matter of context. Derived from the Latin (*con* or *cum*, "with, together" and *texere*, "to weave") the term denotes something that is "woven-together" and forms a thought pattern. Sometimes called "the connection" (also from the Latin, *con*, "with," and *nectere*, "to bind") this latter term presents the idea of joined or linked together. The context, therefore, is "the part of a discourse in which a word or passage occurs and which helps to explain the meaning of the word or passage."[8]

Most Biblical books present a closely knit argument or development, and a verse or passage is like the individual pieces of a jig-saw puzzle or the varicolored threads woven into a pattern. If we would understand the part, we must see it in proper relation to the whole. Only as the pieces of a jig-saw puzzle are fitted properly together does the picture appear. Only as the single threads are woven properly together does the pattern become visible. It is similar in the matter of interpretation of Scripture. Only as a passage is interpreted in relation to that which precedes and follows it can the truth it contains be clearly seen and explained.

The importance of construing a passage in the light of its context can scarcely be overemphasized. Berkhof correctly calls it *"the conditio sine qua non* of all sound exegesis."[9] Yet no single requirement of accurate Biblical exposition is so widely disregarded, especially by those who view the Bible as a collection of proof texts. But anyone, no matter how soundly his views of Biblical inspiration and authority may be, is in danger of ignoring the context, particularly if he unwittingly labors to sustain some Biblically unsound system of interpretation, some mere sectarian dogma, or some ecclesiastical heresy over which time and tradition have cast a halo.

The doctrinal errors upon which the popular cults and sects of our day flourish have arisen to a large extent because the original promulgators of these alleged truths ignored the context of the passages out of which they were taken. Later followers of these teachers embraced these tenets without once testing them rigidly in the crucible of their contextual relationships. Subjection to such a rigorous test would dispose of many of the lopsided teachings and doctrinal aberrations that divide and weaken the professing Church of Jesus Christ today.

Examples of passages misinterpreted in the course of time

---

[8] *Webster's Collegiate Dictionary* (5th ed.; Springfield, Mass., G. & C. Merriam Co., 1941), p. 219.

[9] *Op. cit.*, p. 104.

and these perversions handed down from generation to generation could be cited almost without number. Such errors as salvation by works, baptismal regeneration, sinless perfection and a second work of grace are but a few of the popular distortions of truth widely subscribed to by different Christian sects.

A classic example of an error which has arisen as a result of failing to pay attention to the context is the doctrine of "falling from grace," construed as "losing one's salvation," supposedly the teaching of Galatians 5:4: "Christ is become of no effect unto you, whosoever of you are justified by the law; ye are fallen from grace." However, just a cursory examination of the connection of this passage with the Apostle's closely developed argument in Galatians involving law and grace will disclose that he is not talking at all about "losing one's salvation," if such a thing were possible, but simply describing those who abandon a grace-faith approach for some admixture of law-works as a basis of their acceptance in Christ.

Another example is the error of connecting the baptism of the Holy Spirit (Matt. 3:11; Mark 1:8; Luke 3:16; John 1:32, 33; Acts 1:5; 11:16; I Cor. 12:13; Rom. 6:3, 4; Gal. 3:27; Col. 2:12) with a so-called "second work of grace," or with "the filling of the Spirit," or with an experience of eradication of the sin nature, or with some other experience subsequent to salvation. These numerous errors are the result of failing to see the various references to the baptism of the Holy Spirit in their respective contextual relationships — the prophetic context in the Gospels, the historical-dispensational context in Acts and the doctrinal context in the Epistles. When the context is properly taken into account the error vanishes.[10]

In dealing with a passage it is necessary to take into consideration both the immediate as well as the remote context. Often due consideration of the thought or argument immediately preceding and following a passage is sufficient to

[10] For an exhaustive discussion of this theme see the author's *The Baptizing Work of the Holy Spirit* (Wheaton, Ill., Van Kampen Press, 1953).

furnish an accurate exposition of it. However, frequently a knowledge of the more remote context is demanded and may embrace a whole paragraph, chapter or number of chapters, an entire book, or in its largest sense the relation of that book to the other books of the Bible.

It is accordingly apparent that the context is intimately connected with the scope and plan of a book, and should be studied in conjunction with them. Normally the scope of a writing should be ascertained first, for the precise meaning of the parts of a book are not likely to be clearly or fully apprehended until the general purpose and plan are understood as a whole.[11]

The Epistle to the Romans furnishes a good example. The purpose, expressed in Chapter I, verse 16 is: "The gospel considered as the power of God unto salvation to every believer, to the Jew first and also to the Greek."[12] The purpose of the book is unfolded according to the following plan of development:

I. Doctrinal. The Salvation of God (I-VIII)
   1. Introduction (I:1-17)
   2. The Need of Salvation. The whole world guilty and lost (I:18-III:20)
   3. The Righteousness of God revealed in Justification of the sinner (III:21-V:11)
   4. The Righteousness of God revealed in the Sanctification of the believer (V:12-VIII:39)
II. Dispensational. God's Dealings with Israel (IX-XI)
   1. Israel and God's Sovereignty (IX)
   2. Israel's Unbelief and Failure (X)
   3. Israel's Future Faith and Conversion (XI)
III. Exhortations and Conclusion (XII:1-XVI:13)
   1. The exhortations (XII:1-XV:13)
   2. The conclusion (XV:14-XVI:27)[13]

Proper attention to the scope and plan of the Book of Romans will be found to be of indispensable help in comprehending the smaller sections. The presentation of the need

11 Milton S. Terry, *Biblical Hermeneutics* (New York, Methodist Book Concern, 1911), p. 108.

12 *Ibid.*, p. 111.

13 Cf. A. C. Gaebelein, *The Annotated Bible* (*Romans-Ephesians*) (New York, Our Hope, 1916), pp. 6, 7.

of salvation in the guilt and lost condition of men prefaces the way for the doctrine of justification of the sinner, which in turn prepares the way for the doctrine of the sanctification of the believer. Only in the light of God's dealing with mankind as a whole (chaps. I-VIII) can the dispensational section treating Israel's past, present and future be understood (IX-XI).

Having determined the general scope and plan of a book, the expositor is prepared to trace the connection of a passage in its more immediate context. In this closer scrutiny the connection of a passage should be sought as near as possible. Sometimes, however, a passage does not yield good sense in connection with what immediately precedes. Romans 2:16 is such an example. Although some would connect this verse with verse 15, this is obviously unsatisfactory. The real connection is either with verse 12 or 13, with the intervening verses construed as a parenthesis.

In the matter of establishing the context the expositor must always be careful to look for parentheses, digressions, or anacolutha. The latter is a literary device expressing energy or strong emotion in which one grammatical construction is abandoned in the midst of a sentence in favor of another that is grammatically different (Zech. 2:11; Ps. 18:47, 48; Luke 5:14).

Sometimes an anacoluthon is combined with a parenthesis or a digression. In such a case the expositor must exert special care to discern the connection of thought. This is true of Romans 5:12-21. In Romans 5:12 the Apostle says: "Therefore as sin came into the world through one man and death through sin, and so death spread to all men because all men sinned . . ." (RSV). He would be expected to continue right on with these words: "so also by one, Jesus Christ, righteousness, and through righteousness, life." But instead he breaks off into a parenthesis or digression (vv. 13-17) and resumes his thought in verse 18. But when he takes up his thought again he resorts to an anacoluthon or a changed grammatical construction.

Occasionally when the connection appears to be undeterminable, the passage may contain a reflection on, or an answer to, the thoughts of the persons addressed, in distinction from their words. Our Lord often gave answer to the thoughts rather than the actual words of his hearers, and the connection is psychological. For example, Nicodemus "came to Jesus by night, and said unto him, Rabbi, we know that thou art a teacher come from God: for no man can do these miracles that thou doest, except God be with him." Jesus, evidently reading the heart of Nicodemus and discerning his need, strikes at the root of that need and says to his visitor, "Verily, verily, I say unto thee, Except a man be born again, he cannot see the kingdom of God" (John 3:2, 3).

Other examples of a possible psychological connection are Jesus' replies to the Pharisees on several occasions as he read the evil thoughts of their hearts (John 5:17, 19, 41). Micah 2:12, 13, too, which some commentators have adjudged to be an interpolation because of its apparent lack of connection, is to be explained as psychologically joined to the prophet's warning to the people of prophesying of wine and strong drink that appeared so desirable to them (v. 11). The idea of this seeming good furnishes him opportunity to turn to the real blessings that the Lord would provide for his faithful people as recounted in verses 12 and 13.

Numerous instances also occur in the Scriptures where the authors themselves explain their own words or the words of the speakers whom they introduce, and thus furnish an invaluable aid to the expositor in clarifying the connection. Note, for example, Jesus' great words at the Feast of Tabernacles in Jerusalem: "In the last day, the great day of the feast, Jesus stood up and proclaimed, If any one thirst, let him come to me and drink. He who believes in me, as the scripture has said, Out of his heart shall flow rivers of living water" (John 7:37, 38, RSV). John significantly adds the explanation: "Now this he said about the Spirit, which those who believed in him were to receive; for as yet the Spirit had not been given, because Jesus was not yet glorified" (v. 39).

The wise expositor, so far from ignoring such explanations,

will welcome them, and pay strict attention to them. He will not only realize that the author is best qualified to know what he means in a certain passage, but the reverent interpreter will rest in the confidence that such elucidations are inspired by the Spirit along with the remainder of the text. Examples of such explanatory insertions by the author are found in John 2:21; 7:29; 12:33; Romans 7:18 and Hebrews 7:21.

5. THE EXPOSITOR AND INTERNAL AIDS TO HISTORICAL INTERPRETATION

The chief resources for the historical interpretation of the Scriptures are found in the Bible itself. This fact will not be doubted by the thoroughly sound expositor. He will fully and unqualifiedly subscribe to II Timothy 3:16 and II Peter 1:21 that "all Scripture is inspired (God-breathed)" and that "no prophecy ever came by the impulse of man, but men moved by the Holy Spirit spoke from God."

Accordingly, the faithful Biblical interpreter will have no difficulty in believing that the Bible is reliable in its historical aspects. Realizing that, in distinction from all other writings, it contains absolute truth, he will not balk at preferring its information and the history it contains to that gleaned from other sources. He will welcome the light which other sources may be able to throw on the exposition and illustration of Biblical truth, but the internal evidence of the infallible Word of God itself will always be for him the real fountain-head of truth.

The first question of the devout student of Scripture will always be: What do the Scriptures say? He will deplore the attitude of some professing evangelicals who seem inclined to give more credence to the voice of profane history, to the alleged evidence of archeology, or to the assumptions of modern literary critcism than to the Inspired Oracles of God. He will welcome light from these various sources of knowledge, but where conflict or contradiction occur, he will test alleged evidence with the utmost rigidity before granting its validity.

The expositor will be continuously aware that his great task is to study the Bible evidence itself. He will be impressed with the necessity of comparing passage with passage, chapter with chapter, book with book, historical reference with historical reference. Only a little experience in Bible exposition will teach the expositor the fundamental truth that the Bible is a systematic and progressive revelation of God's plans and purposes for man and the ages and that in a very definite sense is complete in itself. As such, it does not depend upon external helps either historical, archeological or literary in order that its spiritual and moral lessons may be comprehended.

For this reason it soon becomes apparent to the Bible expositor that his predominant task is understanding what the Scriptures themselves say. That this can only be accomplished by comparing Scripture with Scripture soon becomes clear to the conscientious Bible student. One of his chief rules becomes this: *Scripture is illuminated and explained by Scripture.*

For example, our Lord in John 10:34-36 refers enigmatically to the term "gods." "Jesus answered them, Is it not written in your law, I said, ye are gods? If he called them gods, unto whom the word of God came, and the scripture cannot be broken; say ye of him, whom the Father hath sanctified, and sent into the world, Thou blasphemest; because I said, I am the Son of God?" To ascertain what Jesus meant in this passage one has to examine the historical occurrence of this expression "god," as employed of "one to whom the word of God came." When Psalm 82:6 is accordingly scrutinized in the light of Exodus 21:6; 22:8; I Sam. 28:13, there appears the well-established Hebrew usage of applying the term "god" to a judge or prophet, whom God dignified with His word and His authority to bear His own name. Thus comparison of Scripture with Scripture illuminates the sense of the passage in John's Gospel.

In like manner Paul's reference to "Christ our Passover" having been "sacrificed" and his exhortation to "keep the feast" (I Cor. 5:7, 8) is to be illuminated first of all by comparison with the Old Testament historical account of this ancient Hebrew feast (Ex. 12:1-21; Lev. 23:4-14; Deut. 16: 1-8).

Similarly, Jesus' reference to "the kingdom of heaven" being like "leaven which a woman took and hid in three measures of meal, till the whole was leavened (Matt. 13:33) must be interpreted on the basis of the progress of evil and not good if we compare Scripture with Scripture. The symbol of leaven in the Old Testament is always mentioned in an evil sense (Gen. 19:3; Ex. 12:8, 15-20). In the New Testament likewise it is "malice and wickedness" (I Cor. 5:6-8), evil doctrine (Matt. 16:12; Mark 8:15; Matt. 22:23, 29). How incongruous, then, to assign it arbitrarily a good meaning in Matthew 13:33, as many interpreters have erroneously done and thus have violated the significance attached to it in the history of Israelite religious thought and practice.

6. THE EXPOSITOR AND EXTERNAL AIDS TO HISTORICAL INTERPRETATION

Although the Bible as a divine revelation is in a very definite sense complete in itself and does not depend upon external sources in order that its spiritual lessons may be understood, yet outside helps may cast a great deal of light upon the Biblical narratives. When the expositor has exhausted the resources of Scripture and still needs further information, he should turn to the various profane sources at his disposal. These belong to two general categories, historical and archeological, and external aids to understanding the Bible are based upon one or the other of these sources, or more commonly upon a combination of the two.

ORIGINAL HISTORICAL SOURCES

For the Old Testament: A great mass of literary material in the form of clay tablets, stelae (engraved stone monuments), and other types of inscriptions has been uncovered in Egypt, Babylonia, Assyria, Asia Minor and Palestine by modern archeological research. Much of this huge corpus of information, which sheds such abundant light on Biblical backgrounds and customs, has been published by competent scholars and its significance for Biblical studies set forth. New discoveries and the older material that has lain untouched in the museums are continually being published.

ARCHEOLOGY AND THE SCRIPTURES

The following books, among others, contain valuable collections of the earlier inscriptions as they bear on the contents of the Old Testament:

King, L. W. and E. A. Wallis Budge, *Annals of the Kings of Assyria* (London, 1902).

Schrader, E., *Keilinschriftliche Bibliothek* (Berlin, 1889, 1900).

Gressmann, H., *Altorientalische Texte zum Alten Testament* (Berlin and Leipzig, 1926).

Luckenbill, D. D., *Ancient Records of Assyria and Babylonia* (Chicago, 1906-1927).

Rawlinson, H. C., *The Cuneiform Inscriptions of Western Asia* (London, 1861-1884).

Langdon, S., *Oxford Editions of Cuneiform Texts* (1923ff.).

Other important sources include:

Breasted, James A., *Records of Ancient Egypt* (5 vols.; Chicago, 1906-1907).

Knudtzon, J. A., *Die Amarna Tafeln* (1915).

Cowley, A., *Aramaic Papyri of the Fifth Century B. C.* (Oxford, 1923).

Gordon, C. H., *Ugaritic Literature* (Rome, 1949).

Kramer, S. N., *Sumerian Mythology* (Philadelphia, 1944).

Pritchard, James E., *Ancient Near Eastern Texts Relating to the Old Testament* (Princeton, 1950).

Source material of significance for New Testament study are the inscriptions on the papyri and ostraca, particularly those from Egypt and Asia Minor. Important and easily accessible volumes are:

Deissman, A., *Light from the Ancient East* (New York, 1910).

————, *Bible Studies* (Edinburgh, 1903).

Ramsay, Sir William M., *The Bearing of Recent Discovery on the Trustworthiness of the New Testament* (4th ed., London, 1920; reprint, Grand Rapids, Baker Book House).

Kenyon, Sir Frederick, *The Bible and the Ancient Manuscripts* (New York, rev. ed., 1939).

Meecham, H. C., *Light from the Ancient Letters* (New York, 1923).

The Life and Works of Flavius Josephus (Philadelphia, n.d.).

The New Testament Apocrypha.

The writings of Philo.

Works on Old and New Testament archeology include the following:

Driver, S. R., *Modern Research As Illustrating the Bible* (London, 1909).
Rogers, R. W., *Cuneiform Parallels to the Old Testament* (2d ed.; New York, 1926).
Albright, W. F., *The Archeology of Palestine and the Bible* (3d ed.; New York, 1935).
————, *From the Stone Age to Christianity* (Baltimore, 1940).
————, *Archeology and the Religion of Israel* (Baltimore, 1942).
————, *The Archeology of Palestine* (Penguin Books, 1949).
Burrows, Millar, *What Mean These Stones?* (New Haven, 1941).
Barton, George W., *Archeology and the Bible* (7th ed.; Philadelphia, 1937).
Kenyon, Sir Frederic, *The Bible and Archeology* (New York, 1940).

A valuable survey of the general field is:

Finegan, J. W., *Light from the Ancient Past* (Princeton, 1946).

Useful also are:

Adams, J. Mckee, *Ancient Records and the Bible* (Nashville, 1946).
Free, J. P., *Archeology and Bible History* (Wheaton, Ill., Van Kampen Press, 1950).
Unger, Merrill F., *Archeology and the Old Testament* (Grand Rapids, Zondervan Publishing House, 1954).

Books on New Testament archeology include the following:

Caiger, S. L., *Archeology and the New Testament* (London, 1939).
Cobern, C. M., *The New Archeological Discoveries and Their Bearing Upon the New Testament* (9th ed.; New York, 1929).

Bible Dictionaries

Smith, *Dictionary of the Bible* (New York, 1871).
Cheyne, T. K. and J. S. Black, *Encyclopaedia Biblica* (4 vols.; London, 1899-1903).
Hastings, J., *A Dictionary of the Bible* (5 vols.; Edinburgh, 1898-1904).
Vigouroux, F., *Dictionnaire de la Bible* (5 vols.; Paris, 1895-1912).
Fausset, Canon A. R., *Bible Cyclopaedia* (New York, n.d.).
Peloubet, F. N., *Bible Dictionary* (Philadelphia, 1912).
Orr, James, ed., *International Standard Bible Encyclopaedia* (5 vols.; reprint, Grand Rapids, Wm. B. Eerdmans Publishing Co., 1939).
Barnes, Charles R., *Bible Cyclopaedia* (2 vols.; New York, 1903).
Davis, John D., *A Dictionary of the Bible* (1898-1924; reprint, Grand Rapids, Baker Book House).
Gehman, Henry Snyder, *The Westminster Dictionary of the Bible* (Philadelphia, 1944).
Miller, Madeleine and J. Lane, *Harper's Bible Dictionary* (New York, 1952).

BIBLE GEOGRAPHIES AND ATLASES

Smith, George Adam, *Historical Geography of the Holy Land* (New York, 1903).

Thompson, W. M., *The Land and the Book* (London, 1903).

Dalman, Gustav, *Sacred Sites and Ways: Studies in the Topography of the Gospels* (New York, 1935).

Adams, J. Mckee, *Biblical Backgrounds* (2d ed.; Nashville, 1938).

Abel, F. M., *Geographie de la Palestine* (2 vols.; Paris, 1933 and 1938).

Wright, G. E. and F. V. Filson, *The Westminster Historical Atlas to the Bible* (Philadelphia, 1945).

BIBLE HISTORIES

Wade, G. W., *Old Testament History* (5th ed.; New York, 1908).

Cook, S. A., in the *Cambridge Ancient History* (Cambridge, 1923——), Vols. II, III, VI.

Olmstead, A. T., *History of Palestine and Syria* (New York, 1931).

Oesterley, W. O. E. and T. H. Robinson, *A History of Israel* (2 vols.; Oxford, 1932).

Mould, E. W. K., *Essentials of Bible History* (New York, 1939).

Edersheim, Alfred, *The Life and Times of Jesus the Messiah* (2 vols.; 31st ed.; 1940).

Schuerer, E., *A History of the Jewish People in the Time of Jesus Christ* (4 vols.; New York, 1891).

LITERATURE ON HISTORICAL INTERPRETATION

Davidson, Samuel, *Sacred Hermeneutics* (Edinburgh, 1843), pp. 320-333.

Lutz, J. L. S., *Biblische Hermeneutik* (2d ed., 1861), pp. 228-274.

Terry, Milton S., *Biblical Hermeneutics* (New York, Methodist Book Concern, 1911), pp. 129-140.

CHAPTER XV

THE EXPOSITOR AND DOCTRINAL INTERPRETATION

As grammatical interpretation of the Bible is inseparably connected with historical study in sound exegetical method, so both are inextricably bound up with theological interpretation. Because of the unique nature of the Bible as a divine revelation, having God as its Author on the divine side and the Holy Spirit as its only proper Interpreter through men on the human side, the Scriptures cannot be placed on a level with other books. For this reason grammatical-historical interpretation, while basic and indispensable, cannot meet the full requirements for the proper interpretation of the Bible. A third factor, the doctrinal or theological, must be taken into consideration, inasmuch as grammatical-historical exegesis, if followed to its logical conclusion, must inevitably lead to the formulation of doctrines and the systematization of theological truths.

Theological interpretation, which the expositor cannot avoid, thus leads to an extension of the grammatical-historical meaning to its fuller theological significance and, in its final development, to a synoptic view of all the Biblical data on a given subject. Moreover, this type of hermeneutical approach not only finds abundant justification in the nature and inspiration of the Bible as a revelation of divine truth, but also in the emphasis it lays upon doctrine (John 7:16, 17; Rom. 6:17; Eph. 4:14; II Tim. 3:16) and the doctrinal use of the Old Testament by New Testament writers (cf. Rom. 4:3; 10:11; 11:8, 9, etc.).

Doctrinal interpretation also finds full corroboration in practical Christian living. A "non-theological type of Christianity is essentially anemic."[1] In recent years the type of liberalism that scoffed at doctrine and customarily denied the possibility of a Biblical theology, at least of the Old Testament, if not of the New, has demonstrated its real inability to meet human need. On the other hand, the trend in liberal circles toward more emphasis on doctrine, with the success of such doctrinal systems as Barthianism, has proved the hunger in the human heart for a systematic presentation of revealed truth.

However, to safeguard doctrinal interpretation it is essential for the expositor to keep certain fundamental principles in mind. Above all he must constantly remind himself that the Scripture itself is the source of his theology and that the Bible as a doctrinal source-book is a unity. He must also strive to relate properly the Old Testament to the New and differentiate between God's dealing with the believer before and after the Cross. He must respect the silence of revelation on certain phases of revealed truth. He must give proper place to the devotional-practical aspects of the truth he expounds. Finally, he must surround himself with a basic theological library of sound works to stimulate and guide his thinking.

1. THE EXPOSITOR AND THE SOURCE OF THEOLOGY

Every expositor must have a theology. The reason for this is obvious. Since the Bible is a revelation of God's truth, any serious study of it must lead to the formation of doctrines. Although theologians often derive their theology to a large extent from philosophy or from tradition, this can never be the case of the genuine Biblical interpreter. The source of his doctrine and the mainspring of his theology must always be the Bible itself. The grammatical and historical study of Scripture must for him be prior to any system of theological doctrine and the source of the truth he systematically preaches and teaches.

Roman Catholic theology draws heavily upon tradition, while the historical Protestant method is to derive doctrine exegetically from the Bible. However, much of Protestant

---

[1] Bernard Ramm, *Protestant Biblical Interpretation* (Boston, W. A. Wilde Co., 1950), p. 98.

theology contains a large element of traditionalism as opposed to strict Biblicism, as well as a substantial philosophical ingredient. The Biblical expositor, on the other hand, must ruthlessly test traditionalism and reject it if it does not fully tally with Biblical truth, no matter how enshrined it may be in present-day theological thinking.

As far as philosophy is concerned, the expositor, although recognizing the place of the philosophic theologian in his important task of correlating Christianity and secular knowledge, particularly human systems of thought, must, however, carefully avoid building his doctrines upon human philosophy or allowing himself to employ it as an independent source of truth. The Bible expositor must rigidly adhere to his task of expounding the one system of truth as contained in the Bible and guard himself vigilantly against any intrusion of human systems of thought which would becloud or pervert Biblical truth or spoil his message by intermixture of worldly wisdom that in turn could in any sense set aside the Word of God (Col. 2:8).

2. THE EXPOSITOR AND THE UNITY OF THE BIBLE

Perhaps no single factor is more detrimental to Biblical exposition in our day than a widespread failure to recognize that the Bible is a unity, and in order to be adequately interpreted must be treated as such. In many circles this unity is lost sight of in a tendency to emphasize the diversity of the content of the Bible.

In other circles the Old Testament and New Testament are studied apart from one another, with little or no attention paid to their close interrelation. Their theologies are frequently treated separately and in many instances the New Testament is refused its legitimate role as a commentary on the Old Testament. Schools and theological seminaries customarily allocate the Old and New Testament into different departments, a practice doubtless necessary, but fraught with the gravest peril to expository preaching, when the essential unity of the Bible is not kept constantly in mind.

In view of these present-day tendencies in Biblical studies it is not superfluous to stress the fact that the Bible is a unity. A number of characteristics of the Scriptures attest this unity. From beginning to end divine truth bears witness to one God and gives a full revelation of Him. This unifying theme of Scripture centers in the person and work of Christ. The development of this theme constitutes one continuous story – the story of human sin and redemption. This story is progressively unfolded first in type, symbol and prophecy and finally in full manifestation in the person and work of the promised Redeemer.

The great unifying redemptive theme of Scripture with all of its marvelous interweaving of history and prophecy and its rich symbolic and typical detail binds the sixty-six books together in what is in reality one Book. The various books, when properly viewed, are thus to be thought of as one unified volume rather than as separate volumes in a mere literary collection.

Moreover, any serious effort to master the content of the Scriptures and to expound it intelligently depends upon this correct view of its unity. Unless one sees that the story and message of the Bible are like a picture intricately wrought out in mosaics, with each book, chapter, verse and even word forming an indispensable part and each with its own appointed place, he is unlikely to take much pains to try to understand it in any exhaustive sense.

As a result of an inadequate view of the unity of the Bible the student will not only be unable to expound the content of the Bible himself, but will look with distrust, if not with positive hostility, upon those who do attempt expository work, regarding their attempts as bold pretension and their claims' as pure presumption. The theological interpretations of the student with defective views of the unity of Scripture will be unreliable, because partial or distorted, owing to his faulty use of the sources of his doctrines in the Word of God itself.

3. THE EXPOSITOR AND THE RELATION BETWEEN THE OLD TESTAMENT AND THE NEW

Since the Bible is a unity, the precise connection between the Old Testament and the New, which constitute the two

well-defined parts of God's Word, must be carefully set forth
if a great deal of theological error is to be avoided. In describing this relationship in a general sense it may be said
that the Old Testament is the introduction to the New and
the revelation of God's ways and purposes therein revealed.

In other words, the Old Testament by history, type and
prophecy is the *preparation* for the Redeemer set forth in the
New. The Gospels constitute His *manifestation* among men
and His provision for their salvation in His death and resurrection. The Book of Acts gives the account of the preaching
of the Redeemer and the *propagation* of His world-wide
Gospel. The Epistles form the doctrinal *explanation* of the
Gospel. The Revelation embodies the *consummation* of all
the purposes of God in Christ for time and eternity.

It is of the utmost importance for the expositor to keep
constantly in mind that the Old Testament is a vital and
inseparable part of the New and that actually there could
have been no New Testament without it. In fact the interpreter is not on thoroughly sound ground in his definition
of relationship between the two testaments until he is persuaded that the New Testament is to a large extent mean-
ingless apart from the Old Testament.

There is sometimes a tendency to stress the fact that the
New Testament as the capstone of revelation is "the chief
source of Biblical doctrine" and "Christian theology" and
tacitly, at least, to imply its superiority in this respect to the
Old Testament.[2] Although this is undoubtedly true, at least
to a degree, such implied comparisons are unwise to the extent that they lose sight of the unity of the Bible and the
inseparable connection between the Old and New Testament.
Can we validly separate a tree from its roots, or a building
from its foundation, or a body from its head? No more can
we disassociate the New Testament from the Old in our
thinking and have each live or exist in the relationship in
which it was meant to be.

New Testament doctrines, despite the fact that they do
shine forth in the full light of revelation, are nevertheless

[2] Ramm, *op. cit.*, p. 101.

so inextricably bound up with Old Testament truths, although the latter are often set forth in shadows, types and prophecies, that to separate them in any way is to incur the peril of distorting them, or at least forfeiting the sense of their development and full-orbed symmetry.

Several rules of interpretation follow from the intimate relationship which exists between the Old Testament and the New.

(1) *The Old Testament must always be diligently searched for the key to the right interpretation of the New.* Paul's doctrine of the guilt of mankind and the revelation of God's wrath (Rom. 1:18 - 3:20) can only be fully comprehended in the light of man's fall recorded in Genesis 3. The Epistle to the Hebrews with its detailed references to the Old Testament priesthood and ritual is understandable only in the light of the accounts of the Tabernacle and priesthood in Exodus and Leviticus. Our Lord's reference to the abomination of desolation (Matt. 24:15) is comprehensible only as the prophecy of Daniel is searched (Dan. 9:27; 11:31; 12:11).

(2) *The New Testament furnishes an inspired commentary on the Old.* The New Testament is not only *enfolded* in the Old, the Old Testament is *unfolded* by the New. Paul's allegory in Galatians 4:22-31, Jesus' reference to Moses' lifting up the serpent in the wilderness (John 3:14) and the entire Book of Hebrews furnish examples. Another striking instance is Matthew 1:23. Its reference to "the virgin" who "shall bring forth a son . . . Emmanuel" gives an inspired comment on Isaiah 7:14: "Behold a virgin[3] shall conceive, and bear a son, and shall call his name Immanuel" (Is. 7:14). Those with unsound views of inspiration, however, would call this "reading" the New Testament into the Old. But the expositor who is sound in his views of Biblical inspiration is not troubled by charges of this sort.

(3) *The expositor must guard against minimizing the Old Testament.* This is the error of rationalistic critics who rule

[3] Revised Standard Version renders "young woman," rejecting the New Testament comment.

out special divine intervention and miracle in Israel's history and institutions as well as those who regard the Old Testament as a phase of historical development which has had its day and which is not needed since we have the New Testament. It is likewise the mistake of those who refuse a future to Israel in the coming age with the fulfilment of such covenants divinely made to the nation as the Palestinian (Deut. 30:1-10) and the Davidic (II Sam. 7:4-7), and such promises as her national restoration (Ezek. 37:1-28) and millennial worship and glory (Ezek. 40:1 - 48:35).

4. THE EXPOSITOR AND GOD'S DEALING WITH MANKIND IN THE VARIOUS PERIODS OF REDEMPTIVE HISTORY

No single qualification is quite so important to an expositor as the ability to discern the difference between the divine dealings with the human race in the various time periods of redemptive history in which man has been tested in respect of obedience to some *specific* revelation of God's will. Some of these so-called "dispensations," while clearly distinguishable, we believe, from a careful study of Scripture, are nevertheless, it is true, less important than others and are often denied the status of a dispensation without, perhaps, serious detriment to the accurate interpretation of the Bible.

Such less important periods are the dispensations of innocence, conscience, human government and promise. In the *dispensation of innocence* man, created innocent, was placed in a perfect environment and subjected to a simple test of not eating of the tree of the knowledge of good and evil. Nevertheless he disobeyed God's command and fell, thus incurring the judgment of the curse (Gen. 1:28 - 3:13).

In the *dispensation of conscience* (Gen. 3:23 - 7:23), man having come to a personal and experiential knowledge of good and evil as a result of the fall, through that knowledge experienced an awakened conscience. Expelled from Eden and placed under the Adamic Covenant (Gen. 3:14-19), man was accountable to approach God through sacrifice and to act according to the known will of God. The result of this testing was man's almost complete degeneration (Gen. 6:5) and the judgment of the Flood.

In the *dispensation of human government* (Gen. 8:20 - 11:9), commencing after the Flood and continuing to the Second Coming of Christ, man becomes responsible to govern the earth for God. Under the terms of the Noahic Covenant (Gen. 9:1-6) the new and distinguishing revelation of God's will for this era becomes the instituting of human government for the first time, implied in the judicial taking of life (Gen. 9:6). Israel's failure to govern for God ended in the judgment of the captivities and the passing of governmental rule of the earth exclusively into Gentile hands (Dan. 2:36-45; Luke 21:24). Gentile failure to govern the earth for God will be judged at the Second Coming of Christ (Dan. 2:31-49; Matt. 25:31-46). This dispensation therefore still continues at the present time and overlaps other dispensations.

In the *dispensation of promise* another new era in the divine dealing was inaugurated as a result of the call of Abraham and the promises and blessings vouchsafed to him and his posterity under the terms of the Abrahamic Covenant (Gen. 12:1-3). This dispensation, too, overlaps and the promises of it are realized in other dispensations.

Beside these time periods in God's dealings, recognition of which is necessary but less important to accurate interpretation, there exist three others whose clear differentiation from one another is indispensable to rightly handling the Sacred Scriptures. These are the periods of law, grace and the kingdom.

The *period of the law* extended from Sinai to Calvary. Hitherto under God's gracious promise which had prepared a deliverer (Moses), provided a sacrifice for the guilty, and by divine power had rescued the people out of Egypt, Israel at Sinai nevertheless rashly accepted law for grace. "Ye have seen what I did unto the Egyptians, and how I bare you on eagles' wings, and brought you unto myself. Now therefore, *if* ye *will* obey my voice indeed, and keep my covenant, then ye shall be a peculiar treasure unto me above all people: for all the earth is mine: and ye shall be unto me a kingdom of priests, and a holy nation" (Ex. 19:4-6).

What had been freely given under gracious divine promise upon no other basis than faith now becomes conditional[4] upon obedience to the legal or Mosaic Covenant (Ex. 20-23), given strictly to the nation Israel. In choosing to come under law as a method of divine dealing, God's ancient people throughout the weary years of their history from Sinai to Calvary demonstrated that it is impossible for fallen man, even when a member of a religiously privileged nation, to be accepted before an infinitely holy God on a merit-works basis rather than on a grace-faith basis.

The severe discipline of the legal age was meant in the divine economy to serve as a "schoolmaster" to lead the Jew to Christ that he might "be justified by faith" (Gal. 3:24). Through the Jews' example of unbroken infringement during the period of enforcement of the law from Sinai to Calvary, culminating in the crucifixion of Christ and the divine rejection of the nation, the necessity of faith through grace as the sole basis of salvation apart from human merit or works was proved to the entire fallen race — Jew as well as Gentile.

In stressing the importance to correct Bible exposition of differentiating these various periods in the divine dealing, particularly the legal dispensation, it is essential to note that divine grace was manifested in all dispensations, even in the legal. Had the case been otherwise, no one under law could possibly have been saved. Those who were saved in the old economy were saved not by keeping of the law, which merely condemned them before a holy God, but by faith, which, however, did not repose in legal forms and empty ritual, but in a Coming Redeemer toward which these pointed (Rom. 3:25, 26).

Although divine grace is operative in all the dispensations, it is of the utmost import to the expositor to see clearly that there is one period extending from the death and resurrection of the Redeemer to His coming again for His own (John 14:3; I Thess. 4:13-18) that is so signally characterized by the outflow of divine favor as to be most saliently distinguished

---

[4] Cf. the "if" of Exodus 19:5, which expresses the essential character of law as a method of the divine dealing.

as the *"dispensation of the grace of God"* (Eph. 3:2). This new age instead of being confined to one nation, as the Mosaic law was, is universal and involves every kindred, tongue and people. Instead of being an immature and preparatory period, it is dispensationally a coming of age and a period of spiritual maturity (Gal. 3:26, 27). Instead of types the new age brings the antitypes; instead of limited working of the Spirit it introduces the gift of the Holy Spirit and full Gospel salvation (John 7:37-39).

To confuse this period with the Mosaic dispensation, to confound or commingle law and grace, to fail to see God's unique purpose in the age of grace — of visiting the Gentiles to call out a people for His name (Acts 15:14-16) into a wholly new entity, the Church as the Body of Christ (Eph. 1:20-23; 3:1-10) — is to shut out vast sections of the Bible to intelligent exposition, to plunge the plan and purpose of God for this age into confusion, and to cast a barrier of discouragement in the pathway of the aspiring expositor. It is, indeed, to blight the Christian message with legalism and to expose pure Christianity to every type of perversion.

However, it is not only of far-reaching importance to correct Bible exposition for the interpreter to distinguish carefully between the dispensation of law and the present age of grace, it is also imperative for him to see that there is yet another important age succeeding this before the eternal state is ushered in. This is the *kingdom age,* the last of the ordered ages conditioning human life on the earth. To inaugurate this period Christ returns in glory. Israel is then restored, and under Messiah's righteous rule becomes the head of the nations and a world-wide blessing (II Sam. 7: 8-17; Zech. 12:8; Luke 1:31-33).

Failure to differentiate the kingdom age from the present period of grace or from the future eternal state involves most serious consequences for the expositor. By applying the great Old Testament kingdom promises to the Christian Church, the expositor not only confounds the position and purpose of the "Body of Christ" (Eph. 1:20-23) in the divine plan, but submits himself to the necessity of wholesale spiritualizing of the extended Old Testament prophecies of the kingdom and finds himself in a bewildering situation of trying to fit together things that obviously do not belong with one another, a procedure highly discouraging to careful exposition.

On the other hand, relegating kingdom truth to the eternal state may not involve jumping the exegetical hurdles of applying it to the Christian Church; yet in either case, Israel, who figures so prominently in Biblical prophecy, both in the Old Testament and the New, and in whose restoration as a nation in the coming Messianic age the great kingdom promises of the Old Testament will find their fulfilment, is denied her proper place in the future purposes of God. The result of this blunder is that the interpreter is seriously crippled in handling Bible prophecy, which constitutes such a large part of the Sacred Text and centers to such a large extent around Israel in her relation to the Messiah in His first and second advents.

For this reason the interpreter who fails to distinguish between the age of law, of grace, and of the kingdom will inevitably be weak in his ability to deal with eschatology. In addition, this deficiency is bound to affect the interpreter's soteriology, since the important doctrines of salvation are so closely interwoven with the great prophetic truths of the Scriptures dealing with last things.

There can be no reasonable doubt that the Apostle Paul was thinking, perhaps primarily, of the importance of distinguishing the various periods of God's dealings with mankind, as revealed in Scripture, when he exhorted Timothy regarding his diligence and accuracy in studying the Sacred Oracles. "Study to show thyself approved unto God, a workman that needeth not to be ashamed, rightly dividing the word of truth" (II Tim. 2:15).

The phrase "rightly dividing" (*orthotomounta*) actually means "cutting straight," (from *orthos*, "straight," and *temno*, "cut"), and graphically sets forth the figure of teaching "the truth correctly and directly."[5] Used in classical Greek of a surgeon

[5] J. H. Thayer, *A Greek English Lexicon of the New Testament* (New York, American Book Co., 1889), p. 453.

cutting or using the knife, where the least deviation from the right handling might result in death to the patient, and likewise employed of an artisan drawing or cutting a straight line,[6] the word picture presented by the New Testament corroborates the necessity facing the expositor of accurately handling the Word of truth from a dispensational standpoint.

5. The Expositor and the Silence of Revelation

The careful expositor of Scripture must not only train himself to expound *all* that the Bible has to say on a particular subject, but, what is just as important, *only* what the Bible has to say. Constantly the Bible student must seek to avoid two extremes into which he is ever tempted to run. He must shun a shallow superficiality, on the one hand, that refuses to deal with all the revealed facts in the case. On the other hand, he must reject a morbid curiosity that would pry into secrets unrevealed and extend doctrines beyond the Biblical evidence.

There is no doubt that the great majority of expositors sin in not expounding *all* that the Bible has revealed. They lack thoroughness. However, there are many students of the Scripture who trespass in failing to observe the silence of revelation. They have a flare for the sensational, especially in dealing with prophetic themes. They cheapen their message by attempting to answer idle questions and deal with abstruse themes. In their attempts to appeal to the curious mind, they go beyond revealed truth to give unwarranted interpretations to current events and conditions, and they do this under the pretense of Biblical exposition.

Nothing is more detrimental to the expository approach than this bold going beyond the Biblical evidence. Such preaching has given the expository method unfavorable publicity in many places. Men have brought disrepute upon the Word of God by unbalanced statements, notoriously in the field of prophecy. World figures such as Kaiser Wilhelm, Hitler, Mussolini and Stalin have been widely identified with "the Antichrist." World War I and II have been frequently

[6] J. H. Whiton, *A Lexicon abridged from Liddell and Scott's Greek English Lexicon*, XX Ed., (New York, Harper & Brothers, 1883), p. 698.

connected with Armageddon. The establishment of the Israeli state in Palestine has been wildly interpreted on the alleged basis of Biblical predictions.

Abuses could be cited almost *ad infinitum* in every field of theological thought besides eschatology. In the field of pneumatology Joel's reference to the "early" and "latter rain" has been connected upon the most nebulous evidence with manifestations of the Spirit in this church age. In the matter of the Godhead, preachers have sometimes gone beyond the evidence of the Bible either to the extreme of a crude tritheistic definition of the Trinity or in the other direction of a flat denial of the personal distinctions in the Godhead. Again, men have unwisely tried to answer every problem connected with such questions as divine sovereignty and human free will, forgetting that there are areas of revelation where God is purposely silent.

The reliable expositor, if he is to gain personal assurance and command the confidence of his hearers, must cultivate a sense of discernment with regard to the silence or reticence of revelation. In addition, he must humbly acknowledge his own ignorance where the Bible is silent. Speaking when God is silent or speaking exhaustively where God is reticent can only be traceable to human pride.

It is not difficult for the humble and discerning student of Scripture to see that there are many areas of divine truth that God has seen fit to veil from man. Examples exist in theology proper, as well as in anthropology, Satanology, demonology, soteriology, ecclesiology, pneumatology and eschatology. But is the problem of the silence of revelation really important? The real problem in this connection lies not in man's not knowing but in his realization that he does not know.

One important result of a sound and thorough theological education is that the student becomes aware not only of what he does know, but of what he does not know. He becomes conscious of the propriety of the fact that if God is reticent on certain aspects of divine truth, men ought not attempt to speak or desire to know beyond what is written.

He is willing to ask himself humbly, "May that which is unrevealed not lie outside the realm of legitimate knowledge and, for man in his present sinful state, be nothing more than idle curiosity?"

6. The Expositor and Matters of Faith

Closely connected with the recognition of the silence or reticence of revelation and its implications in theological interpretation is the principle governing matters of faith. The expositor, if he is to do his most effective work, must always remember that what is *not* a matter of doctrinal revelation cannot be made a matter of faith. This is the historic Protestant position as opposed to Romanism, which adds other voices including tradition to the Biblical revelation. The Protestant position is fundamental to valid Biblical interpretation.

The grave danger of men speaking when God is silent is that the word of man becomes mixed with the Word of God and appropriates to itself the authority that only the Word of God should have. This principle is operative in all doctrinal declarations that go beyond revealed truth.

A good illustration of man's tendency to go beyond "Thus saith the Lord" is offered by the subject of evil supernaturalism. This theme is developed voluminously in Scripture, yet many phases of the subject are characterized by a chaste reticence which is disappointing to carnal curiosity. As a result, men have gone far beyond the limits of revelation and in the name of Christianity and ostensibly on the basis of the Bible conjured up the hobgoblins, witches and other gross superstitions of medieval times.[7] Then, too, much that is said about hell goes far beyond the explicit revelations of Scripture.[8]

Another example of going beyond the limits of revelation is the matter of Christian liberty. Many legalistic interpreters

[7] See the present author's, *Biblical Demonology* (Wheaton, Ill., Van Kampen Press, 1951), pp. 3-6; 155-157.

[8] For example, Jonathan Edwards' famous discourse, "Sinners in the Hands of an Angry God." Dante's "Inferno" or Milton's "Paradise Lost" are also classic examples of human imagination going beyond (or contrary to) divine revelation.

in applying the practical truths of Scripture to the life of today in the matter of separation fail to see that the utmost care must be exercised not to place human interpretations on the same par as explicit Bible teachings and enforcing these as tests of faith and fellowship. Failure in this regard has resulted in lopsided views of sin. More deep-seated sins of the spirit are frequently condoned while the seriousness of certain comparatively innocent types of carnality is magnified out of all proportion (II Cor. 7:1). Many otherwise able expositors are badly crippled in their usefulness by failure in this regard and unwittingly place themselves in a narrow sphere which is productive of a spirit of criticism and judgment of others.

7. The Expositor and the Devotional-Practical Aspect of Doctrinal Interpretation

The successful interpreter of Scripture must capture the predominantly practical and devotional nature of the Bible and bring its great truths face to face with the urgent everyday problems and needs of his hearers. No teacher, no matter how profound his exegetical theorizings or philosophizings may be, or how extensive his knowledge of the letter of Scripture or his grasp of theology, is a true expositor if he does not bring the truth he expounds to grips with the practical life of his auditors.

The expositor may not consider himself an evangelist, but he must persistently "do the work of an evangelist" (II Tim. 4:5), always keeping his unsaved hearers separated from his saved hearers in his thinking, and pressing upon them the claims of the Gospel of grace. On the other hand, he must constantly bear in mind the everyday needs of his saved hearers, and urge upon them the practical aspects of Christian living for their edification as well as instruction.

The importance of continually emphasizing the practical character of Scripture and of bringing its practical claims to bear upon the believer and the unbeliever alike, without the expositor's confusing them in his own thinking and appeal, is tremendous. The harm wrought by failure of many interpreters of Holy Scripture in this pivotal matter is incalculable.

One does not have to go far to find the theoretical type of Bible teacher, correct in his exegesis, but spiritually cold and unevangelistic and seemingly removed from the vital needs of not only the unsaved, but of the saved as well. This type of exposition, which may be styled an *intellectual Biblical* approach, errs in neglecting the practical and devotional nature of the Scriptures, and results to a great degree in spiritual barrenness. It discusses prophecy and the coming of the Lord, but fails to inculcate a love for "His appearing" (II Tim. 4:8). It discourses with meticulous accuracy on our position in Christ, but fails to convict the unbeliever of his lost condition or to inspire the believer "to set" his affections "on things above and not on things on the earth" (Col. 3:1). It gives critics of the Bible conference and the prophetic meeting and the enemies of Bible exposition in general just cause for censure.

Almost as appalling as the coldly intellectual expositor is the interpreter who, although he is fervent in his spiritual appeal and comparatively accurate in his presentation of truth, yet falls into the same snare as the coldly intellectual expositor of failing to differentiate as clearly as he ought between the saved and the unsaved. Much of his zeal is thus nullified, because misdirected.

The result of this common, present-day malpractice is that the unsaved get the erroneous impression that the glorious position of the believer together with his responsibilities as a son in God's family, is for them. As a result of such preaching the unsaved are not only mistakenly encouraged in a false security, but unwittingly urged on to discharge responsibilities which are utterly beyond them as unregenerate individuals. The confusion and harm of this evil are tragic.

But the competent expositor, in his constant aim to emphasize the intense practicality of the message and meaning of the Bible, must not only carefully distinguish between the saved and unsaved in his audience, but must also have clearly in his mind *to whom the Scripture he is expounding is addressed*

— whether to "the Jews, Gentiles or the Church of God" (I Cor. 10:32). Failure to do this and to apply any promise in the Bible indiscriminately and without thought to whom it is primarily directed, is productive of as much confusion and harm as failure to distinguish between the saved and the unsaved.

This, however, does not mean that because great sections and far-reaching promises, especially of the Old Testament, are addressed to a suffering remnant of godly Israelites during the future tribulation period,[9] or to Israel established as a nation in the millennial kingdom,[10] or to the redeemed in the eternal state,[11] that such passages may not have an application to our day and may not be used in a practical way to win the lost or edify the saved. It does mean, however, that the *expositor* must know to whom the passage is actually addressed if he is to avoid serious errors in dealing with it or have any real success in expounding it.

It is possible, for example, to use Ezekiel's vision of the dry bones (Ezek. 37) in preaching spiritual resurrection or regeneration (Eph. 2:1) to the unsaved. But unless the preacher comprehends the precise meaning of this vision in its context, and sees that it actually is not speaking about resurrection at all, either physical or spiritual, but of the future national resuscitation of the nation Israel and its restoration to Palestine in the age to come, he is exposed to all kinds of fallacious exegesis.

If the preacher uses the vivid imagery of the dry bones to portray passing from spiritual death to spiritual life, he must realize this is not an exposition of the passage and must be extremely careful to point out the real meaning of it to his audience, if only briefly, and indicate plainly that his treatment of it is in the nature of a special application only.

What is true of Ezekiel's vision of the dry bones is also true of the great kingdom prophecies of the Old Testament, such as the rule of the millennial King (Is. 11), the revival of the land (Is. 35) or the exaltation of Jerusalem as the

[9] For example, Ps. 45:1, 2, 7-9; Is. 41:10-20.
[10] Is. 2:1-5; 11:1-16; 35:1-10.
[11] Is. 65:17; 66:22; Rev. 21:1-8.

capitol of the millennial earth (Is. 60). These splendid prophecies may be used to preach evangelistically to the lost or devotionally to the saved of this age. But the expositor must never convey the impression that such use of them constitutes an exposition much less a fulfillment of them.

Every preacher ought to be careful to give at least a short explanation of the scope of these great passages and their actual contextual meaning. He can do this without diminishing their essential practicality. In fact, he should train himself to treat these great sections of the Word of God exhaustively in their true contextual meaning and yet make them practical and "down-to-earth" in their application to the everyday problems of our present age. This he must discipline himself to do if he is going to qualify as an expositor.

Because a passage treats of divine warning or promise to a Jew in a coming age is no proof that it cannot present a spiritual challenge to a believer in this age. The best and most effective expository work will always give proper balance to the devotional and practical aspects of the grammatical, historical and theological exegesis of the Word of God.

8. THE EXPOSITOR AND A BASIC THEOLOGICAL LIBRARY

Indispensable to the work of an expositor is a collection of sound and illuminating commentaries and theological volumes to stimulate and guide his thinking. This part of an expositor's library need not be large, but it must be carefully chosen. A few really good works are much better than a large indiscriminate mixture of sound and unsound volumes, which will only serve to confuse the student.

Extreme caution must be exercised to select not only those volumes that are grammatically and historically accurate, but in addition those that display spiritual insight and show facility in "rightly dividing the Word of truth," the latter being of special importance.

Although the expositor ought to cultivate assiduously his own interpretive gifts, based upon a thorough study of the grammar of the original languages, together with the history of Biblical backgrounds, and these in turn grounded upon complete reliance on the tuition of the Holy Spirit, yet he must also avail himself of the truth and inspiration God has given through specially talented men of the past and the present. The works of these Spirit-taught men will enable a diligent student to master the whole gamut of Biblical revelation, a task too great for a lifetime if one had to discover every phase of revealed truth for himself.

The expositor who would be competent within the compass of a ministry of thirty or forty years must humbly realize that "others have labored" and he has "entered into their labors" (John 4:38). Accordingly, he will not disdain to avail himself of the best helps he can secure to aid him in his mastery of the Word.

Inasmuch as suggestions for commentaries have been given in connection with grammatical-historical exposition,[12] only a list of useful volumes on theology are herein listed. Some of these are more strictly systematic, with more pronounced philosophical, psychological and other features. Others are more pronouncedly Biblical, and hence more valuable to the expositor.

SYSTEMATIC THEOLOGY

Calvin, John, *Institutes of the Christian Religion* (Basel, 1536; reprint, Grand Rapids, Wm. B. Eerdmans Publishing Co.).

Cooke, William, *Christian Theology* (London, Partridge and Oakley, 1848).

Venema, Hermannus, *Institutes of Theology* (Edinburgh, T. & T. Clark, 1850).

Wardlaw, Ralph, *Theology* (2 vols.; Edinburgh, Adams & Charles Black, 1856).

Watson, Richard, *Theological Institutes* (2 vols.; New York, Carlton and Philips, 1856).

Dick, John, *Lectures on Theology* (Cincinnati, Applegate & Co., 1864).

Martensen, H. L., *Christian Dogmatics* (Edinburgh, T. & T. Clark, 1866).

Mueller, Julius, *The Christian Doctrine of Sin* (Edinburgh, T. & T. Clark, 1868).

Smeaton, George, *The Doctrine of the Atonement* (Edinburgh, T. & T. Clark, 1868; reprint, Grand Rapids, Zondervan Publishing House).

Crawford, T. J., *The Doctrine of the Scriptures Respecting the Atonement* (London, W. Blackwood, 1871).

[12] See Chapter XIII.

Hodge, Charles A., *Systematic Theology* (New York, Scribner's, 1872; reprint, Grand Rapids, Wm. B. Eerdmans Publishing Co.).

Hodge, A. A., *Outlines of Theology* (New York, A. C. Armstrong, 1878; reprint, Grand Rapids, Wm. B. Eerdmans Publishing Co.).

Laidlaw, R. A., *Bible Doctrine of Man* (Edinburgh, T. & T. Clark, 1879).

Oehler, Gustav Friedrich, *Old Testament Theology* (New York, Funk & Wagnalls, 1883; reprint, Grand Rapids, Zondervan Publishing House).

Peters, George N. H., *The Theocratic Kingdom* (3 vols.; New York, Funk & Wagnalls, 1884).

Alexander, W. Lindsey, *A System of Biblical Theology* (Edinburgh, T. & T. Clark, 1888).

Miley, John, *Systematic Theology* (2 vols.; New York, Methodist Book Concern, 1892-1894).

Strong, Augustus H., *Systematic Theology* (New York, A. C. Armstrong, 1899).

Shedd, W. G. T., *Dogmatic Theology* (2 vols.; Edinburgh, T. & T. Clark, 1889; reprint, Grand Rapids, Zondervan Publishing House).

Gerhart, E. V., *Institutes of the Christian Religion* (2 vols.; New York, A. C. Armstrong and Funk & Wagnalls, 1891).

Clarke, W. M., *An Outline of Christian Theology* (New York, Scribner's, 1898).

Davidson, A. B., *Theology of the Old Testament* (Edinburgh, T. & T. Clark, 1904).

Mullins, E. Y., *The Christian Religion in Its Doctrinal Expression* (Nashville, Baptist Sunday School Board, 1917).

Warfield, B. B., *Biblical Doctrines* (New York, Oxford University Press, 1929).

————, *Studies in Theology* (New York, Oxford University Press, 1932).

Thomas, W. H. Griffith, *Principles of Theology* (New York, Longmans Green and Co., 1930).

Burrows, Millar, *Outlines of Biblical Theology* (Philadelphia, Westminster Press, 1946).

Boettner, L., *Studies in Theology* (Grand Rapids, Wm. B. Eerdmans Publishing Co., 1947).

Chafer, Lewis Sperry, *Systematic Theology* (Dallas, Dallas Seminary Press, 1947).

Baab, Otto, *Theology of the Old Testament* (Nashville, Abingdon-Cokesbury Press, 1949).

Heinisch, Paul, *Theology of the Old Testament* (Collegeville, Minn., Liturgical Press, 1950).

Literature on Doctrinal Interpretation

Angus, J. and S. G. Green, *The Bible Handbook* (New York, Fleming Revell, 1908; reprint, Grand Rapids, Zondervan Publishing House), pp. 215-275; 358-378.

Chafer, L. S., *Systematic Theology* (Dallas, Dallas Seminary Press, 1947), I: 114-119.

Berkhof, L., *Principles of Biblical Interpretation* (Grand Rapids, Baker Book House, 1950), pp. 133-166.

Ramm, Bernard, *Protestant Biblical Interpretation* (Boston, W. A. Wilde Co., 1950), pp. 97-124.

Chapter XVI

THE EXPOSITOR AND FIGURATIVE LANGUAGE

The literatures of all lands and languages abound in figurative expressions. The Bible is no exception to this universal fact, but an ideal illustration of it. Being predominantly an Oriental book, on the human side the Bible is a product of the Semitic mind, which customarily expressed itself in emphatic and lively forms. Even the New Testament, written in Greek and to a large extent influenced by Greek thought and culture, nevertheless was authored by Semites and to a large degree reflects the figurative and symbolic language found in the Old Testament.

Since the language of the Bible is frequently highly figurative, it is of the utmost importance for the expositor to comprehend the basic elements of figurative speech and to see to what extent such language is to be interpreted literally. Moreover, the interpreter must appreciate the fact that figures add color, life and emphasis to language and that all great literature that would strike the imagination and appeal to the heart of humanity, as the Bible does, must employ them in greater or lesser degree.

A figure may be defined as "a mode of speaking or writing in which words are deflected from their ordinary signification."[1] The actual deflection or turning from the original meaning to another for the sake of giving life or emphasis to an idea is called a *trope* (from Greek *tropos,* "a turn," from *trepein,* "to turn").

Such figurative or tropical usage of words is common in our

[1] Webster's *New Twentieth Century Dictionary* (New York, Publishers Guild, 1942), p. 655.

language, as when we call a stupid fellow "an ass" or a shrewd man "a fox." Compare Amos' denunciation of the wanton, oppressive women of decadent Samaria as "cows of Bashan" (Amos 4:1) and our Lord's designation of the cunning Herod as a "fox" (Luke 13:32). Figures of this type are calculated to strike the imagination and stick in the memory. They distill into a lively expression the essence of an idea and lend power and appeal to the speaker or writer's style.

1. GENERAL PRINCIPLES FOR DISTINGUISHING BETWEEN LITERAL AND FIGURATIVE LANGUAGE

It is important that the expositor acquaint himself with the numerous figures of speech used in Scripture to be able to determine whether a particular word or passage is to be construed as tropical or literal. If an interpreter knows the types of figures in general use in rhetoric, the various tropes will normally be easily recognizable as such, and the meaning will usually be clear from the context.

A golden rule of interpretation in dealing with any Biblical passage, figurative or otherwise, is this: *When the plain sense of Scripture makes common sense, seek no other sense; therefore, take every word at its primary, usual, literal meaning, unless it is patently a rhetorical figure or unless the immediate context, studied carefully in the light of related passages and axiomatic and fundamental truths, clearly points otherwise.*

It is always important to search for a literal meaning before accepting one that is figurative. Although the Bible makes extensive use of figures, especially in poetical and prophetical sections, its underlying thought and teaching are literal, even in the most highly wrought figurative sections. When due recognition is made of all bona fide rhetorical figures occurring in a passage, these stylistic devices are to be thought of as merely throwing into bolder relief the basic literal meaning which the figures are emphasizing.

Figurative language is, therefore, to be thought of as an ally and not an enemy of literal interpretation and as a help to it and not a hindrance. If it cannot be proved that a word or passage fits into the category of one of the numerous figures recognized in rhetoric, it must not be assumed that it is nevertheless a figure. It may be, but it must be taken in its literal sense, unless that sense does not make common sense. In other words, if the literal proves to be *absurd* or in any way *inconsistent,* either with other parts of the sentence or with the nature of the subject discussed, "we may conclude with tolerable certainty that the language is figurative."[2]

The test of consistency is, accordingly, of great importance in distinguishing between literal and figurative language. If the expositor is in doubt that the literal meaning is intended, he should ask himself several questions. Is the literal meaning *consistent* with the general context? With parallel passages? With the general historical or doctrinal subject of which it forms a part? Is it consistent with the divine purpose for Jew, Gentile and the Church in the ordered ages of God's redemptive plan? Is it in agreement with the custom of a writer or class of writers with respect to a free use of figures or their employment in the discussion of particular subjects?

If under these searching tests the literal meaning is found to be consistent, *it should be preferred to a figurative or less usual signification.*[3]

A good illustration of the sound principle of preferring the literal to the figurative meaning of a word, when the literal meets the test of consistency, is furnished by the widely occurring name of Zion in the Psalms and prophecies of the Old Testament.[4] Many expositors have construed Zion in these passages to be a figure of the Christian Church when it has a prophetic significance and not to refer to a literal future city of Jerusalem at all. But this turns out to be a pure assumption in the light of the full witness of God's Word.[5]

---

2 Clinton Lockhart, *Principles of Interpretation* (2d ed., rev.; Ft. Worth, S. H. Taylor, 1915), p. 157.

3 *Ibid.,* p. 160.

4 Ps. 2:6; 48:2; Is. 4:5; 60:14, etc.

5 Rollin Thomas Chafer, *The Science of Biblical Hermeneutics* (Dallas, Bibliotheca Sacra, 1939), pp. 79f.

In many passages of Scripture it is clear that the Church, the Body of Christ, is a distinctive New Testament revelation and not a subject of Old Testament prophecy at all (Eph. 3:1-10), except as concealed in Old Testament types, which were not to be revealed until after New Testament events gave significance to their meaning. Hence, "Zion and Jerusalem mean Zion and Jerusalem, not the Church."[6]

2. VARIOUS FIGURES OF SPEECH USED IN SCRIPTURE

The literary quality of Scripture is of an exceedingly high caliber. Yet this high evaluation as literature is not a detriment, but rather an asset, to its truly remarkable appeal to the human heart, lettered as well as unlettered. No small part of the attractiveness of the Bible is due to its arresting style which in large measure is the result of the many figures of speech that adorn its sacred page, making its message live and glow with meaning.

Outstanding among Biblical figures of speech is the *simile* or imaginative comparison (from the Latin *similis*, "like" or "similar"). In this common rhetorical device two things are likened to each other, which however different in other respects they may be, yet have some strong point or points of resemblance. In this figure the formal comparison is made by the use of such comparative adverbs as *like, as, so,* etc. Examples are numerous. "The wicked are like the troubled sea, when it cannot rest, whose waters cast up mire and dirt" (Is. 57:20). Of the godly happy man, however, it is said that "he shall be like a tree planted by the rivers of water that bringeth forth his fruit in its season" (Ps. 1:3).

The *metaphor,* on the other hand, (Greek, *meta,* "over," and *pherein,* "to bear"), is an implied likeness, in which the formal adverb of comparison used in the simile is omitted and in the process a word is transferred from an object to which it properly belongs to another to which it does not really belong. Our Lord's words in Matthew 5:13 are a metaphor. "Ye are the salt of the earth." Stated as a simile, which would be less direct and forceful, the saying would be, "Ye are like

[6] C. I. Scofield, *Correspondence Course,* Vol. I, p. 128.

the salt of the earth." In Jeremiah 2:13 two metaphors are found. "They have forsaken me, a fountain of living waters, and hewed them out cisterns, broken cisterns, that can hold no water."

Besides the simile and the metaphor, which deal with a comparison either explicit or implied, there is a large class of figures of speech involving some apparent absurdity or inconsistency, by which the attention of the reader is arrested and in the solution of which a fact or truth is forcefully impressed upon him. Included under this type of figure are the *paradox*, the *oxymoron*, *irony*, *personification*, *paranomasia*, *anthropomorphism*, *anthropopathism*, *hyperbole*, *litotes*, *synecdoche* and *metonymy*.

The *paradox* (Greek, *para*, "beyond" and *doxon*, "opinion," from *dokein*, "to think, suppose") is a statement that is seemingly absurd or contrary to received opinion, which is calculated to arrest attention and emphasize the truth or fact it contains. An example is found in Matthew 13:12: "But whosoever hath not, from him shall be taken away even that which he hath." The apparent absurdity is contained in the thought of taking something from one who has nothing. But the figure simply stresses that the little the person may have will be taken from him.

Other famous paradoxes are: "Whosoever will save his life shall lose it" (Mark 8:35). "As unknown, and yet well known; as dying, and, behold, we live; as chastened, and not killed: as sorrowful, yet always rejoicing; as poor, yet making many rich; as having nothing, and yet possessing all things" (II Cor. 6:9, 10).

The *oxymoron* is a figure involving an apparent inconsistency between a noun and its modifier (Greek *oxymoron*, "a striking saying," which at first blush seems foolish, from *oxys*, "sharp," and *moros*, "stupid"). Proverbs 12:10, which describes "the tender mercies of the wicked" as being "cruel," is an example. The emphasized idea is that the tenderest mercies a wicked man may have are still harsh.

Matthew 6:23 is another example of oxymoron: "If the light that is in thee be darkness, how great is that darkness."

How can light be darkness? The truth thrown into bold relief in this instance is that if the spiritual light governing the higher life be darkened, what will be the state of the region of life governed by the lower nature — the realm of the passions and appetites — which is naturally dark and needs the presence of that light to keep it at all in check?

Irony is a type of sarcasm or satire that holds up to ridicule some sin or folly by using language opposite in meaning to what is actually meant (*eiron*, "a dissembler in speech," from *eirein*, "to speak"). Thus Elijah taunts the Baal worshipers in their prayers to a non-entity: "And at noon Elijah mocked them, saying, Cry aloud: for he is a god; either he is musing, or he has gone aside, or he is on a journey, or perhaps he is asleep and must be wakened" (I Kings 18:27, RSV).

Job makes use of irony in berating his overweening friends. "No doubt ye are the people, and wisdom shall die with you" (Job 12:2). The Apostle Paul also quite frequently employs this device as in I Corinthians 4:8: "Already ye are filled! Already ye have become rich! Without us you have become kings!" That the Apostle is speaking ironically appears in the appended clause: "And would that you did reign, so that we might share the rule with you!" (RSV).

Personification is a widely used figure in which inanimate things are given animate characteristics and things without personality are endowed with personal attributes. Thus Isaiah describes the physical restoration of Palestine in the millennial age in terms of an effective personification. "The wilderness and the dry land shall be glad; and the desert shall rejoice, and blossom as the rose" (Is. 35:1, ARV). Again: "The mountains and the hills shall break forth before you into singing; and all the trees of the field shall clap their hands" (Is. 55:12, ARV).

A *paranomasia* is a pun or play upon words (Greek, *para*, "beside," and *onomos*, "name"). A notable example is Matthew 16:18 where there is a play upon Peter (*petros*, "a small rock or stone," and *petra*, "a ledge of rock"). "Thou art Peter, and upon this rock I will build my church." Similarly in Philippians

3:2, 3 there is a play upon concision (*katatome*) and circumcision (*peritome*): "Beware of the concision: for we are the circumcision, who worship by the Spirit of God" (ARV). In Matthew 8:22 by means of paranomasia Jesus contrasts the spiritually dead with the physically dead. "Follow me; and leave the dead to bury their own dead." Isaiah uses a type of paranomasia more commonly known as *assonance* in which words with similar consonants are combined with words with different vowels: "And he looked for judgment (*mishpat*), but behold oppression (*mispach*); for righteousness (*tsedaqah*), but behold a cry (*tse'aqah*)" (Is. 5:7).

An *anthropomorphism* is the attribution of human physical characteristics to God (*anthropos*, "man," and *morphe*, "form"). This manner of speaking of God, except as deity assumed angelic form before the incarnation of Christ, or in the case of the actual assumption of humanity by the Son, is a figurative accommodation to human forms, since a spirit, and "God is a Spirit" (John 4:24), does not have human members. Examples of anthropomorphisms are found in God "smelling" (Gen. 8:21), stretching forth his "hands" (Is. 65:2), "walking" (Gen. 3:8), and having protective "wings" (Ruth 2:12).

Anthropopathy (*anthropos*, "man," and *pathos*, "feeling") is the ascription of human passions to God, such as "wrath" (Rev. 15:1), "jealousy" (Zech. 8:2), mirth or laughter (Ps. 2:4), repentance or change of mind (Gen. 6:6) and joy (Judg. 9:13). In dealing with these particular expressions, especially the wrath or the jealousy of God, it is necessary to realize that a figure is being employed that must not be violated. It must be understood that God does not literally exercise the passions of men. His wrath is simply the necessary reaction of His infinite holiness where His grace and mercy are spurned. His jealousy is simply the expression of His zeal and faithfulness toward the object of His love. To literalize these figures is to misunderstand them.

Hyperbole (*hyperbole*, "an overshooting, excess," *hyper*, "over," and *ballein*, "to throw") is an exaggeration for emphasis. It is a widely used device often characteristic of the Bible and of graphic literature in general. John, the apostle, makes use of this figure in the last verse of the Fourth Gospel. "And there are also many other things which Jesus did, the which if they should be written every one, I suppose that even the world itself would not contain the books that should be written" (John 21:25, ARV).

The Psalmist employs hyperbole when he describes his sorrow in this fashion: "I am weary with my groaning; every night make I my bed to swim; I water my couch with my tears" (Ps. 6:6). Poetic hyperbole also describes Saul and Jonathan as "swifter than eagles" and "stronger than lions" (II Sam. 1:23).

Hyperbole must not be construed as falsehood. It has no intention to deceive. It merely seeks to emphasize a fact by overstatement. If it is properly used, it becomes a useful tool in making language live and glow with meaning.

Litotes (from *litos*, "plain, simple") is the use of a weaker for a stronger expression, or the emphasizing a fact by denying its contrary. In a sense it is the opposite of hyperbole. Whereas in the latter the emphasis is secured by an overstatement, in the former it is attained by an understatement. This effect is secured by resorting to the negative of the opposite. The prophet effectively employs it in accentuating Messiah's meekness: "A bruised reed will he not break and a dimly burning wick will he not quench" (Is. 42:3). The sense of this passage is that the coming Redeemer would not only not crush an already cracked twig, hence very easily broken, but would protect and restore it. A flickering wick, easily extinguished, he will not only not put out, but fan it into a flame.

Paul's assertion concerning his political status that he was "a citizen of no mean city" (Acts 21:39) is the emphatic equivalent that he was a citizen of a very illustrious city.

Synecdoche (Greek, *synekdechesthai*, "to receive jointly") is the use of a part for the whole, the whole for a part, a genus for a species, a species for a genus, or a singular for a plural. Thus "all the world" is employed in Luke 2:1 for the Roman Empire, to emphasize its vast extent. In Matthew 12:40 three days and three nights designate a period less than seventy-two actual hours. In Mark 16:15 a genus is used for a species: "Go ye into all the world and preach the gospel to the whole creation" (RSV). Species for genus is illustrated in Romans 1:16: "Salvation to everyone that believeth; to the Jew first and also to the Greek," where the expression "Greek" denotes not a comparatively small class in the Gentile world, but the whole Gentile world.

Metonymy (Greek, *meta*, suggesting "change," and *onoma*, "a name") is the use of one word for another, as the effect for the cause, the cause for the effect, the abstract for the concrete and the container for the thing contained. Metonymy of cause and effect is illustrated by the expression "Moses and the prophets" (cause) which stands for the writings (the effect) of which these men were authors (Luke 16:29; 24:27). Job uses "arrow" (cause) for "a wound caused by an arrow" (effect) when he says, "My *arrow* is incurable" (Job 34:6).

In I Samuel 15:29 an effect is used for its cause. "The Strength of Israel will not lie nor repent; for he is not a man, that he should repent." The word "Strength" (effect) is used for the God of Israel (cause) because He was the source of Israel's resources. In Romans 3:30 the abstract is used for the concrete where "circumcision" denotes the Jews and "uncircumcision" the Gentiles, and in Romans 11:7 where "election" denotes the "remnant according to the election of grace."

Illustrations of the use of the container for the thing contained are found in Psalm 23:5: "Thou preparest a table before me in the presence of mine enemies"; Deuteronomy 28:5: "Blessed shall be thy basket and thy kneading trough"; and I Corinthians 10:21: "Ye cannot drink the cup of the Lord, and the cup of devils: ye cannot be partakers of the Lord's table, and of the table of devils." In these instances "table, basket, kneading trough and cup" are used for that which they contained or for that for which they were used.

Besides figures involving comparisons, as similes and metaphors, and those containing elements apparently inconsistent, there are some which involve omissions. These must be clearly understood by the expositor in order that he may be able to supply what is omitted to arrive at the full meaning intended by the author. The context and the purpose of the writing must naturally be carefully considered and only what is essential to express the evident intent of the author must be supplied.

The most common form of omission is called *ellipsis* (Greek, *en*, "in," and *leipein*, "to leave"), which is the leaving out of 'one or more words, obviously understood, but necessary to make the passage grammatically complete. This literary phenomenon is frequent in the Bible, especially in the Old Testament. Occasionally it may be the result of the falling out of a word or words in the course of the transmission of the text, but in the majority of cases it is a rhetorical device for the sake of emphasis through the medium of brevity.

Psalm 19:3, 4 furnishes an example:

> No speech, and no words —
> Not heard — their voice;
> In all the earth went forth their line
> And their words to the end of the world.

The translation, *"there is* no speech nor language *where* their voice is not heard,"* is an attempt to fill in the elliptically expressive form of the original. Genesis 3:22, 23 furnishes another example: "Then the Lord God said, Behold the man has become like one of us, knowing good and evil; and now, lest he put forth his hand and take also of the tree of life, and eat, and live forever (——), therefore the Lord God sent him forth from the garden of Eden, to till the ground from which he was taken."

A special kind of ellipsis is *aposiopesis* (Greek, *apo*, "from," and *siopao*, "be silent"), consisting of a sudden breaking off of an utterance under great emotion, as if one were unwilling or unable to express his mind. Moses' impassioned utterance in Exodus 32:32 is an example: "But now, if thou wilt forgive their sin — and if not, blot me I pray thee, out of the book which thou hast written." Other examples occur in Luke 19:42 and Ephesians 3:1, 2.

The *pregnant construction* is another variety of rhetorical device that gains emphasis by an omission. In this figure a proposition is joined with an expressed verb, while in reality it belongs to an unexpressed verb, which, however, is comprehended in the other verb as its consequent. An instance is Psalm 74:7: "They have cast fire into thy sanctuary, they have *defiled* the dwellingplace of thy name *to the ground.*" The thought is, of course, to be completed in supplying some expression such as "by burning it to the ground." "He [the Lord] will save me into His kingdom" (II Tim. 4:18), says Paul. He means "save me *by bringing me* into His kingdom."

Zeugma ("yoke") consists of two nouns that are joined or "yoked" to one verb, though only one of them really suits the verb. In I Corinthians 3:2 Paul uses this device. "Milk I caused thee to drink, and not meat." Of Zecharias it is said: "And his mouth was opened immediately, and his tongue" (Luke 1:64). What is meant is "and his tongue was loosed."

These various figures of speech are of the utmost importance in giving the Bible a vivid and compelling style. Use of these striking ways of saying things is no small part of the secret of the Bible's universal appeal as literature. To recognize these basic forms of speech and to distinguish the essential thought from the peculiar mode of expression in which it may be couched, constitutes an indispensable part of the training of an expositor.

LITERATURE ON FIGURATIVE LANGUAGE

Hervey, G. W., *A System of Christian Rhetoric* (New York, Harper & Brothers, 1873), pp. 381-511.

Terry, Milton S., *Biblical Hermeneutics* (New York, Methodist Book Concern, 1911), pp. 157-176.

Angus, J. and S. G. Green, *The Bible Handbook* (New York, Fleming Revell, 1908, reprint, Grand Rapids, Zondervan Publishing House), pp. 215-223.

Lockhart, Clinton, *Principles of Interpretation* (2d ed., rev.; Ft. Worth, S. H. Taylor, 1915), pp. 156-190.

Chapter XVII

THE EXPOSITOR AND THE INTERPRETATION OF PARABLES

The study of the principles of correct interpretation of parables is very important for the work of an expositor. This is true not only because of the extensive use of parabolic teaching by our Lord in his earthly ministry but also because this method of inculcating truth is peculiarly subject to abuse, even by otherwise cautious interpreters.

Although the Old Testament only occasionally employs parables, as in Isaiah 5, and New Testament use is confined to the life and ministry of our Lord, as catalogued by the synoptists Matthew, Mark and Luke, the examples in the Gospels are so prominent by their position and significant in their meaning, especially in their prophetic ramifications, that the student must exercise the utmost diligence in correctly expounding them. Error in interpreting them will result in serious mistakes in setting forth the meaning of other passages.

1. DEFINITION OF A PARABLE

In its etymological meaning the word "parable" (from *paraballein, para,* "beside" and *ballein,* "to throw") signifies a similitude or likeness in which one thing is cast "by the side of another for the sake of comparison."[1] In this broadest connotation of the term it is practically identical with a simile. In some of our Lord's parables there is such a simple comparison drawn in a single verse, in Matthew 13:13: "The kingdom of heaven is like unto leaven, which a woman took,

---

[1] J. H. Thayer, *A Greek-English Lexicon of the New Testament* (New York, American Book Co., 1889), p. 478.

and hid in three measures of meal, till the whole was leavened."[2]

In its more usual and technical sense, however, the word "parable" signifies "a narrative moving within the sphere of physical or human life, not professing to communicate an event which really took place, but expressly imagined for the purpose of presenting in pictorial figure a truth belonging to the sphere of religion, and therefore referring to the relation of man or mankind to God."[3]

These various features serve to differentiate the parable from other similar figurative narratives as well as from actual history. Sometimes, however, difficulty arises as to the question of whether a certain narrative is historical or purely imaginative, and hence whether or not it is to be classified as a parable and interpreted as such.

The account of the rich man and Lazarus in Luke 16:19-31 is an example. The similarity of this story to a parable has led many expositors to classify it as such and to interpret it accordingly. But this is a mistake, inasmuch as the narrative is not said to be a parable. It rather possesses every feature of an actual occurrence, including the description of two men in life, in death, and in life after death. Besides, names of definite individuals, like Lazarus and Abraham, are given, which would not be possible in a genuine parable.

Moreover, there are serious consequences in construing as a parable what is not really a parable but an actual historical happening. For example, this practice allows the exegete to ignore the important eschatological revelations in this passage (Luke 16:19-31) concerning life after death in the pre-Cross period under the excuse that, as a parable, only the features that constitute the substance of the story are to be interpreted. The result in this case would be a definite loss.

2. TYPES OF PARABLES

The bulk of parables in the Bible are those of Jesus recorded in Matthew, Mark and Luke. These divide themselves

---

[2] Cf. also Matthew 13:44 and verses 45, 46.
[3] Siegfried Goebel, *The Parables of Jesus* (Edinburgh, T. & T. Clark, 1913), p. 4.

into two general classes — symbolic and typical. The first class forms by far the largest number.

The *symbolic* parable is based upon the fact of the essential harmony between the natural and the supernatural realm, between the physical and the spiritual, so that by virtue of this divinely established correspondence "states and relations, incidents and operations, belonging to the former sphere of life, mirror something of a like kind in the latter sphere."[4] In this manner the visible becomes the symbol of the invisible, the earthly of the heavenly, the physical and material of the spiritual, and the temporal of the eternal.

The symbolic parable accordingly sets forth spiritual truth under the image of man's relations to the material world about him. Thus our Lord uses such human activities as sowing, reaping, fishing and sheep-herding as representations of similar incidents and operations in the sphere of God's kingdom. Earthly treasures, for example, are made to represent spiritual blessings. An earthly feast is used to picture gospel privilege. Relations such as exist between king and subjects, master and servants, proprietor and stewards, father and son, bridegroom and bride, creditor and debtor are made to portray similar relations between God and man; or to set forth some phase of God's redemptive or prophetic program.

Alongside of symbolic parables are the *typical* variety. These illustrate the teaching they set forth not by means of symbolic clothing but by direct example. Under this classification are to be included the Good Samaritan (Luke 10:30-37), the Rich Fool (Luke 12:16-34) and the Pharisee and the Publican (Luke 18:9-14). In all these examples there is a comparative setting, side by side, of characters drawn from everyday life, with moral-spiritual truths to be taught. To achieve a didactic purpose a particular case is introduced in the form of an artificial history by way of comparison with the general truth intended to be taught.

In the typical parable the specific story recounted so substantiates the principle being inculcated that the truth in question is intuitively recognized. The chief persons of the

[4] *Ibid.*, p. 5.

typical parable, after whom it is named, are not symbolic images, but the representatives of a moral and spiritual disposition. For example, the folly of the rich man in laying up treasure and forgetting God when death lurked so near at hand (Luke 12:16-34) gives an obvious moral to the narrative by the application of what is recounted of a particular case to all cases of a like kind. The same is true of the pride and self-righteousness of the Pharisee, or the humility and contrition of the Publican (Luke 18:9-14), or the kindness of the Samaritan as contrasted with the selfishness of the Priest and Levite (Luke 10:30-37).

The Old Testament contains an example of both the symbolic and the typical parable. The parable of the Vineyard (Is. 5:1-7) may be classified as symbolic, whereas the parable of the rich man who took a poor man's only lamb to make provision for a guest (II Sam. 12:1-6), as used by the prophet Nathan to rebuke David for his sins of murder and adultery, constitutes the typical variety.

3. THE PARABLE AND THE ALLEGORY

The parable and the allegory, although often quite similar, are not identical. The former is essentially a comparison, and as such is often simply an extended simile, introduced by such a comparative expression as "like," or "as." Even when the comparison is not formally stated, and is merely analogical, the idea of placing one thing beside another for the purpose of comparison is prominent, and the figure is not far removed from a simile.

The allegory (*allos*, "other," and *agoreuo*, "to speak in the *agora* or assembly") as a figurative discourse in which the principal subject is described by another subject resembling it in its properties and circumstances, partakes more of the character of an extended metaphor. Whereas the parable confines itself to that which is real, and in its imagery does not go beyond the limits of probability, or what might be actual fact, the allegory by contrast gives expression to greater flights of the imagination. In illustrating spiritual and moral truth it resorts to the direct personification of ideas or attributes and in so doing readily makes use of what may actually be improbable or impossible. The improbable or impossible element, however, is easily recognized by the reader as a part of the figurative device used to set forth the truth or moral lesson in question more graphically.

Thus the allegory in Psalm 80:8-15 presents Israel as a vine taken out of Egypt, planted in Palestine, and so blessed that its branches extended to the Mediterranean Sea and its shoots to the Euphrates River. Israel's idolatry is pictured moreover as causing the walled vineyard (Palestine) to be broken down and ravaged by wild beasts.

It is impossible, of course, in reading this allegory to imagine that a real vine is meant. What vine could extend to the Mediterranean and send out shoots to the Euphrates? The reader acquainted with the fortunes of ancient Israel, however, can readily discern under the allegorical dress a plain chapter from the actual history of God's ancient people.

Paul's well-known allegory in Galatians 4:21-31 differs from the usual type in presenting a historical rather than a purely imaginative narrative. An episode in the life of Abraham is employed to present analogies bearing upon the attitude of Jews and Gentiles toward the Gospel of Christ. Hagar, the bondwoman, personifies unconverted Jews in bondage to the Mosaic law. Her son, Ishmael, cast out from Abraham's family, stands for Jews rejected by God because of unbelief. Sarah and her son Isaac represent Christians enjoying the liberty of the Gospel in complete acceptance with God.

4. The Parable and Other Literary Types

Other forms of figurative teaching besides the allegory bear some resemblance to the parable. Among these is the fable (from the Latin *fabula*, "a story"), which may be defined as a tale designed to instruct or amuse and in which animals and sometimes inanimate objects are introduced as speakers and actors.

Jotham's fable of the trees (Judg. 9:8-20) is the oldest example of this literary type and as beautiful as any made since.[5] It was spoken after the death of Gideon, the great judge of Israel, when Abimelech, one of Gideon's lesser sons by a maidservant, conspired against his brothers, slew them, except Jotham, the youngest son, who escaped. Standing on the heights of Mount Gerizim Jotham propounded the fable of the trees to the foolhardy men of Shechem who were supporting Abimelech as king.

"The trees went forth on a time to anoint a king over them; and they said unto the olive tree, Reign thou over us. But the olive tree said unto them, Should I leave my fatness wherewith by me they honour God and man, and go to be promoted over the trees?" Likewise valuable trees like the fig and the vine declined the regal offer. But the worthless bramble accepted on the condition that all the other trees come and put their trust in its shadow.

The representation of the trees as reasoning and speaking as men clearly marks Jotham's discourse as a fable. Moreover, the fable is clearly distinguished from both the allegory and the parable. The latter figures never use the inanimate and brute creation as actors and speakers, as does the former.[6] The allegory, however, does employ direct personification of ideas and attributes, as we have noted, and accordingly, like the fable is more boldly imaginative than the parable, which, on the other hand, confines itself to that which may actually be a fact, or at least to that which is of possible or probable occurrence.

Besides the fable the *riddle* and the *enigma* are sometimes confused with the parable. These latter literary forms, while similar to parabolic teaching in serving to conceal a truth from those who have not spiritual penetration to comprehend it, may make much use of the metaphor, but never, like the parable, form a narrative or assume to set forth a formal comparison.[7]

The celebrated riddle, "Out of the eater came forth meat,

[5] Jehoash's fable of the thornbush and the cedar (II Kings 14:9) is another Scripture example.

[6] Cf. "Parables," in *Smith's Dictionary of the Bible*, ed. by H. B. Hackett (Boston, 1887), Vol. III, p. 2328.

[7] Milton S. Terry, *Biblical Hermeneutics* (New York, Methodist Book Concern, 1911), p. 189.

and out of the strong came forth sweetness" (Judg. 14:14), can only be understood in the light of Samson's finding honey in the carcass of a lion (Judg. 14:8, 9). As in this case, the riddle deals essentially with earthly things, and is especially designed to exercise human ingenuity.

On the other hand, the enigma is concerned with higher and more sacred truth, which it serves both to conceal and throw into sharp relief. A good example is the mystic number of the Beast, 666, (Rev. 13:8). A general knowledge of Biblical prophecy and Scriptural numerics, moreover, is necessary for the proper interpretation of this enigma. Many of the proverbs of the Old Testament (cf. Prov. 26:10) as well as the sayings of Jesus are enigmatic (cf. Luke 22:36; John 21:18). But the proverb in general, as well as the riddle and the enigma, differs from the parable in being much more terse and pointed.

5. RULES FOR THE INTERPRETATION OF PARABLES

The proper interpretation of parabolic literature is of the greatest importance to the expositor. This fact is true not only because parabolic teaching figures so prominently in the ministry of our Lord Himself, but also because many of His parables have a very practical bearing upon character and conduct and, in many instances, touch upon vital eschatological and prophetic themes indispensable to the general understanding of the divine plan of the ages.

a. *The general nature of the parable as a form of literature must be understood.* This literary genre is commonly considered to have three parts — the occasion and scope (often called the *root* or *basis*), the similitude or figure in the form of an imagined episode or story (the *bark* or *covering*), and the moral or spiritual lesson taught (the *marrow* or inner substance and core).[8]

Into these three parts of a parable a number of elements enter. There is an *earthly* element which ties into the occasion and scope and the closely connected similitude. Hence a parable takes the form of an illustrative story employing

---

[8] *Ibid.,* p. 191.

some everyday event, custom or possible occurrence. The actual illustrative material in the parable emphasizes the *earthly* aspect, and parables accordingly deal with such perennially interesting common events as marriages, feasts, household affairs, business transactions, fishing, farming, sheepherding and worshiping. Their remarkable didactic value, moreover, lies in the graphic hominess of their appeal and the factuality and familiarity of their illustrative dress.

Beyond the earthly element, interwoven in the actual similitude, is the *spiritual* ingredient contained in the lesson or message the parable is designed to teach. This is the point or purpose of the whole and is the result of the *analogical* relationship the earthly element sustains to the spiritual element. It is this analogy between the earthly and spiritual elements that gives the parable its distinctive illustrative and argumentative force.[9]

It is quite essential for the expositor to comprehend clearly the general nature of the parable as a potent didactic device. Especially is it necessary for him to see the twofold level (the earthly and the spiritual) on which it operates. Unless these various elements that enter into the construction of a parable are taken into account, and carefully interpreted in the light of their proper relation to one another, the expositor will be seriously handicapped in dealing with the parabolic literature of the Bible.

b. *The historical occasion and purpose of the parable must be determined.* Fundamental to the interpretation of a parable is an inquiry into the contextual relationships. Why, when, where and under what circumstances it was spoken and similar considerations are prerequisite to any intelligent interpretation of its meanings. If these basic contextual features are neglected, the expositor may well despair of arriving at a satisfactory interpretation.

For example, to understand the seven parables of "the kingdom of the heavens" recorded in Mathew 13, it is necessary not only to connect Jesus' teaching with the immediate con-

[9] Cf. Bernard Ramm, *Protestant Biblical Interpretation* (Boston, W. A. Wilde Co., 1950), p. 178f.

text of His ministry from the boat as he spoke by the side of the sea (vv. 1-3), but, what is much more important, to place this pivotal turning point in our Lord's career in the larger context of Matthew's Gospel. The king and the message of His kingdom having been rejected by the Jews (Chaps. 1-12), and a new message of rest and service offered to such in the nation as were conscious of need (11:28-30), the king now turns to the new age which will be ushered in as a result of His death and resurrection and which will extend to His second advent (Chap. 13).

Failure to note carefully the historical occasion of these seven parables as dealing with this present age and to discern their purpose in setting forth the general character of this new era as a period of seed-sowing, of mingled wheat and tares, of the progress of the leaven of evil, of the hiding and rejection of Israel in the field of the world, of the formation of the pearl, the Church of Christ, and of the mixture of the good fish and the bad in the dragnet, will result in serious misinterpretation of this important section of eschatological revelation.

It is always of the utmost importance in interpreting parables to follow rigidly any clues in the context which will aid in elucidating the parable's meaning. These clues act as signposts to keep the expositor on the highway of correct interpretation and to guard him from wandering in some side road of fanciful exegesis. A good instance of this is furnished in the triad of parables in Luke 15, consisting of the parable of the lost sheep, the lost coin and the lost son. Frequently these well-known parables are expounded with little regard for the historical occasion that called them forth. But the interpretive context in Luke 15:1, 2 is indispensable to their proper exposition. "Now the tax collectors and sinners were all drawing near to hear him. And the Pharisees and the scribes murmured, saying, This man receives sinners and eats with them" (RSV).

In the light of the context it becomes quite apparent that, whatever application interpreters have made of these parables (and they have been multifarious), Jesus intended them to be a justification of his eating with publicans and sinners and meant them to teach that God's redemptive love and forgiveness in Christ extended to this hated and sinful segment of the population, so despised by the religionists of that day.

Likewise, Jesus directed the parable of the Pharisee and the Publican "to some who trusted in themselves that they were righteous and despised others" (Luke 18:9). This interpretive lead must be followed if the parable is to be kept on a sound exegetical basis. The same is true of the parable of the unrighteous Judge (Luke 18:1-8), which is definitely said to teach that men "ought always to pray and not to lose heart" (v. 1).

Besides the historical occasion and the definite statement of the purpose of a parable, it is often necessary to search carefully to see how much of it is actually interpreted for the reader. Jesus, for example, frequently interprets His parables. Such is notably the case in the parables of "the kingdom of the heavens" in Matthew 13. The parable of the Sower (vv. 3-9) is explained in verses 18-23. The parable of the tares (vv. 24-30) is explained in verses 36-43.

In addition, valuable interpretational leads for the exposition of all seven of these parables are given in verses 10-17. These pivotal comments, so often ignored, are indispensable to a full understanding of the scope and meaning of our Lord's teaching recorded in this chapter. These explanatory verses tell us that Jesus, in revealing the nature and course of this present age between His first advent in humiliation and His second advent in glory, was giving truths that were hidden from Old Testament "prophets and righteous men" (v. 17).

Old Testament prophets indeed saw the first and second advents, but in one blended and indistinguishable view. The new period to be taken up with the formation of the Church, the Body of Christ, by the outcalling of the Gentiles (Acts 15:14, 15; Eph. 1:19-23; 3:1-10) was, however, hidden from them (I Pet. 1:10-12; Rom. 16:25). In the parables of the "mysteries of the kingdom of the heavens" Christ first gives the introductory revelation of these great truths which later are to be fully revealed through the Apostle Paul (Eph. 3: 5, 6).

c. *The similitude or literal narrative constituting the parable as a figure of speech must be carefully distinguished.* Since the interpretation of parabolic literature hinges on the analogy between the earthly element contained in the similitude and the spiritual truth to be taught, the features of the former must be thoroughly analyzed. If a parable deals with a narrative framework which has to do with farming, sheepherding, management of property, fishing, or some other phase of ancient Jewish or Graeco-Roman life, the expositor must spare no pains to acquaint himself with the customs involved.

Adequate knowledge of the manners and local color of Bible times is of great importance because ancient usages frequently are completely incomprehensible to our modern world and many times the whole point of a parable may hinge on the correct understanding of the events and practices used as illustrations in the similitude. Unless the expositor becomes conversant with the particular ways of life alluded to, he will be seriously handicapped in the full elucidation of the parable which he is expounding. Moreover, the spiritual or prophetic truth the parable is designed to teach will be obscured or distorted in proportion as its natural imagery and human story are misunderstood. The best Bible dictionaries, commentaries and special works on Bible manners and customs, accordingly, must be consulted.[10]

d. *The spiritual or prophetic truth taught by the parable must be accurately discerned.* Since the spiritual truth or frequently the prophetic revelation to be inculcated constitutes the marrow and inner substance or core of the parable, it is of supreme importance. All the other constituent elements — the historical occasion, the purpose (the root) and the literal story or similitude (the bark) are secondary. The primary thing is the truth conveyed and not the vehicle of its convey-

[10] Cf. Edward Cone Bissell, *Biblical Antiquities* (Philadelphia, American Sunday School Union, 1888); Alfred Edersheim, *The Life and Times of Jesus the Messiah* (New York, Longmans Green & Co., 1940), Vols. I, II; Fred H. Wight, *Manners and Customs of Bible Lands* (Chicago, Moody Press, 1953).

ance, the spiritual lesson presented and not the literary medium of its presentation, the prophetic revelation and not its figurative dress.

For this reason, the expositor must exercise the greatest caution in distinguishing the spiritual or prophetic truth taught from the similitude of the parable and its relevant and essential imagery from that which is merely accidental. It is wise always to look for the one central truth the parable is slanted to teach. While some parables such as the Sower and the Wheat and the Tares[11] have several points to teach and the details of the imagery are given such significance by our Lord Himself (cf. Matt. 13:3-23; 36-43), yet most of the parables present one essential truth and the details of the imagery merely fill out the similitude and are not to be pressed for meaning. Failure to observe due restraint in this phase of parabolic interpretation has led many otherwise capable expositors to magnify the irrelevant and non-essential often to the point of pure fancy and to the degree that the central truth of the parable is wholly obscured.

This practice of failing to differentiate the similitude or figurative dress of a parable from the truth it is designed to set forth and attaching significance to the non-essential details of the bark or figurative drapery is commonly called making a parable "walk on all fours." It is an exegetical fallacy productive of much arbitrary and farfetched interpretation and must be avoided by the careful expositor.

Isaiah's parable of the Vineyard (Is. 5:1-7), for example, has frequently been abused by expositors who have unduly pressed into meaning many details of its imagery which are merely ornamental and designed only to make the similitude more graphic and interesting. For instance, the tower in the vineyard is made to stand for Jerusalem (Grotius) or the temple (Bengel); the winevat, the altar (Chrysostom); and the gathering out of the stones, the expulsion of the Canaanites together with their stone idols (Grotius).

11 For an interpretation of these parables see R. C. Trench, *Notes on the Parables of Our Lord* (New York, Fleming Revell, n.d.; reprint, Grand Rapids, Baker Book House), pp. 55-87.

But such unwarranted handling of the parable distracts from its real meaning and these details of the Lord's care of His vineyard, the house of Israel (v. 7), merely indicate the complete provision He had made for the safety and prosperity of His people Israel.

The same exegetical caution must be exercised in interpreting the parable of the Wicked Husbandmen (Matt. 21: 33-44), in which our Lord appropriates the same imagery that Isaiah employs in his parable. Here, as in Isaiah, special meanings must not be sought in the hedge, the winepress and the tower. Nor should the expositor seek to identify each servant sent with some particular Old Testament prophet. In view of the overstraining these details have received from interpreters in general constant emphasis must be laid on the fact that at most the details are incidental rather than important.

However, in the matter of determining what parts of a parable are significant and what portions are purely embellishing accessories to the story, no precise rules can be laid down. Spiritual discernment and common sense "are to be cultivated and matured by a protracted study of all the parables, and by careful collation and comparison."[12]

In addition to determining what parts of a parable are significant and what portions are merely accessory the interpreter needs to exercise great caution in the doctrinal and theological use of parables. That parables do teach doctrine can scarcely be denied. But doctrine deduced from them must be clearly indicated by the historical context and must be in agreement with the analogy of faith and the plain teaching of Scripture in general. The honest interpreter must ever be alert against the temptation of reading his own theological preconceptions into parables.

Particularly in the realm of prophecy and eschatology the parabolic portions of the Scripture have been doctrinally abused. An instance of this is furnished by the parable of the Ten Virgins. Many interpreters[13] have erred in introducing the

[12] Terry, *op. cit.*, p. 198.
[13] Cf. Trench, *op. cit.*, pp. 192-208.

Church of Christ into this parable whereas the whole historical context of the Olivet Discourse (Matt. 24 and 25) shows that it is Israel exhorted to be ready for the coming of her Messiah-King at His second advent that is the subject of the parabolic teaching. In the parable of the Good and Evil Servants (Matt. 24:45-51) Messiah is the "Lord of the household." In the parable of the Ten Virgins He is the Bridegroom, who having been married to His Bride, the glorified Church in heaven (Rev. 19:7, 8), is seen returning with her to the earth to deliver His people Israel and establish them in the blessings of the millennial kingdom.

The theme is the need for watching on the part of the nation Israel (25:13). The ten virgins of whom five were wise and five foolish represent the nation in its spiritual condition as manifested in its Messianic hopes at that time. The five wise with oil in their lamps represent the believing remnant looking for their soon-coming Messiah. The foolish, who had no oil in their lamps, are the unbelieving Israelites, who are not ready to welcome their Messiah and who are excluded from the Messianic kingdom, symbolized in parabolic language by being shut out from the marriage feast (Matt. 25:10).

In introducing believers of this age into the parable of the Ten Virgins many expositors are given an occasion to read unsound theological notions into their interpretations. Accordingly, some interject Arminian ideas into the circumstance of the parable that asserts that "the door was shut" against the foolish virgins. Others misuse it to teach what is commonly known as "a partial rapture." According to this vagary only the most spiritual believer will be taken to be with Christ when He appears. Others will be left behind to endure the rigorous sufferings of the time of judgment upon the earth.

These errors not only clash with the general testimony of Scripture but with revealed truth concerning God's grace as well. Those who purport to draw such teachings from this parable not only grossly misuse it, but unwittingly cast immeasurable dishonor upon the grace of God, which is magnified in Scripture not because it saves the worthy or the deserving, but the completely unworthy and meritless.

In similar manner the parable of the Talents (Matt. 25:14-30), as in the Ten Virgins and other portions of our Lord's great eschatological treatise given in the Olivet Discourse, is concerned with Israel's relation to her coming king. The reference to "the days of Noah" (Matt. 24:37-39), the separation by judgment of two working in the field and at the mill (24:40-42), the parable of the "goodman" of the house (24:43, 44), and the parable of the good and evil servants (24:45-51), all have the same purpose of enjoining Israel at the end of the age to *watch* and be *ready* for Messiah's return.

The elements of moral and spiritual value set forth in these parables represent such works as are required for admission into the Messianic kingdom (cf. Matt. 5:1 - 7:29; 19:28-30; Luke 3:8-14). The good servant is found by the returning King faithfully caring for the household, the wise virgins had oil in their lamps, the dutiful servants are found to have increased their talents.

But the wicked and slothful one-talent man is cast "into outer darkness" (Matt. 25:30), that is, he is excluded from the blessings of the Messianic kingdom just as the foolish virgins are similarly shut out by being barred from the marriage feast. To apply these parables to the message of free grace proclaimed through faith in Christ in this present church age is to introduce contradiction and confusion and to subject these passages to doctrinal misuse.

LITERATURE ON PARABLES

Plumptre, E. H., "Parable," in *Smith's Dictionary of the Bible*, ed. by H. B. Hackett (Boston, 1887), III, p. 2327.

Fausset, A. R., "Parable," in *Bible Cyclopaedia* (New York, George Doran, n.d.), p. 538f.

Trench, R. C., *Notes on the Parables of Our Lord* (New York, Fleming Revell, n.d.).

Taylor, W. M., *The Parables of Our Saviour* (New York, A. C. Armstrong, 1896).

Terry, Milton S., *Biblical Hermeneutics* (New York, Methodist Book Concern, 1911), pp. 188-213.

Goebel, Siegfried, *The Parables of Jesus* (Edinburgh, T. & T. Clark, 1913).

Schodde, G. H., "Parable," in *International Standard Bible Encyclopedia* (Grand Rapids, Wm. B. Eerdmans Publishing Co., 1939).

Dodd, C. H., *The Parables of the Kingdom* (London, Nisbet & Co., 1936).

CHAPTER XVIII

THE EXPOSITOR AND SCRIPTURAL TYPOLOGY

The study of the principles of correct interpretation of Scriptural typology is indispensable for the work of an expositor. It is even more important than a study of the proper interpretation of parables. Whereas parables occur only occasionally in the Old Testament, and in the New Testament are confined to the ministry of our Lord, Messianic and redemptive types form the warp and woof of the Old Testament and their fulfillment or antitypes constitute the warp and woof of the New Testament.

Although the interpretation of Scriptural typology has doubtless sometimes been overdone and typical significance attached to that which is not a valid type or to details of valid types to which significance ought not to be attached, yet the greatest transgression against this most rewarding field of Bible study is apparently not committed by those who overdo in the matter, but by those who "underdo," who as the result of extreme caution completely bypass many bona fide types. Indeed, the most successful expositor will be the one who discerns most clearly that the grand subject of the Bible and its central unifying theme are the person and work of Jesus Christ, the Redeemer, and that everywhere He is to be traced in type, symbol, promise and prophecy. Playing no small role in this truly remarkable setting-forth of Messiah's person and work from eternity past to eternity future are the types and symbols of Holy Scripture.

202 PRINCIPLES OF EXPOSITORY PREACHING

1. THE DEFINITION OF A TYPE

A type (Greek *typos*, "a blow, mark of a blow, pattern, impress," from *typtein*, "to strike") is an allegorical or symbolic representation of some person, event or thing. The fulfillment of the type is called the *antitype*. Angus and Green distinguish between an allegory and a type, the former being defined as "a double representation in *words*" the latter as "a double representation in *action;* the literal being intended and planned to represent the spiritual."[1] The "representation in action" (the literal) occurs in the Old Testament and constitutes a prefigurement of events, persons and things in the New Testament (the spiritual).

Often a type is definitely prophetic, and A. B. Davidson is substantially correct when he says that "typology is a species of prophecy."[2] This is certainly the case when types deal with the first and second advent of Christ, which Old Testament prophets saw clearly, but in blended view. Hence the typology of the tabernacle, the priesthood, the set feasts of Israel and many other features of the old economy are prophetic of the person and work of Christ in His first or second advent.

A type, however, is not necessarily a prophecy, because its typical import may not be made known in the age in which the type itself appears. Indeed, much of the typology of the Old Testament prefigures events and truths which deal with the period between the two advents of Messiah, and which constitute an interval which was unrevealed to Old Testament seers (Matt. 13:11-17). Hence, this new age with its distinctive purpose of calling out the Church was unrevealed in Old Testament prophecy as well as in Old Testament typology. In fact, the New Testament Church, "the revelation of the mystery," was as the Apostle declares, "kept secret since the world began" (Rom. 16:25) and was "in other generations . . . not made known unto the sons of men, as it hath now been revealed unto his [Christ's] holy apostles and prophets in the Spirit" (Eph. 3:5, ARV).

[1] J. Angus and S. G. Green, *The Bible Handbook* (New York, Fleming Revell, 1908; reprint, Grand Rapids, Zondervan Publishing House), p. 221.
[2] *Old Testament Prophecy* (Edinburgh, T. & T. Clark, 1905), p. 210.

This mystery of the New Testament Church, involving the divinely disclosed truth hidden in Old Testament times, that Jew and Gentile were to be baptized into a wholly new spiritual entity, the Church, the Body of Christ (I Cor. 12:13; Eph. 1:22, 23) and into the risen and glorified Christ Himself (Rom. 6:3, 4; Gal. 3:27; Col. 2:12), was nevertheless prefigured typically in various persons, events and institutions set forth in the Hebrew Scriptures. Thus Eve (Gen. 2:23) becomes a type of the Church as the Bride of Christ (John 3:28, 29; II Cor. 11:2; Eph. 5:25-32), as does also Rebekah in the account of Abraham's seeking a bride for His son Isaac, type of Christ, the bridegroom (Gen. 24:1-67).

In similar manner the Feast of Pentecost (Lev. 23:15-22) typifies the formation of the New Testament Church at Pentecost (Acts 2) by the baptism of the Holy Spirit (Acts 1:5; 11:16; I Cor. 12:13). The two loaves which were baked in the celebration of this ancient feast clearly speak of Jew and Gentile made one "in Christ" by the Spirit's baptizing work (Rom. 6:3, 4), and the "new meal offering" (Lev. 23:16) prepared for the occasion adumbrates this new spiritual entity.[3]

Thus, it may be said, that a type is not always prophetic. Although always designed by God to prefigure some subsequent development of truth in the course of the history of redemption, it is of the utmost importance in understanding general scriptural typology to realize that such typical meaning was at best only partially known to the age in which the type was instituted and in many cases, as with the New Testament Church, was completely unknown. Not until the antitype appeared, often many centuries or even millennia later, and progress in revelation had made the type humanly recognizable, did it become invested with its God-ordained significance as illustrative of the divine dealing.

Correctly understood, there is no stronger proof of the divine inspiration of the Bible than typology. It is in reality the divine redemptive program of the ages deftly woven into

[3] Cf. the present author's *The Baptizing Work of the Holy Spirit* (Wheaton, Ill., Van Kampen Press, 1953), pp. 114f.

the warp and woof of Holy Writ by the finger of God Himself. Until the expositor has this exalted view of Biblical typology and is eager to know God's redemptive ways with mankind, past, present and future, he will never truly appreciate the marvels of Scripture types nor be fully equipped to expound their wonders.

2. ESSENTIAL CHARACTERISTICS OF TYPES

As a "preordained representative relation which certain persons, events, and institutions of the Old Testament bear to corresponding persons, events, and institutions in the New,"[4] a genuine type always contains certain unmistakable elements. Knowledge of these distinguishing features is indispensable not only for recognizing a bona fide type, but is fundamental as well to its correct interpretation.

First, a type possesses the elements of *reality* and intrinsic *dignity*. It consists of a person, event or an institution that is actual and not fictional, real and not imaginary. Accordingly, a type has its origin in history and not in myth or legend. Moreover, the historical fact or incident furnishing the basis of the type is not trivial, but of exalted dignity and worth. In every case it is a suitable vehicle to be a prefigurement of the benefits to come to mankind by virtue of the mediatory sacrifice of Christ. Recognition of this characteristic of a Scripture type is necessary if the exposition is to avoid construing as typical that which is not really meant to be a type or in interjecting what is trifling into the interpretation of a bona fide type. Although the antitype normally refers to something higher and nobler than the type, the type itself, if genuine, is never an unworthy medium for the conveyance of truth.

Secondly, a type possesses the element of *similarity*. There must be some significant point of resemblance or analogy between the Old Testament citation and the New Testament counterpart, as Adam in his representative character and relation to the human race is a type of Christ (Rom. 5:14) or as Moses as a prophet was a type of "the Prophet" that was

---

[4] Milton S. Terry, *Biblical Hermeneutics* (New York, Methodist Book Concern, 1911), p. 246.

to come (Deut. 18:15, Acts 3:22). The aspect of likeness must be substantial, not superficial. It must be easily and naturally recognizable by the seeker after spiritual truth. If it is not readily discernible to the Spirit-taught mind that is conversant with God's redemptive plan as it affects the various ages, it must be avoided. The reliable expositor will deal unsparingly with that which is strained and artificial or that which is trifling or superficial in matters of typology.

Thirdly, a type contains the element of *dissimilarity*. It is fully as important to recognize this ingredient as the element of similarity. Frequently a type illuminates truth by contrast. It is not uncommon for the dissimilar elements to furnish as much instruction as the similar aspects. Adam, for instance, furnishes a contrasting type of Christ as well as a comparative type. In I Corinthians 15:45-47 the "first man Adam" is said to have been "made a living soul" (Gen. 2:7), that is, he derived life from God, his Creator. On the other hand, "the last Adam" is declared to be "a life-giving Spirit." So far from deriving life He was the fountain and the giver of life to others (John 1:4; 10:10). In origin the first man was of the earth, earthy; the Second Man is "the Lord from heaven." Each is the head of a creation, Adam of the old, and Christ of the new. These also are in contrast. In Adam all die; in Christ all will be made alive (I Cor. 15:22). The Apostle Paul draws another impressive typical contrast between Adam and Christ in Romans 5:12-21.

Although the elements of dissimilarity may often be instructive, there is a common error to be avoided of attaching typical significance to these aspects when they merely constitute the historical or geographical background essential only to the existence of the type. A case in point is the tabernacle. While Israel's ancient worship was designedly typical and richly instructive of the person and work of the Messiah to come, all the boards, sockets, and curtains are not to be construed as prefiguring redemptive truths.

The Levitical priesthood most assuredly is typical of present-day Christians (Rev. 1:6; I Pet. 2:5, 9). But certainly every article of priestly clothing is not to be deemed typical of something pertaining to the followers of Christ. The high priest is typical of Christ (Heb. 3:1), but clearly the Aaronic type can go only so far in its imperfection and falls short of its antitype. To contrast the type with its antitype is legitimate. But to force the surrounding area of dissimilarity into the typology when it is purely essential background material, is to open the door to the unsuitably trivial and to do violence to the type.

Fourthly, a type possesses evidence of *divine designation*. This indication of purpose and appointment by God to represent the thing typified may be implicit or explicit. Two extremes, however, are to be avoided. First, the extravagance of some, who granting that divine designation may be explicit as well as implicit, have run to excess in seeking for types in every incident and event, however trivial, recorded in Scripture. Second, the barren reserve of others, who denying that a type may be implicit, have unduly contracted the typical element of Scripture asserting that "just so much of the Old Testament is to be accounted typical as the New Testament affirms to be so, and no more."[5]

The true approach to the identification of types lies midway between these two extremes. Types are not only those "expressly declared" to be such "by Christ or by His apostles," as Bishop Marsh contends,[6] but also includes those that may be inferred to be such by reasoning "from typical wholes to typical parts."[7] This is the method of Cocceius of the seventeenth century as later reinterpreted by Patrick Fairbairn of the nineteenth century.[8] Accordingly, Fairbairn is right in maintaining with Marsh "that Scripture is the sole rule, on the authority of which we are to distinguish what is properly typical from what is not," but he corrects Marsh's too narrow view by insisting that "in this, as well as in other things, Scripture

[5] See "Type" in the *International Standard Bible Encyclopaedia*, ed. by J. Orr (reprint, Grand Rapids, Wm. B. Eerdmans Publishing Co.), V, p. 3030.

[6] Bishop Herbert Marsh, *Lectures on the Criticism and Interpretation of the Bible* (London, 1842), p. 373.

[7] Bernard Ramm, *Protestant Biblical Interpretation* (Boston, W. A. Wilde Co., 1950), p. 144.

[8] Patrick Fairbairn, *The Typology of Scripture* (New York, Funk & Wagnalls, 1900; reprint, Grand Rapids, Zondervan Publishing House), Vol. I, pp. 9-23.

may indicate certain fundamental views or principles, of which it makes but a few individual applications, and for the rest leaves them in the hand of spiritually enlightened consciences."[9]

New Testament writers most certainly have not exhausted Old Testament types. The truth is they have merely taken samples from the great storehouse where many more are found (I Cor. 10:11). If this fact is not true, "nothing is more arbitrary than the New Testament use of types, for there is nothing to distinguish them from a multitude of others of the same class."[10]

Moreover, any attempt to rescue typology from too narrow views, such as the Marshian, which reduce its content unwarrantedly, "if in any measure successful," as Fairbairn says, "will also serve to exhibit the unity of design which pervades the inspired records of both covenants, the traces they contain of the same divine hand, the subservience of the one to the other, and the natural dependence alike of the Old upon the New, and of the New upon the Old."[11]

The expositor, on the other hand, who refuses to be sidetracked into the opposite extreme of extravagant handling of types, will also render the cause of sound Bible exposition great service. Nothing is better calculated to destroy confidence in the validity and trustworthiness of the Bible than methods of interpretation that wrest Scripture out of the sphere of the natural and the historical and place it in the realm of the arbitrary and fanciful.

3. VARIETIES OF TYPES

Principal types of the Old Testament fall into five general categories. These include typical persons, events, institutions, offices and actions. Typical *persons* comprise Old Testament characters whose lives and experiences illustrate some principle or truth of redemption. Cain is a type of the natural man, destitute of any adequate sense of sin or atonement (Gen. 4:3; II Pet. 2:1-22; Jude 11). Abel is a type of the spiritual man

[9] *Ibid.*, p. 24.

[10] W. G. Moorehead, "Types," in *International Standard Bible Encyclopaedia*, ed. by J. Orr (reprint, Grand Rapids, Wm. B. Eerdmans Publishing Co., 1939), V, p. 3030.

[11] Fairbairn, *op. cit.*, p. 24.

whose sacrifice of blood (Gen. 4:4; Heb. 9:22) evidenced his confession of sin and his faith in the interposition of a substitute (Heb. 11:4). Enoch, "translated that he should not see death" (Gen. 5:24; Heb. 11:5), is a type of the saints to be "caught up" before the Great Tribulation (I Thess. 4:14-17), while Noah, preserved through the flood (Gen. 7:1), is a type of the remnant of Israel preserved through this time of trouble (Jer. 30:5-9). Similarly, Abraham, Isaac, Jacob, Joseph, Moses, Joshua, David and many other Old Testament saints are typical of some aspect of the Messiah or some phase of redemption.

Typical *events* include such important occurrences as the flood, the exodus from Egypt, the wilderness wandering, the pillar of cloud and fire, the giving of manna, the supply of water from the rock, the lifting up of the brazen serpent, the conquest of Canaan, the war with the Amalekites, and numerous other happenings. The Apostle Paul says that such events happened to Old Testament believers "typically (*tupikos*); and they were written for our admonition, upon whom the ends of the ages are come" (I Cor. 10:11).

Typical *institutions* include the whole Levitical ritual in which lambs and other animals were slain and blood sprinkled to make atonement for sin (Lev. 17:11). These are prefigurative of "the Lamb of God" who would take away the sin of the world (John 1:29; Heb. 9:28; I Pet. 1:19). The entire ancient calendar of set sacred feasts in ancient Israel is typical of phases of God's redemptive plan. The weekly sabbath (Lev. 23:1-3) pictures the rest of faith into which the believer is to enter (Heb. 4:9, 10). The Passover (Lev. 23:4, 5) portrays Christ our Redeemer (I Cor. 5:6-8). The Feast of Unleavened Bread (Lev. 23:6-8) portrays the holy walk of the redeemed (I Cor. 5:6-8). The Feast of Firstfruits (Lev. 23:9-14) sets forth Christ risen (I Cor. 15:23). Pentecost (Lev. 23:15-22) adumbrates the formation of the Church (Acts 1:5; 2:1-4; I Cor. 12:13) and the present age of the outcalling of the Gentiles (Lev. 23:22; Acts 15:14, 15). The Feast of Trumpets (Lev. 23:23-25) points to Israel's future regathering (Joel 2:1 - 3:21). The Day of Atonement (Lev. 23:26-32) looks forward to Israel's repentance and conversion previous to Christ's second advent. The Feast of Tabernacles (Lev. 23:33-44) closes the sacred cycle and presents restored Israel in full millennial blessing (Zech. 14:16-19; Rev. 21:3).

Typical *offices* include prophets, priests and kings. Every Old Testament prophet, particularly Moses (Deut. 18:15-18), as a medium of divine revelation and a God-sent messenger, was a type of Christ, the Prophet par excellence (John 6:14; 7:40). The Levitical priests, and especially the high priest, in the performance of their sacred duties, were types of Him who through His own blood entered into the Most Holy Place once for all, thereby obtaining eternal redemption (Heb. 4:14; 9:12). The sons of Levi in general prefigure present-day believers as "priests to God" (Rev. 1:6). The kingship also typified Christ as a coming king. Melchizedek, "king of righteousness and king of peace" (Heb. 7:2), David, Solomon, and indeed every other to whom God might have said, "I have set my king upon my holy hill of Zion" (Ps. 2:6), by his holy office preannounced the eventual coming of the "King of kings and Lord of lords" (Rev. 19:16). Thus Christ the Lord unites in Himself the combined offices of prophet, priest and king and fulfills the types of previous dispensations.

Typical *actions* include Jonah's experience with the great fish, which was a prophetic type of our Lord's burial and resurrection (Matt. 12:39). The prophets performed many symbolical-typical actions. Isaiah walked naked and barefoot for three years as a prophecy that Assyria would bring down Egypt and Ethiopia to shameful defeat (Is. 20:2-4). Jeremiah hid a linen girdle by the Euphrates, which was ruined when he was later told to fetch it, and this constituted a prophetic sign that Jerusalem and Judah's pride would likewise be marred (Jer. 13:1-11). Zechariah was instructed to make crowns of silver and gold for the head of Joshua, the high priest, which action was prophetic of the millennial role of Messiah as a King-Priest, reigning over the earth (Zech. 6:9-15).

4. RULES FOR THE INTERPRETATION OF TYPES

Typology assumes such an important place in Bible exposition that the reliable interpreter cannot afford to neglect

this phase of his training. Although in the interpretation of
types "we use the same rules as in interpreting parables and
allegories properly so-called,"[12] a number of specific suggestions may be set down, which will be helpful.

*a. Make certain your general approach to the subject of
typology is sound.* Begin with a thorough study of the New
Testament teaching on the subject. Such allusions to types
as occur in the Pauline epistles (cf. I Cor. 5:6-8; 10:11) and
so profusely in the Epistle to the Hebrews will facilitate
locating the great typical areas of the Old Testament. These
will be found to be principally in the Pentateuch and less
frequently elsewhere.[13] This reveals the whole of which the
parts are typical.

Reject any extreme position on typology, either the extravagance which sees the most recondite truth in the simplest, most commonplace circumstance or the ultra-conserva-
tism which accounts only so much of the Old Testament
typical as the New Testament specifically affirms to be so.

*b. Ascertain the real points of similarity between the type
and its antitype.* This having been done, all novel and far-
fetched analogies must be uncompromisingly rejected. A case
in point is Melchizedek, a type of the eternal priesthood of
Christ (Gen. 14:18-20; Ps. 110:4; Heb. 7:1-25). The elements of similarity between type and antitype are these:
Melchizedek was both king and priest, as was Christ. He
was timeless — being *presented* without recorded parentage,
genealogy or death — as Christ's priesthood is perpetual and
timeless. He was superior to Abraham and the Levitical
priests prefiguring Christ's priestly dignity. His priesthood
was not legally constituted like the Levitical, but was without
successor or limitation, pointing to Christ's inviolable and
unchangeable priesthood.

However, many expositors have not confined their interpretations of the teachings of this type to the elements of
similarity. As a result, a vast amount of unprofitable theo-
rizing has accumulated around it, particularly concerning the

[12] Angus and Green, *op. cit.,* p. 227.
[13] Cf. Rollin Thomas Chafer, *The Science of Biblical Hermeneutics* (Dallas,
Bibliotheca Sacra, 1939), p. 82.

identity of Melchizedek of the Genesis narrative. But despite the statement in Hebrews 7:3 that the ancient king-priest was "without genealogy, having neither beginning of days nor end of life" there is no reason to suppose, if the real points of likeness between the type and the antitype are carefully kept in mind, that he was other than a human being. He simply is *presented* in the sacred record without ancestry, without descendants and unconnected with any line of priests to furnish a picture of an everlasting king-priest, realized antitypically in Christ. To insist that Melchizedek was supernaturally born and did not die, or to make him a theophany, is to go beyond the real points of resemblance between the type and the antitype and to attempt futilely to trace all imaginable analogies.

c. *Determine also the points of contrast between the type and its antitype.* Notable difference between type and antitype are frequently enlarged upon by New Testament writers. Moses and Christ are so contrasted in Hebrews 3:1-6. The important point of analogy is Moses' faithfulness as an apostle and servant of God, based upon the statement in Numbers 12:7 that he was faithful in all the house of God. But the writer develops the type by contrast, showing that Christ is worthy of far greater glory than Moses inasmuch as our Lord is builder of the house and as such has more honor than the house. Moreover, Moses was faithful only as a servant in the house, but Christ as a son over the house.

The writer to the Hebrews also enlarges expansively upon the contrast of the Aaronic priesthood to Christ, the great High Priest. These and other types illustrate the importance of noting unlikenesses as well as likenesses between the type and the antitype. They also demonstrate that the type is inferior to the antitype, inasmuch as the shadow is inferior to the substance. For this reason perfection is not to be expected in Old Testament types and they are not to be pressed for exhaustive analogies.

d. *Rigidly test each type.* Expositors are always liable to yield to the temptation of interpreting as typical what is not really typical, or interpreting details of valid types typically which are merely part of the geographical or historical background, and ought not to be included in the typical interpretation at all. Two simple tests can be applied to overcome this danger. First, many such alleged types do not involve clearly the same moral or spiritual principle as their alleged antitypes and must be rejected as types. Second, in many cases alleged types will be found unsuitably trivial in their character, and must be excluded from the typical category on the basis of sound spiritual discernment.

Accordingly, while there is undeniably a very rich and highly instructive typology clustering about the ancient tabernacle, it is an extravagance to be avoided to see mystery and mysticism in every cord and pin of the ancient structure. Whereas the altar of burnt offering, the laver and many other parts of the tent most clearly do prefigure redemption to come, many details, however, do not carry special principles, and are not to be forced into the type.

For example, to find in the brass of the brazen serpent a metal inferior to gold or silver and to construe this as indicative of the outward meanness of the Saviour's appearance, or to imagine that it was cast in a mold, not wrought by hand, and thus to prefigure the divine conception of Christ's human nature, or to surmise that it was fashioned in the shape of a cross to portray more precisely the manner in which Christ was to suffer, is to interject pure suppositions that, as Terry says, "are far-fetched, misleading," and are "to be rejected."[14]

e. *Interpret types on the basis of clearly revealed doctrine.* Doctrine may be illustrated by types, but not established by it, except where there is clear New Testament witness. The Book of Hebrews, it is true, proves doctrine from types. But we may well hesitate to do so, since we are not inspired. On the other hand, clearly revealed doctrine is to be employed always to guide the interpretation of a type. If a typical interpretation is at variance with plain truth, it must be summarily rejected.

What is even more important is the fact that typology

[14] Terry, *op. cit.*, p. 251.

THE EXPOSITOR AND SCRIPTURAL TYPOLOGY   213

must be interpreted in accordance with the divine plan of
the ages. Interpreters who reject premillennial eschatology
and who frown upon sound dispensational distinctions find
themselves greatly embarrassed in those phases of typology
that deal with the future restoration of Israel as a millennial
nation. The Feast of Trumpets (Lev. 23:23-25), the great
Day of Atonement and the Feast of Tabernacles (Lev. 23:
26-44), for example, are divested of their real meaning if
misapplied to the Church of this age. No single factor is quite
so important to interpretation of Scripture typology as a
keen perception of God's redemptive program as it begins
in eternity past and reaches to eternity future.

5. Types and Symbols

Both types and symbols "are outward representations of
spiritual truths."[15] As such they are emblems, representing
one thing to the eye and another to the understanding. The
symbol (*synbolle*, "a throwing together, a comparison," from
sun, "with," and *ballein*, "to throw") may represent something either past, present or future, having in itself "no
essential reference to time,"[16] and as such be illustrative of
what already exists. The type, on the other hand, has a
necessary time relationship and is definitely prefigurative of
something future from itself. It has a mystical or spiritual
meaning, and is confined to divine revelation as contained
in the Word of God. Symbols on the other hand are not
confined to sacred truth, but are also common outside of the
Bible, often being constituted common signs among men,
as the lion denoting kingliness or courage, the olive or the
laurel representing peace, or the color white denoting purity,
etc.

With these distinctions in mind it is easy to see that Adam
in his representative character and connection with the race
was a prefigurement or type of Christ (Rom. 5:14) and not
a symbol. Likewise it is evident that the "coats of skins"
with which God clothed sinning man are typical (not symbolic) of "Christ made unto us righteousness" (I Cor. 1:30).

---

[15] Cf. Angus and Green, *op. cit.*, p. 221.
[16] Terry, *op. cit.*, p. 246.

On the other hand, the rainbow is a symbol of God's covenant mercy and faithfulness (Gen. 9:13-16; Ezek. 1:28; Rev. 4:3). The bread and wine of the Lord's Supper are symbols of His broken body and shed blood (Luke 22:19, 20). The pillar of cloud and of fire that guided Israel of old was a symbol of God's directing presence (Num. 9:15-23).

The apocalyptic visions of Ezekiel and Daniel and particularly of John in the Book of Revelation are largely symbolic. The golden lampstands of Revelation 1:12-20, for instance, are symbols of then-existing churches; and the stars, of the ministers of those churches (v. 20). The seven-sealed book (Rev. 5:1) is an emblem of Christ's redemptive title deed to the earth. His opening the book and loosing the seals (Rev. 5:1 - 8:1) is a symbolic typical action in which the symbol foreshadows something to take place in the future. In such cases the symbol merges into the type when the temporal element appears and the emblem prefigures an event yet to occur or a truth yet to be revealed.

Important among Bible symbols are numbers. For instance, one is the number of unity and deity (Deut. 6:4; Zech. 14:9). Three, for example, is the number of completed unity — the triune God (unity in trinity), the tripartite nature of man (I Thess 5:23). Four is a world number — the four winds (Dan. 7:2), the four corners of the earth (Rev. 7:1), the four world empires summing up Gentile earth sovereignty (Dan. 7:1-7) and four cherubic living creatures who watch over the earth (Rev. 4:8; 5:8).

Six is the number of manifested evil; trebled, the number of the beast-superman, 666, the acme of human wickedness (Rev. 13:18). Goliath, the Philistine giant, type of all opposers of God and of God's people, was six cubits in height and had six fingers and six toes (I Sam. 17:4; II Sam. 21:20). Nebuchadnezzar's idolatrous image was sixty cubits high and six broad (Dan. 3:1).

Seven is the number of completeness and fullness. God celebrated a finished creation by resting on the seventh day (Gen. 2:2, 3). The sabbath day, the seventh year, and the Jubilee year after seven sevens of years were all significant among the Jews. In Revelation appear seven churches, denoted by seven lampstands or light bearers (Rev. 1:12), seven spirits, representing the one Holy Spirit (4:5), seven lamps bespeaking fullness of light (4:5), seven seals indicating a complete closing (5:1), seven trumpets (8:1) and seven bowls of wrath (16:1) poured out by "seven angels" and containing "the seven last plagues" in which are "filled up the wrath of God" (15:1).

In like manner, other numbers are symbolically significant. Twelve stands for the rule of God. The twelve tribes of Israel were to be the instrument of God's theocratic rule in the old dispensation. In the New Jerusalem of the eternal state (Rev. 21:9-21) the blessing of God's complete rule is everywhere apparent in the predominance of the number of divine sovereignty — twelve gates, twelve foundations, twelve thousand furlongs its dimensions each way. Likewise, upon earth, according to our Lord's promise, the twelve apostles are to "sit upon twelve thrones, judging the twelve tribes of Israel" (Matt. 19:28).[17]

Beside numbers, colors also figure prominently in Scripture symbolics. Blue stands for that which is heavenly (Ex. 25:4; 39:22), purple for royalty (Mark 15:20), scarlet for sacrifice (Heb. 9:19), white for purity (Is. 1:18), black for death (Rev. 6:5, 6) and hell (Jude 13), and red for blood and war (Rev. 6:5).

Metals are also symbolically significant in Scripture. Gold signifies deity (Rev. 1:13), silver, redemption (Ex. 38:27), brass, judgment (Num. 21:9; John 3:14, 15), iron, strength (Dan. 2:41; 7:7) and clay, weakness (Dan. 2:42).

LITERATURE ON SCRIPTURAL TYPOLOGY

Marsh, Herbert, *Lectures on the Criticism and Interpretation of the Bible* (London, 1842).

Muenscher, Joseph, "On Types and the Typical Interpretation of Scripture," in *The American Biblical Repository* (Jan., 1841).

Jukes, Andrew, *Law of the Offerings in Leviticus* (8th ed., New York, Nisbet, 1870), Vols., I-VII.

---

[17] For a general discussion of the significance of numbers in the Bible see F. W. Grant, *The Numerical Bible: The Pentateuch* (5th ed.; New York, Loizeaux Brothers, n.d.), pp. 8-20; E. W. Bullinger, *Number in Scripture* (London, 1894).

Thomson, Wm. H., *Christ in the Old Testament* (New York, Harper & Brothers, 1884).

Moorehead, W. G., *Studies in the Mosaic Institutions* (New York, Fleming Revell, c. 1895).

Spurgeon, C. H., *Types and Emblems* (New York, Sheldon, n.d.).

Soltau, Henry W., *The Tabernacle, the Priesthood and the Offerings* (London, Morgan, n.d.).

Fairbairn, Patrick, *The Typology of Scripture* (2 vols.; New York, Funk & Wagnalls, 1900; reprint, Grand Rapids, Zondervan Publishing House).

Davidson, A. B., *Old Testament Prophecy* (Edinburgh, T. & T. Clark, 1905), Chaps. XIII, XIV.

MacIntosh, C. H., *Notes on the Pentateuch* (6 vols.; New York, Fleming Revell, n.d.).

Coates, C. A., *Outline Studies: Genesis-Deuteronomy* (5 vols.; Kingston-on-Thames, n.d.).

Ridout, S., *Lectures on the Tabernacle* (New York, Loizeaux Bros., 1914).

Chafer, L. S., *Systematic Theology* (Dallas, Dallas Seminary Press, 1947), I:xxix-xxxii; III:116-126; IV:136-141; VI:47-56.

Calloway, T. W., *Christ in the Old Testament* (New York, Loizeaux Bros., 1950).

Chapter XIX

THE EXPOSITOR AND BIBLICAL PROPHECY

The interpreter without doubt faces his most serious expository problems in the field of Biblical prophecy. These difficulties are of such a nature that they have divided Christian teachers and preachers into hostile camps. Rationalistic critics commonly deny the supernatural predictive element in prophecy altogether and labor to explain it away by liberal theories or, failing that, grant only a "brilliant intuition."[1] Roman Catholics identify the kingdom of God with their concept of the visible church, which according to their assumption, fulfills many of the Old Testament prophecies. Jews around New Testament times claimed a future literal fulfillment of those same prophecies in themselves at some future time.

Among Protestant expositors three schools of prophetic interpretation exist. Premillennialists follow a predominantly literal method of prophetic interpretation, believing that after this present church age, God will again take up with the Jews, reinstating the nation in divine favor and fulfilling in them the ancient covenants and promises. Amillennialists, on the other hand, reject the literalistic method of premillennialists and pursue a spiritualizing approach to Old Testament prophecy, believing that references to the future Messianic kingdom over Israel find their fulfillment in the Christian Church of this age. Postmillennialists are between the literal and the spiritual, believing that Christ will return after the millennium.

[1] Cf. Robert Pfeiffer, *Old Testament Introduction* (New York, Charles Scribner's Sons, 1941), p. 423.

1. The Importance of Prophecy in Biblical Exposition

The vast amount of confusion and disagreement that prevails among Christian scholars in the realm of interpretation of prophecy and the tendency in many quarters to ignore or neglect this segment of Biblical truth, however, cannot obscure its far-reaching expository significance. The comparative importance of predictive prophecy as it stands in relation to other phases of revealed truth is demonstrated by the fact "that at least one-fifth of the Bible was, at the time it was written, an anticipation of the future."[2] Much of this extended revelation has been fulfilled, particularly in the first advent of our Lord. A large part of it, however, still remains to be fulfilled, principally in connection with the second advent.

It is quite obvious that the preacher or teacher who minimizes or ignores the predictive portions of the Word, or who, as in some cases, is actually hostile toward prophetic preaching, and who defends his position on the ground of presenting essential soteriological truth, runs the grave risk of distorting the truth he is presenting by separating it from the prophetic and eschatological framework with which it is so frequently inextricably connected in the Sacred Text.

On the other hand, no matter how much practical salvation truth the expositor may present, or how accurately he may set it forth, in failing to give prophetic truth its proper place, he shuts himself off from the realm of full-orbed Bible exposition. It is inevitable that such handling of the Word should result in serious disadvantage, both to the preacher and to those to whom he preaches, inasmuch as it keeps both from God's full message for man.

Our Lord most certainly intended that His disciples should know the prophetic Word and laid emphatic stress upon the Holy Spirit's ministry in instructing them in this phase of divine revelation. "I have yet many things to say unto you, but ye cannot bear them now. Howbeit when he, the Spirit of truth, is come, he will guide you into all truth . . . he

[2] L. S. Chafer, *Systematic Theology* (Dallas, Dallas Seminary Press, 1947), Vol. I, p. xxxii

will show you things to come" (John 16:12, 13). Thus in most intimate connection with the Spirit's tuition in "all truth" our Lord mentions the prophetic Word, which He describes as "things to come." It is therefore impossible to be instructed by the Spirit "into all truth" and not fully embrace the important category of "things to come."

Although this basic fact is plainly set forth by our Lord Himself, and no element in the preparation of an expositor is more indispensable than a thorough grounding in an unabridged systematic Biblical theology, which includes a complete study of prophecy and eschatology, yet it is precisely at this point that authors of works on systematic theology fail and seminary curricula fall short.

The average text on systematic theology includes scant reference to typology and rarely contains more than a superficial summary of eschatology. In fact, the latter is customarily treated as an alien, as though it did not intrinsically belong to the subject at all, but is merely to be tacked on to round it out and give it a logical conclusion. Over against this severe curtailment of eschatology there must be a drastic expansion of the doctrine of last things if Biblical exposition is to be rescued from this serious hindrance to its development.

Since no given moment of time is a fixed point of division between things past and things future, eschatology, as the systematic arrangement of "things to come," should, as Lewis Sperry Chafer says, "include all in the Bible which was predictive at the time it was uttered."[3] When eschatology in this manner is expanded in theological text books and in the seminary classroom, this branch of systematic theology at least will fulfill its worthy purpose of equipping men for an expository ministry.

2. THE THEMES OF FULFILLED AND UNFULFILLED PROPHECY

In preparation for the high calling of a preacher of the Word of God the student must be thoroughly grounded in the distinction between fulfilled and unfulfilled prophecy. A

[3] *Ibid.*, p. xxxiv.

knowledge of the literal and minute fulfillment of fulfilled prophecy will be vastly beneficial in strengthening the student's faith in the inspiration and inerrancy of the Word of God and the certainty of the fulfillment of unfulfilled prophecy. Such knowledge will act as a powerful impetus to the study of the predictive Word in general and whet the appetite for an understanding of God's redemptive plan as it comprehends the ages from eternity past to eternity future. The student who is aroused concerning the wonders of fulfilled prophecy will normally be stirred up to search out the wonders of unfulfilled prophecy.

The major features of *fulfilled* prophecy include the moral and spiritual future · of Noah's sons (Gen. 9:24-27), Israel's servitude in Egypt (Gen. 15:13-16) and restoration to Canaan (Gen. 46:4); the future of Jacob's sons (Gen. 49:3-27); the Seventy-Year Captivity in Babylon (Jer. 25:1-14; 29:10); a partial restoration under Cyrus the Great (Is. 44:28; 45:1); the coming and ministry of John the Baptist (Is. 40:3-5); the birth of Christ (Mic. 5:2; Is. 7:14); the offices of Christ (Deut. 18:15-18; Ps. 110:4; Ps. 10:16); the ministries of Christ (Is. 42:1-4; 49:1-7); the sufferings and death of Christ (Ps. 22:1-21; Is. 53:1-8); the burial and resurrection of Christ (Ps. 16:10; Is. 53:8-10); the ascension of Christ (Is. 52:13; John 14:3; 16:7); the present age and the formation of the Church (Matt. 16:18) by the Spirit's baptism (Matt. 3:11; Mark 1:8; Acts 1:5; 11:16); the destruction of Jerusalem (Luke 21:24) and the character and course of this age (Acts 15:14, 15).

The major features of *unfulfilled* prophecy include the last days of the Church (II Tim. 3:1-10); the out-taking of the Church (I Thess. 4:13-18) and the first resurrection (I Cor. 15:53); the judgment of the believer's works (II Cor. 5:10; I Cor. 3:11-15); the marriage of the Lamb in heaven (Rev. 19:7-9); the great tribulation on earth (Jer. 30:5-7; Matt. 24:21; Rev. 7:14); the man of sin (Dan. 7:8; II Thess. 2:3; Rev. 13:1-10); the day of the Lord (Mal. 4:1; II Thess. 2:3; Rev. 4:1 - 19:16); the second advent of Christ (Rev. 19:11-16); the battle of Armageddon (Rev. 16:13-16); the destruction of

Babylon (Rev. 17 and 18); the judgment of the nations (Joel 3:2-8; Matt. 25:31-46); the regathering of Israel (Ezek. 37: 1-28; Matt. 24:31); the binding of Satan (Rev. 20:1-3) and the establishment of the kingdom (Is. 11:1-8; Rev. 20:4); the last revolt (Rev. 20:7, 8); the doom of Satan (Rev. 20: 10); the great white throne judgment of sinners (Rev. 20:11-14); the new heavens and earth, and the eternal state (Rev. 21:1 - 22:21).

In addition to the indispensable distinction between fulfilled and unfulfilled prophecy the student in preparation for the high vocation of expounding the Word needs a thorough orientation in the *great time periods* of Scripture, particularly the difference between the old dispensation and the new, the Mosaic or legal age and the period of grace (John 1:17; Eph. 3:2), the unique feature of the New Testament Church formed by the baptism of the Holy Spirit (Matt. 3:11; Mark 1:8; Acts 1:5; I Cor. 12:13) at Pentecost (Acts 11:16) as contrasted with the nation Israel (Rom. 11:1-36), the peculiar nature of the "gospel of the kingdom" as preached by John the Baptist and Jesus (Matt. 3:2; 4:17), and the Apostle Paul's "gospel of the grace of God" (Eph. 3:1-12) together with the contrasts between the Jews, the Gentiles and the Church of God (I Cor. 10:32) during this age.

Innumerable details of truth are comprehended in this immense body of Scripture. But it is not more than every preacher must be acquainted with "if he is to fulfill his high and holy appointment as an expositor of the Word of God."[4] When predictive prophecy is slighted, a large segment of revealed truth with its wise instruction and sanctifying power is sacrificed. In addition a great deal of detail, which God has designed to demonstrate his unchanging faithfulness and the glory of His Word, is ignored. As a result the knowledge of the divine plan and purpose, "which alone underlies intelligent cooperation with God in service, becomes impossible."[5]

Accordingly, men who depreciate prophecy, or who pre-

4 *Ibid.,* p. xxxv.
5 *Ibid.*

clude an adequate treatment of it by erroneous presuppositions or unworkable eschatological hypotheses, fall into various wrong emphases, inaccuracies of statement and misguided aims. They talk of "bringing in the kingdom" or "converting the world," forgetting that God's revealed purpose for this age is not world conversion or the establishment of the kingdom, but a taking out of a people from both Jew and Gentile for His name (Acts 15:14, 15) to form the Church, the body of Christ (Eph. 1:19-23).

They discourse on the "brotherhood of man and the fatherhood of God," ignoring the fall and the need for personal regeneration through faith in Christ. They utterly confound the unsaved of this age, whom the Bible names as "Jews and Gentiles" with the saved, "the church of God" (I Cor. 10:32). Consequently, very frequently morality is preached to the unsaved instead of regeneration, works instead of faith, a social gospel instead of the Gospel of the grace of God, Communistic doctrines instead of pure Christianity. The evils of neglecting any portion of God's Word are multitudinous, and the Church of God has suffered irreparable harm by its neglect and ignorance of Bible prophecy.

3. THE BIBLICAL CONCEPT OF PROPHECY

The Bible presents the predictive element of Scripture as a supernatural phenomenon transcending human limitations. The prophet when he uttered predictions or in general declared the Word and will of God is represented as speaking under the power of the Holy Spirit. Similarly divination, the heathen counterpart of prophecy (Deut. 18:9-14) and a Satanic imitation of it, in its inspirational aspects at least, is demoniacally inspired and calculated to deceive.[6] Accordingly, God's people, while encouraged in heeding the true prophets of God and solemnly warned of the peril of false prophets, were given the far-reaching promise of the Prophet par excellence – the Messiah Himself (Deut. 18:15-18; Acts 3:22, 23).

Scripture plainly presents prediction as a manifestation of

---

[6] Cf. the present author's discussion of prophecy and divination in *Biblical Demonology* (2d ed.; Wheaton, Ill., Van Kampen Press, 1953), pp. 119-142.

God's power glorifying His person, exalting His redemptive work in Christ and setting forth the divine character of His revealed Word. Were there but one or two fulfilled prophecies, such as that of the Virgin birth (Is. 7:14) to occur in Bethlehem of Judah (Mic. 5:2), the supernatural character of the Scriptures would be attested by the sacred history which records their fulfillment. But when these predictions run into the thousands, which concern the Persons of the Godhead, men, angels, nations, events and destinies, with each one occurring in its precise time and place, the evidence is incontestable for the wisdom and power of God, the grace and glory of the foretold Redeemer, the wonders of His prophesied redemption and the divine character of the Word which reveals these marvels.

Scripture also presents the predictive Word as a response to man's need. Apart from divine revelation man does not know what a day may bring forth. To the omniscient God, however, the end is known from the beginning. "Known unto God are all his works from the beginning of the world" (Acts 15:18). Through the Word man's need for guidance is supplied and especially through the predictive Word the believer's life and service are immeasurably benefited. What could be more stimulating to faithfulness and diligence in God's work than a knowledge of the things God has prepared for those who love Him (I Cor. 2:9) and a realization of the rewards for sacrificial service Christ will dispense to them (II Cor. 5:10)? What could be more comforting to the Christian in times of sorrow and bereavement than to know Christ has gone away "to prepare a place" for us, that where He is there we may be also (John 14:3)?

It is, therefore, quite apparent that Scripture conceives prophecy to be immensely valuable to the believer. In view of these values and the wonders of predictions now fulfilled it would appear that men would grasp after every word of divine prediction yet unfulfilled, searching into its significance and glorying in the additional light it affords. That the opposite is true is all the more inexplicable in consideration of these facts.

General neglect of Biblical prophecy by those who have been appointed to preach and teach the whole counsel of God is tragic. In reality it means that this most potent stimulus to godly living and serving to a large degree has been withheld from the people, and with what harm who can imagine? It scarcely need be said that "the preacher who persistently and consistently avoids prophetic themes is committing a wrong which only heaven can estimate."[7] The same may be said for textbooks on systematic theology which make no adequate attempt to account for such a vast and vital segment of divine revelation, and for seminaries that use such textbooks and teach such an abbreviated eschatology and so influence the student to pursue the same course.

4. RULES FOR THE INTERPRETATION OF PROPHECY

Interpretation of the prophetic portions of the Bible does not differ radically from the interpretation of other parts of the sacred revelation. The same essential rules that govern all sound exegesis will, of course, apply to the exposition of the prophecies. However, certain special hermeneutical principles have particular significance for this type of Biblical literature and must constantly be kept in mind by the expositor who would adequately handle the prophetic portions of the Bible.

a. *Select a workable system of prophetic interpretation.* This is obviously of first consideration and is of fundamental importance. Moreover, it is necessary for the expositor to be thoroughly persuaded in his own mind that the system he has adopted is the correct one, for obviously premillennialism, postmillennialism and amillennialism cannot all three be right. Although little unanimity of choice can reasonably be expected upon a subject of such highly controversial nature as this is, it nevertheless remains true that no student of Bible prophecy can be thorough and honest in his work and not be persuaded his system is the right one. He may be deceived in the matter, but he will of necessity have firm convictions if diligence and depth mark his expository efforts.

7 Chafer, *op. cit.,* IV, p. 285.

Because a thorough and sincere student may be deceived in the matter of the correctness of the system of interpretation he espouses, it is of the utmost importance that he be willing to subject his views to rigid testing — not only logically and theologically — but, above all, Scripturally. This is necessitated by the plainly observable fact that in any system of intepretation, whether in prophecy or some other field of theology, there are always strong personal and environmental predisposing factors, such as: the preachers the interpreter has heard, the instruction he has had, the books he has read, the denomination he serves, the creedal or traditional doctrines (which may be far from Biblical) by which he is influenced.

In view of these facts it is imperative that the expositor of prophecy should approach his subject as free from bias and as open-minded as possible. He dare not allow himself to be blinded to the inadequacies of any particular system because it may be enshrined in some creedal statement to which he or his denomination may subscribe, and therefore made sacrosanct. Nor may he safely subscribe to it purely on the grounds of its antiquity and its adoption by great names in the history of the Church.

Traditionalism and creedalism may be notoriously unreliable guides to truth, as may be demonstrated from a simple study of the history of the Church, both of the Roman Catholic and Protestant wings. Moreover, the seeker after truth must continually remind himself of the persistence of error and the blind tenacity with which it is frequently held by its adherents, particularly when canonized by tradition, intrenched by ecclesiastical recognition and propagated in theological textbooks.

But the expositor must test his system of prophetic interpretation in other ways besides examining it for bias or traditional or creedal error. In addition to scrutinizing it carefully theologically, he must rigidly test it logically.[8] He must enquire whether it is based on sound inductive reason-

[8] Cf. Chapter X, "The Expositor and the Laws of Logic."

ing[9] or whether it is largely deductive.[10] If deductive, he must be absolutely sure the universal propositions from which its conclusions are arrived at are capable of being *inductively* sustained from *all* Scripture evidence available, or whether they take into account only *part* of the evidence. Premillennial, amillennial and postmillennial views must face this searching test, and be "found wanting" in proportion as they fail to meet it.

In selecting a system of prophetic interpretation the sincere seeker after truth must be assured that nothing short of prayerful and exhaustive searching of the Holy Scriptures, coupled with a meticulous systematization of *all* the evidence he encounters there under a *sound inductive method of logic,* with complete reliance upon the Holy Spirit's guidance, will suffice to assure him of the right choice. For, after all, to the genuine expositor the only question that really matters is, What does the Scripture actually teach on the subject? The moment he allows himself to be swayed by any other consideration he steps down from the lofty eminence comprehended in the apostolic command, "Preach the Word," and begins to walk on a lower plane.

b. *Determine the background of the prophecy.* Having settled upon the correct system of interpretation, the expositor is in a position to cultivate to the fullest advantage the large prophetic portions of the Word. Fundamental to this task is a knowledge of the historical background of the prophet and his prophecy.

Since the Bible contains history that is wedded to prophecy, and since the latter has its origin in the local historical situation, a study of history is the starting point in any study of prophecy, whether didactic or predictive, fulfilled or unfulfilled. The good interpreter will not content himself until he has thoroughly acquainted himself with the names, historical events, archeological sidelights and political or social conditions underlying the prophetic portion he is expounding.

[9] Cf. Chapter XI, "The Expositor and Inductive Reasoning."
[10] Cf. Chapter XII, "The Expositor and Deductive Reasoning."

The same will apply to all geographical references and allusions to customs and material culture of the day.

To achieve this purpose the best Bible histories, commentaries, dictionaries, and works on Biblical archeology and customs will be consulted. The solid factual basis of the history and local color behind the prophecy thereby gained will prove indispensable to exposition of the prophecy and act as a deterrent against extreme or farfetched interpretations. Even more important, such background study will aid the expositor in distinguishing the prophecy from the contemporary historical situation, which gave it rise. This is frequently of very great moment, for it is not always obvious what element of a prophecy is purely local or temporal. To confound the historic and local with the prophetic inevitably leads to confusion of interpretation.

The famous prophecy of the virgin birth of Christ is an example. "Therefore the Lord himself shall give you a sign; Behold, a virgin shall conceive, and bear a son, and shall call his name Immanuel. Butter and honey shall he eat, that he may know to refuse the evil, and choose the good" (Is. 7:14, 15). In these two verses Christ is immediately in the foreground. But in verse 16 there is a sudden shift to the local contemporary situation. "For before the child shall know to refuse the evil, and choose the good, the land that thou abhorrest shall be forsaken of both her kings." The child in this verse is not Immanuel, but evidently Isaiah's own infant son, Shear-jashub, whom he was divinely instructed to take with him as a part of the sign to wicked King Ahaz (Is. 7:3). Similarly, the vision of the cleansing of Joshua, the high priest (Zech. 3:1-7), does not become Messianic till verse 8, nor his symbolic crowning (Zech. 6:9-11) till verse 12.

c. *Observe the context of the prophecy.* This rule governing context, of course, is fundamental to the interpretation of any passage of Scripture, but applies with special force to prophetic portions, which frequently suffer from careless mishandling in this respect. The problem commonly exists even where chapter and verse divisions are fortunate, but where the expositor is simply dilatory in adequately scrutinizing that which precedes and succeeds the prophecy under consideration. The difficulties are increased, however, for the unwary student when chapter and verse divisions are unfortunate. This frequently occurs in prophetic sections.

Interpreters of the famous fifty-third chapter of Isaiah, which so marvelously foretells the vicarious sufferings, death, burial, resurrection, ascension and present intercession of our Lord, commonly place their exposition of this great prophecy at serious disadvantage by completely ignoring Isaiah 52: 13-15, which forms an introductory summary to the fifty-third chapter and thus is inseparably connected with it and is actually a vital portion of this great poem.

Similarly the transfiguration of Jesus (Matt. 17:1-13) really begins at Matthew 16:28. Because the chapter division here is infelicitous, many interpreters have completely ignored this verse as a vital part of the context and consequently have failed to see that this important event constitutes a prophetic vision or foreview of the future millennial kingdom. "Verily, I say unto you, There be some standing here, which shall not taste of death, till they see the Son of man coming in his kingdom" — the "kingdom" being in its prophetic aspect and having reference to the Messianic rule to be set up on the earth at the return of the King in glory (Matt. 24:29 - 25:46; Luke 19:12-19; Acts 15:14-17).

But the interpreter of prophecy must not only pay attention to the immediate context of the prophecies he attempts to expound. He must also constantly keep in mind the more remote context, especially the over-all divine prophetic plan of the ages, and *must relate each individual prophecy to that plan in its full sweep from eternity past to eternity future.*

On the other hand, the expositor who refuses to believe that God has such a plan or that it is revealed in Scripture, or who, believing that there is such divine purpose, will not take pains to search it out, will make little real progress in the exposition of Biblical prophecy. The reason for this is not far to find. The predictive element of Scripture, especially if all that was future at the time of writing is taken into account, as should be the case, constitutes a vast and complex body of material. Unless there is some unifying purpose and divine design to bind together each prophetic passage, to coordinate each reference, to produce prophetic harmony and to provide for logical systematization, this welter of material must remain an unsolved jigsaw puzzle, or at best one that is only partially solved, with many of the pieces not fitting together. The secret to placing the parts together in an orderly design is a knowledge of the divine plan of the ages as revealed in the prophetic Scriptures.

When once God's plan of the ages as revealed in the Scripture is comprehended, the otherwise impossible task of harmonizing the prophetic Word becomes possible. Recurring Old Testament themes of fulfilled prophecy can be minutely traced in their fulfillment in the New Testament and illuminatingly placed in God's revealed program of redemption.

Recurring themes of unfulfilled Old and New Testament prophecy likewise can be collected, compared, systematized and illuminatingly placed in God's revealed plan as it pertains to the future. Such oft repeated Old and New Testament subjects as the great tribulation (Jer. 30:5-7; Matt. 24:21; Rev. 7:4), the man of sin (Dan. 7:8; II Thess. 2:3; Rev. 13:1-10), the day of the Lord (Mal. 4:1; II Thess. 2:3; Rev. 4:1 - 19:16), the second advent of Christ (Dan. 7:13; Zech. 14:4; Matt. 24:30), the judgment of the nations (Joel 3:2-8; Matt. 25:31-46), the regathering of Israel (Ezek. 37:1-28; Matt. 24:31) and the establishment of the kingdom (Is. 11:1-16; Mic. 4:1-4; Rev. 20:4) when collected and compared amazingly explain and supplement each other, and when properly placed into their larger prophetic context immeasurably clarify details and add to a more complete understanding of the whole prophetic plan.

d. *Determine upon the normal literal approach, rather than the mystical, as the sound method of prophetic interpretation.* Despite the confusion created by the disagreement of conservative scholars over the interpretation of Old Testament prophecy, there does not seem to be a single cogent reason why the expositor should abandon the *normal* method of interpreting language in general and which is also applicable to Scripture exposition in general, when he encounters Biblical prophecy. This *normal* approach, constituting what is aptly called "the golden rule of interpretation," which was discussed in connection with the expositor and figurative language,[11] because of its extreme importance, especially in connection with prophetic exposition, is repeated at this point: *When the plain sense of Scripture makes common sense, seek no other sense; therefore, take every word at its primary, usual, literal meaning, unless it is patently a rhetorical figure or unless the immediate context, studied in the light of related passages and axiomatic and fundamental truths, clearly points otherwise.*

If this *normal* rule for interpreting language in general, Biblical as well as non-Biblical, is followed in prophecy and the literal interpretation is taken as the limiting guide, then the premillennial view is inescapable. This is true because the Old Testament speaks over and over again of a future Israelite theocracy with its capital at Jerusalem (Is. 60:1-22; Zech. 8:1-23; 14:16-20), with Messiah manifested in righteousness and universal peace (Mic. 4:1-4; Is. 11:1-16) and with Israel exalted as the nation of spiritual blessing (Is. 35:1-10; Zech. 8:23).

These plain statements, embraced in innumerable and extended Old Testament passages, and comprehended in the various covenants and promises made to ancient Israel, such as the Palestinian (Deut. 30:1-10), the Davidic (II Sam. 7: 4-17) and the New (Jer. 31:31-40; Heb. 8:8-13) can only have literal meaning in a future beyond the present church age and subsequent to the second advent of Christ, for Christ is personally manifested as the Messiah-King-Priest in these magnificent prophetic portraits. In this case, moreover, the amillennial position is ruled out because this theory assumes that the prophetic language is not to be interpreted *normally*, but *mystically*, and accordingly, that the prophets do not mean what they say. When they refer to "Israel," "Jerusa-

[11] See Chapter XVI.

lem" or "Zion," they do not mean "Israel," "Jerusalem" or "Zion," but the Church of the present day. Hence this view spiritualizes (more correctly "mysticalizes") these great prophecies. Postmillennial interpretations are likewise impossible because Messiah is present in the Old Testament portraitures, and accordingly, He must come before the millennium to establish it.

If one is prepared arbitrarily to abandon the *normal*, literal, "golden-rule" method of interpreting language when he comes to prophecy and to grant what must always appear to many interpreters as a violent assumption, that in prophetic literature "Israel" means "the Church," then the amillennial position is allowable. In such a case, Old Testament Jewish prophecies are *completely* spiritualized ("mysticalized") to the Church and are now in process of fulfillment.

If Old Testament prophecies are *partly* spiritualized ("mysticalized") postmillennialism is the result. The elements of universality and the earthly character of the Old Testament passages are granted, but they are transferred from Israel to the Church, the progressive extension of which over the entire world is looked for.

The interpreter of prophecy, therefore, is to be a *literalist*. This does not mean, however, that he denies that prophecy contains *figurative* language or makes use of *symbols*, or that great spiritual truths are taught therein. "His position is simply, that the prophecies are to be *normally* interpreted (i.e., according to the received laws of language) as any other utterances are interpreted — that which is manifestly literal being regarded as literal, and that which is manifestly figurative being so regarded."[12]

The amillennialist (or the postmillennialist) is sometimes referred to as a *spiritualist* in contrast to the premillennialist, who is a literalist. But these terms are scarcely accurate. The amillennialist is rather an interpreter of prophecy "who holds that certain portions are to be *normally* interpreted,"

12 E. R. Craven in Lange's Commentary (reprint, Grand Rapids, Zondervan Publishing House), *Revelation*, p. 98.

while "other portions are to be regarded as having a *mystical* . . . sense."[13]

Thus, for example, "spiritualists" would interpret the famous Messianic prophecy of Christ riding into Jerusalem on an ass (Zech. 9:9) normally. "Jerusalem" in this case means Jerusalem and "Zion" means Zion. However, in Zechariah 14:17 in connection with a reference to worship in the millennial kingdom the language is "spiritually" ("mystically") interpreted and Jerusalem is construed as referring to the Church of this age. "And it shall be, that whoso will not come up of all the families of the earth unto Jerusalem to worship the King, the Lord of hosts, even upon them shall be no rain."

It is thus apparent that the essential difference between the systems of prophetic interpretation is not the difference between *literal* and *spiritual,* but between *normal* and *mystical.*[14] *Literal* is not opposed to spiritual, but to *figurative.* *Spiritual,* on the other hand, is opposed to *material.* Since much of prophecy is highly figurative and filled with symbols, particularly apocalyptic books, such as Daniel and Revelation, it is impossible for any interpreter to be a complete literalist. It is quite possible for him, however, to interpret these sections *normally,* that is, as he would interpret *any* literature, and he should do so, taking into account, of course, figures as figures and symbols as symbols. This, on the other hand, is quite distinct from a mystical interpretation, which assumes the passage is dealing with something entirely different from what the plain indication of the words suggest.

e. *Determine the correct relationship between the form of the prophecy and the ideas conveyed by it.* This difficult question constitutes the crux of prophetic interpretation.[15] It is at this point the lines are drawn. The amillennial school, for instance, in general maintains that no more detailed fulfillment is to be expected of Old Testament prophecies,

---

[13] *Ibid.*
[14] *Ibid.*
[15] Cf. A. B. Davidson, *Old Testament Prophecy* (Edinburgh, T. & T. Clark, 1905), p. 181-183.

which were to be fulfilled after the advent of Christ and the establishment of Christianity, than the broad realizing of the ideas. The Jewish dress in which the ideas are clothed must be stripped away. There is no correspondence to be expected between the form of the prediction and the form of the fulfillment, because the only way the Old Testament prophet could visualize the ideal or true religion of God was in terms of the ancient Jewish economy in which he lived. When this economy passed away, the imagery of the Jewish commonwealth became a "prophetic husk" that must now be stripped off to lay bare the true kernel of prophecy.

The postmillennial school holds that some part of the form of the prophecy may be realized in the fulfillment of its main ideas. A millennium is granted, but the universal and earthly character of it is transferred to the Church.

In contrast to these systems the premillennial school teaches that the ideas of the prophecy will find fulfillment *precisely* in the form in which they are expressed in the prediction. To the premillennialist the Jewish coloring of the prophecy is most emphatically not simply a kind of glass through which the Old Testament prophet saw. It rather points to a future earthly Messianic kingdom to be brought about by the second advent of Messiah, the regathering and restoration of Israel in a millennial age that will intervene before the eternal state is introduced.

Although this view comprehends the correct relationship between the form of the prophecy and the ideas conveyed by it, it must be guarded against an extreme literalism which would violate the *normal* interpretation of figurative and symbolic language or reduce elevated poetic sections, such as the highly wrought portrait of millennial peace and blessing in Isaiah 11:6-9 or of the restoration of Palestine and its people in Isaiah 35:1-10, to a prosaic insistence upon details.

Nor must this view be permitted to be similarly misdirected to maintain that the ideas of the prophecy will find fulfillment *absolutely exactly* (instead of "precisely") in the form in which they are expressed in the prediction. This position is unwarranted and would lead to absurdities. It fails to take into account the limitations of the Old Testament (and the New as well) both in the matter of ideas and forms to express them, limitations which are due to continued progress in arts and inventions since the Scriptures were written.

Accordingly, there are, for example, no Biblical words to describe modern weapons of warfare, modern modes of travel, or modern ways of living. In prophecies involving these concepts and referring to events still future, it would be unreasonable to expect imagery other than that with which the prophets were familiar and equally unreasonable for the modern expositor to impose a rigid literalism on their ancient modes of expression. The *normal* approach would be to construe their ancient counterparts in terms of their modern equivalents.

Thus in Zechariah 9:10, containing a prophecy of Christ's victories at His second advent in glory, "the chariot," "the war-horse," and "the battle-bow" are equivalent to their modern counterparts, the tank, the guided missile and machine gun, or the like. Likewise, in Isaiah 60:6-9, which embraces a prophecy of a general travel exodus to millennial Jerusalem, the "camels" (v. 6) would stand, no doubt, for some modern means of land transportation, like the automobile, while those "that fly like a cloud and like doves to their windows" (v. 8) would clearly point to air transportation. The "ships of Tarshish" (v. 9) would accurately portray the modern as well as the ancient mode of sea traffic, which will evidently still be used in millennial times.

Although the premillennial view of expecting fulfillment of Old Testament prophecies *precisely* in the form in which they are expressed in the prediction is to be guarded against an extreme and unwarranted literalizing on the one hand, it must at the same time be guarded against contamination from an unwarranted spiritualizing ("mysticalizing") on the other.

Opponents of premillennialism often criticize its literal,

that is, *normal* approach to interpretation and cite the fact that at least a portion of Old Testament typology is spiritually ("mystically") fulfilled in the New Testament Church. This is true, but it must never be forgotten that a type is *not* necessarily a prophecy, because its typical significance may be completely unrevealed in the age in which the type appears, as in the case with the New Testament Church. In contrast a prophecy can never be unrevealed. The very fact of its being a prophecy comprehends revelation and consequent knowledge of that revelation. For this reason the argument against literal or normal interpretation of prophecy based on the spiritual ("mystical") fulfillment of typology loses its force.

When Old Testament typology is taken out of alleged cases in which the New Testament "spiritualizes" the Old Testament, there is little left to furnish a valid argument against the *normal* or literal treatment of Old Testament prophecies. However, under inspiration there is no reason why a New Testament writer might not attach a mystical meaning to a bona fide Old Testament prophecy. This, however, is no valid argument for handling all kingdom or millennial prophecies of the Old Testament in this manner.

LITERATURE ON THE INTERPRETATION OF PROPHECY

Brook, J. H., *Till He Come* (Chicago, 1891).

Beecher, W. J., *The Prophets and the Promise* (New York, Crowell, 1905).

Davidson, A. B., *Old Testament Prophecy* (Edinburgh, T. & T. Clark, 1905).

Kirkpatrick, A. F., *Doctrine of the Prophets* (3d ed., London, Macmillan & Co., 1906).

Blackstone, W. E., *Jesus Is Coming* (New York, Fleming Revell, 1908).

Kellogg, S. H., *Are the Premillennialists Right?* (New York, Fleming Revell, 1923).

Masselink, W., *Why a Thousand Years?* (Grand Rapids, Wm. B. Eerdmans Publishing Co., 1930).

Feinberg, Charles L., *Premillennialism or Amillennialism?* (Grand Rapids, Zondervan Publishing House, 1936).

Chafer, L. S., *The Kingdom in History and Prophecy* (Chicago, Bible Institute Colportage Assoc., 1936).

Reese, Alexander, *The Approaching Advent of Christ* (London, Marshall, Morgan & Scott, n.d.).

Hamilton, F. E., *The Basis of Millennial Faith* (Grand Rapids, Wm. B. Eerdmans Publishing Co., 1942).

Allis, Oswald T., *Prophecy and the Church* (Philadelphia, Presbyterian & Reformed Publishing Co., 1945).

Jones, Russell Bradley, *The Things Which Shall Be Hereafter* (Nashville, 1947).

Chafer, L. S., *Systematic Theology* (8 vols., Dallas, Dallas Seminary Press, 1947).

Rowley, H. H., ed., *Studies in Old Testament Prophecy* (New York, Charles Scribner's Sons, 1950).

Walvoord, John F., "Millennial Series," *Bibliotheca Sacra* (Oct., 1950-Jan., 1954).

Young, E. J., *My Servants the Prophets* (Grand Rapids, Wm. B. Eerdmans Publishing Co., 1952).

CHAPTER XX

HOW TO EXPOUND ANY PASSAGE IN THE BIBLE

Although competent expositors of the Word of God cannot be produced in a single day any more than a towering oak can grow into height overnight, any preacher, no matter how far short he has fallen of the expository ideal, can take immediate steps to correct this failure and embark upon an expository career that will yield him returns far beyond his fondest expectations. But no minister is likely to take these simple steps necessary to begin such a career unless he acquires at least a general idea of what expository preaching is and unless, being challenged by the appalling need for such a ministry, he is brought to realize the vast benefits which will accrue both to him and to those who hear him as a result of the prosecution of it.

Nor will a minister be challenged to expository endeavor who is not persuaded that the very words of Scripture are the inspired oracles of God and who will not allow himself to be progressively sanctified by that Word as his hearers are. But once he has caught the vision of the glory of the Word in its saving and sanctifying power, and begins to realize the various qualifications necessary for a ministry of Bible exposition, he will not allow anything to stand in the way of his complete development for his work as an expositor, not only spiritually but technically and doctrinally as well.

The wise student of the Word (and the expositor must first and foremost be a student of the Word) will soon perceive, however, that to begin his expository career, he does

not have to wait until some future time when he has acquired or developed all these qualifications. He will see that
his job as a minister is to "preach the Word," being "instant
in season and out of season," and that no matter how ill-
prepared he may be for his task, by following a few simple
rules he may embark upon an expository approach at once,
removing his deficiencies as he goes ahead. Following these
suggestions of procedure will set the student on a course
that, if prayerfully and industriously pursued, will eventually
result in his being able to expound any passage in the Bible.

1. To Expound Any Passage in the Bible the Book in Which the Portion Occurs Must First Be Carefully Analyzed

This is the absolute starting point for the preacher who has
never cultivated exposition and who is seriously lacking in
knowledge of the content of the Bible. The reason for this
procedure is apparent. If the student lacks the more general
knowledge involved in becoming acquainted with the purpose, theme and logical development of the argument of
a book, he can scarcely be able to deal with the more specific requirements presupposing the details of the argument.
If the whole is obscure, the parts that bear a vital relationship to it and to one another because of their mutual connection with the whole, can scarcely be evident.

The only way to become acquainted with the books of
the Bible in their order to one another and their individual
content and logical development is by studious Bible reading.
Expository preaching is born in the cradle of Bible study
and prayer. The preacher who would start an expository
ministry must begin it in prayer and Bible reading. He
must pray over the Word. He must read the Word — read
it voluminously, read it believingly, read it as the very Word
and will of God and therefore intended by God to be understood by men. Read it as possessing divine plan and purpose. Read it with expectant determination to discover that
plan and purpose.

But beyond all consideration of *how* he must read, the

expositor *must simply read the Word.* The *how* is important, but the actual reading is more important. No student who is unwilling to read the Word will ever make a successful start in a career of expounding it.

On the other hand, the student who does read the Word will make much more rapid progress if he uses the proper aids to guide him in his study. Essential to this phase of his work are analytical introductions and outlines to the individual books.[1] These will prove of inestimable value in helping the student to see the meaning of a book as a whole and also to visualize the relation of its constituent parts to it and to one another.

If the student, for instance, wishes to choose a particular passage from Paul's letter to the Galatians to expound, he should first read and reread the entire letter, consulting the best introductions and analyses, thereby becoming thoroughly familiar with the subject matter of the book as a whole and with the constituent parts as they are connected with one another and with the whole. The following analysis of the Epistle by W. Graham Scroggie will prove suggestive:[2]

> Introduction: (1:1-10)
> I. A Personal Narrative (1:11 - 2:21)
>   (Paul vindicates his apostolic authority)
>   1. His claim to divine illumination (1:11, 12)
>   2. His conduct before his conversion (1:13, 14)
>   3. His commission at his conversion (1:15, 16a)
>   4. His course after his conversion (1:16b-17)
>   5. His contact with the Apostles (1:18 - 2:10)
>   6. His controversy with Peter at Antioch (2:11-16)
>   7. His conclusion of the whole matter (2:17-21)
> II. A Doctrinal Argument (3:1 - 5:1)
>   (Justification is by faith in Christ alone)
>   1. The Doctrine Expounded (3:1-29)

[1] See, for example, William G. Moorehead, *Outline Studies in the Books of the Bible* (New York, Fleming Revell, 5 vols., 1893-1910); G. Campbell Morgan, *The Analyzed Bible* (New York, Fleming Revell, 10 vols., 1907—); W. Graham Scroggie, *Know Your Bible,* Vol. I (analytical) Old Testament, Vol. II (analytical) New Testament (London, Pickering and Inglis, 1940); also Scroggie's *A Guide to the Gospels* (London, Pickering and Inglis, 1948); J. Vernon McGee, *Briefing the Bible* (Wheaton, Van Kampen Press, 1949); J. Sidlow Baxter, *Explore the Book,* 6 vols., (London, Marshall, Morgan and Scott, 1951).
[2] *Know Your Bible,* II, pp. 159-161.

        a. Proved from past Christian experience (3:1-5)
        b. Proved from the covenant of God with Abraham (3:6-18)
        c. Proved from the general scope of the law itself (3:19-24)
        d. Proved from our present Christian standing (3:25-29)
     2. The Doctrine Enforced (4:1 - 5:1)
        a. A legal illustration (4:1-20)
        b. An historical illustration (4:21 - 5:1)
III. A Practical Exhortation (5:2 - 6:10)
   (Enter into the full consequences of your emancipation)
     1. The Effective Subversion of Liberty (5:1-12)
        a. The peril of circumcision (5:2-6)
        b. The hindered and the hinderer (5:7-10)
        c. The persecutions of the Apostle (5:11, 12)
     2. The Highest Expression of Liberty (5:13-15)
        a. Love is the spirit of the Law (5:13, 14)
        b. A solemn warning (5:15)
     3. The Abiding Secret of Liberty (5:16-26)
        a. Contrasts (5:16-18)
        b. Catalogues (5:19-23)
        c. Conclusions (5:24-26)
     4. The Practical Outcome of Liberty (6:1-10)
        a. Exhortations to sympathy (6:1-5)
        b. Exhortations to liberality (6:6-10)
Conclusion: (6:11-18)

Having thus familiarized himself with the Epistle to the Galatians by a careful study and analysis of the entire book, the student is now in a position to go a step farther and deal with some passage within the book. The whole being comprehended, the parts may now be dealt with.

2. TO EXPOUND ANY PASSAGE IN THE BIBLE THE PORTION SELECTED MUST BE SUBJECTED TO CAREFUL EXEGESIS

Analysis of the entire book in which the passage occurs is to be followed by exegesis of the particular passage. Analysis gives the "connection" or context, so essential to correct exposition. Exegesis (from Greek, *ex,* "out," and *egeisthai,* "to lead, guide") brings forth the actual meaning of the passage by defining the words it contains and relating them to one another by means of the rules of grammar, the facts of history and the truths of Biblical theology — all in the light of the scope and plan of the book.

It is precisely at this vital point that the untrained or inadequately trained minister faces his greatest obstacle to expository work. The expositor needs to know ancient history, Biblical theology, church history, homiletics, the Bible itself, and other studies in a standard seminary course, but especially does he require a knowledge of the original languages of Scripture. For it is in the Hebrew and Greek original text that exegesis properly takes place. It is there that words are defined in their etymological meaning or in their developed use (*usus loquendi*). It is in this realm that idioms are clarified, rare words or words occurring but once are defined, synonyms distinguished, and important points of grammar and syntax are set forth casting light upon the passage being studied.[3]

So important is a knowledge of the languages of Scripture to sound exegesis that every preacher without such training is under a tremendous responsibility to correct this deficiency, if at all possible. However, in many instances, and for various reasons, it is impossible for men to acquire this basic preparation. In such cases, although an extremely serious handicap will always exist, particularly in the sphere of exegesis, there is no reason why an expository ministry should not be cultivated with all diligence. By the use of reliable translations and commentaries, by diligent study of the English Bible, sound Biblical theology, ancient history and archeology and kindred disciplines, remarkable success and blessing will attend the expository efforts of men who, lacking formal training, will, nevertheless, earnestly strive to be faithful in preaching the Word.

Such expositors, deficient in equipment fundamentally essential to an interpreter of the Word of God, will, however, be shut up to secondary sources, and must continuously be wary of the accuracy or soundness of these sources, not being able to check them with the original languages. Also such students of the Word must be constantly alerted to error and false doctrine, particularly aberrations like "translation theology," since they lack a knowledge of the original languages and accordingly are rendered unable to check their

---

[3] See Chapter XIII, "The Expositor and Grammatical Interpretation."

interpretations by the Hebrew and Greek text, which is in reality the fountainhead of revealed truth.

But let it be assumed the preacher possesses a working knowledge of Biblical languages and kindred theological disciplines. Having analyzed the book from which he is to expound a passage, he is now ready to proceed to the exegesis of the passage from the original language.

a. *The first step in exegesis is philological.* Suppose the expositor selects Galatians 3:25-29. He must begin by translating this section from the original language, ascertaining the accurate meaning of all the words contained in it with the aid of the best Greek lexicons. This preliminary exegetical exercise is of the utmost importance, for unless the expositor knows the definition of each term in the passage and precisely how it is used, he will be unable to grasp the import of the passage as a whole, no matter what care he may exercise in other phases of his exegesis. This procedure involves noting the primitive root or etymological signification of the word, its current or developed usage, and then determining in which sense it is employed in the passage being dealt with.

A good example of an etymological use is furnished by our passage in the term "schoolmaster" in the Authorized Version; "tutor" in the American Revised; "custodian" in the Revised Standard (Gal. 3:24, 25). The Greek word will be found to be *paidagogos* (from *pais,* "child," and *agogos,* "leader, conductor," from *ago,* "to guide, accompany"). The meaning of this expression, transparent from its etymology, is a "child-tender." It is at once apparent to the student of the Greek that none of the English renderings is satisfactory for the simple reason that no such a person as the *paidagogos* exists in our modern social life, and unless the student is able to see the meaning of the original term in its root idea, he is likely to have very inadequate or even erroneous notions concerning its significance in this passage.

A good illustration of the employment of a word with a later or developed meaning is supplied by the difficult and much controverted word "baptize" (*baptizo*). "For as many of you as were baptized into Christ did put on Christ" (Gal. 3:27). Exegesis of this passage requires that the student search out *all* the meanings of this word, such as (1) "dip, immerse," (2) "ceremonially cleanse, or purify by washing," (3) "administer the rite of baptism," (4) "to bring into organic union or under the power of anything which is capable of effecting a change."[4] Having thus traced the meaning, and noted its Biblical and extra-Biblical use, the student must decide what use the word has here. The decision seems inescapable that the usage in this passage is not etymological or original, but developed and later.

In similar fashion every significant word must be dealt with in the passage under consideration. Any synonyms or antonyms, whether actually occurring in the text or required to illuminate the particular expression that does occur must be carefully defined and contrasted. Thus the use of "sons" (*huioi*) verse 26 ("For ye are all sons of God, through faith, in Christ Jesus") calls for immediate clarification by definition in the light of its synonym "children" (*tekna*). Especially is this point imperative because the Authorized Version employs the wrong synonym, rendering the verse: "For ye are all the *children* of God by faith in Christ Jesus."

A simple check of the Greek words will at once show how unfortunate the choice of the word "children" was, inasmuch as the very point to be brought out is that the Christian is no longer in the condition of "children" (*tekna*, "born-ones," from *tikto*, "to bring forth children") but in that of fully grown-up sons.[5] Antonyms in the passage calling for similar careful treatment are "Jew" and "Greek," "bond" and "free," "male" and "female" (v. 28).

In addition, in dealing with the philological aspect of his exegesis, the student must be aware of special idioms, rare words, and words occurring but once. Such difficult expressions must be painstakingly handled. The expositor who

[4] Cf. Merrill F. Unger, *The Baptizing Work of the Holy Spirit* (Wheaton, Van Kampen Press, 1953), p. 78; James W. Dale, *Classic Baptism* (Philadelphia, Presbyterian Board of Publication, 1867), p. 354.

[5] Cf. W. Sanday, in *A New Testament Commentary for English Readers*. Ed. by C. J. Ellicott, Vol. II, p. 448.

avoids them or any phase of his philological task, can never do first-class work.

b. *The second step in exegesis is grammatical.* The student who has acquired an accurate and comprehensive knowledge of the words in a passage is now ready to relate them to one another by the laws of grammar to bring out the meaning of the section as a whole. The contributions of the study of Hebrew and Greek grammar to the clearer understanding of the sacred text are exceedingly rich and well-nigh incalculable. No phase of ministerial training, if appreciated and cultivated, can prove quite so rewarding to the student insofar as the independent discovery of truth is concerned, as well as the refutation of error.

To cite but a few examples from the passage under consideration the following grammatical notes may be mentioned. The "all" (*pantes*) of verse 26 ("For ye are *all* sons of God by faith in Christ Jesus") is stressed by its being placed first in the sentence and is equivalent to the quantitative expression, "As many" (*hosoi*) of verse 27. Similarly in verse 28 ("For *ye* are *all* one in Christ Jesus"), special emphasis is laid on this pronoun "ye" (*humeis*) by its insertion as a separate pronoun (which is not done except in emphatic style) with "all" (*pantes*), indicating that the Galatians were themselves a signal instance of the power of the Gospel to make men one in Christ. Again in verse 29 the word "ye" (*humeis*) is for the same reasons emphatic ("And if *ye* are Christ's [*humeis Christou*] then are ye Abraham's seed"). The use of *humeis Christou* rather than *Christou este* "lays stress apparently on the wonderful transformation of men who had been aliens from the people of God into members of Christ."[6]

Another significant grammatical point which may be noted is the use of two aorist tenses in verse 27, the second of which is evidently coincident with the first. The American Revised Version accordingly renders the passage correctly: "For so many of you as were baptized into Christ *did put on Christ*."

[6] Frederic Rendall in *The Expositor's Greek Testament* (Grand Rapids, n.d.), Vol. III, p. 175.

Thus Greek syntax points out the truth that the Spirit's baptism here set forth is identical with the truth expressed in the figure "did put on Christ," and not merely concomitant with it, as the Authorized Version might lead us to conclude: "For so many of you as have been baptized in Christ have put on Christ."

c. *The third step in exegesis is historical.* The philological and grammatical study of the Hebrew or Greek of a passage of the Bible is indispensable to ascertaining its real meaning but it is not enough. The historical examination of the passage is also essential. In the original as well as in translations there are obviously questions of a historical nature that must be studiously considered if the meaning of the passage is to be made clear. Some of these questions, such as plan and scope of a book and the context, will have been largely settled in the analysis of a particular book. Other problems, however, such as who the author of the book is or who is the speaker in a certain passage, if there is a speaker, what customs, events or persons are referred to, etc., call for careful scrutiny.

The passage in Galatians offers an excellent example of an historical allusion that must be known if the section is to be clearly understood. This is the reference to the Greek "pedagogue" or "child-tender," which has already been considered in connection with its etymological meaning. However, the philological study of this word can help only so far, in this instance. History must supply the remaining necessary information, for the Apostle uses the reference to the Greek pedagogue to illustrate the position of true believers under the Law before the coming of Christ, and unless history sheds light on the subject, the illustration can at best be obscure.

But history fully clarifies this reference. The *paidogogos* was a confidential dependent, "usually a slave or freedman, to whom boys in a family were committed, whose duty it was to attend them at their play, lead them to and from the public school, and exercise a constant superintendence over their conduct and safety."[7] As a term applied figuratively to the Mosaic Law as dealing with men in a mere state of childhood and tutelage (Gal. 3:24, 25) the expression, illuminated by history, becomes very instructive.

The passage in Galatians offers a second important example of historical allusion vital to the comprehension of its meaning. This is the figure of "putting on Christ" (Gal. 3: 27). The Greek or Roman youth upon passing from boyhood to manhood marked the important transition by a change of dress from the boyish tunic to the adult male toga. The youth hitherto subject to domestic rules and regulations now passed out of this preparatory stage into the privileges and responsibilities of citizenship. In like manner the believer in this age is baptized into Christ and thus is freed from the spiritual immaturity of the legal age.

3. To Expound Any Passage in the Bible the Portion Selected Must Be Prayerfully Interpreted

Interpretation (from Latin, *interpretari,* "to explain, elucidate," from *interpres,* "an agent between two parties")[8] construes the particular Scripture under consideration in the light of the belief and judgment of the expositor. This phase of exposition takes up where exegesis leaves off, so that exegesis must precede interpretation, and the latter, if it is to be sound, must be solidly grounded in the former. In fact, careful scientific exegesis furnishes the only sure foundation for reliable interpretation, and interpretation to the extent that it is not founded upon sound exegesis of the Biblical text is worthless, except as the Spirit of God may sovereignly over-rule in the life of the interpreter.

Whereas exegesis is philological, grammatical and historical, interpretation is largely doctrinal and theological. Exegesis presents the meaning of a passage according to the signification of words, the laws of grammar and the facts of history. It deals with God's Word scientifically, arriving

---

[7] Thomas Sheldon Green, *A Greek-English Lexicon to the New Testament,* 11th ed. (New York, James Pott, 1911), p. 134.

[8] The interpreter is thus a mediary between God and men, as far as revealed truth as contained in the Word of God is concerned.

at its meaning precisely as one would arrive at the meaning of any other piece of literature. Interpretation, on the other hand, goes beyond exegesis, inasmuch as the Bible transcends other literature, being unique in having God as its Author and the Holy Spirit as its Interpreter.

If grammatical-historical exegesis were sufficient to understand the Bible, there would be no need for the teaching ministry of the Holy Spirit, and all men, regardless of their spiritual experience, could comprehend Scripture on the basis of mere human scholarship. This being emphatically not the case (John 16:12-16; I Cor. 2:11-16), grammatical-historical study under the guidance of the Holy Spirit inevitably leads to the formation of doctrines and a workable system of systematized theology.

Elucidating and explaining the facts and truths brought to view as a result of exegesis in the light of the doctrines and theology of the expositor constitute interpretation. Moreover, reliability in this vital phase of the expository process depends upon two factors: first, the interpreter's thoroughness and accuracy in exegesis, and second, his gift of spiritual discernment, coupled with humble dependence on the Holy Spirit to use that gift.

Galatians 3:25-29 offers several unusual illustrations of the fact that grammatical-historical exegesis can go only so far when interpretation must take over. For instance, the Apostle's use of the figure of the Greek pedagogue as applied to the Mosaic or legal age when men were, in a dispensational sense, in a state of childhood and tutelage, calls for interpretation in the light of one's comprehension of the essential difference between the age of law, extending from Sinai (Ex. 19:4-6) to Calvary (Matt. 27:51), and the age of grace (Eph. 3:2), stretching from Pentecost to the glorification of the Church (I Thess. 4:13-18). Unless the expositor clearly understands the difference between these two time periods in the redemptive program, his interpretation of the Apostle's words concerning the Greek pedagogue is going to be inadequate or even positively erroneous, no matter how flawless his exegesis of this passage may be.

Of greater interpretational significance, however, is the Apostle's allusion to baptism in this passage: "For as many of you as were baptized into Christ did put on Christ" (Gal. 3:27, ARV). No matter how exhaustively the expositor of this passage has dealt with the term *baptizo,* philologically, as well as grammatically and historically, the difficult problem of interpretation still remains whether this reference is to ritual baptism in water or real baptism by the Holy Spirit.

How shall this vexing problem be settled? The answer is, It can only be resolved, as numerous other similar problems in the Bible, by a sound doctrinal and theological interpretation that is the result of the correct view of the Bible as a unity and as the source of theology. Only such a view of the sacred revelation will admit of a complete systematizing of *all* Bible doctrines and an *unabridged* Biblical theology that deals inductively and fully with *all* phases of divine revelation, omitting no field of doctrinal investigation nor any part of a particular field. Such an attitude toward the Bible, attested by study and thorough systematizing of its teachings, alone will suffice to furnish an adequate doctrinal and theological basis for interpretation.

Accordingly, before an interpreter can with any degree of assurance dismiss this reference as merely water baptism, he is under obligation at least to make a systematic study of Spirit baptism, and honestly face the question whether this reference, despite the majority of commentators, is not after all an allusion to an operation of the Spirit of God and not a ritual performed by man.

But a study of the baptizing work of the Holy Spirit (Matt. 3:11; Mark 1:8; John 1:32, 33; Acts 1:5; I Cor. 12:13) is one of the notable omissions of systematic theology. Although a doctrine of far-reaching importance (Rom. 6:3, 4; Col. 2:10), the basis of the believer's position (Eph. 1:3, 6, 7) and possessions "in Christ" (Eph. 1:19-23; Col. 3:1-4),[9] this theme is completely ignored in the ordinary systematic theology or Bible commentary, and treated as if it were non-

[9] Cf. Merrill F. Unger, *op. cit.,* pp. 1-136.

existent. Hence the average interpreter is not challenged with the claim of this passage to identification with Spirit baptism rather than with water baptism.

However, when the various references to a baptism that puts the believer "in" or "into Christ" (Rom. 6:3, 4; Col. 2:10) and into Christ's Body, the Church (I Cor. 12:13), are collated, it is found that all these passages refer to Spirit baptism, for that alone can put us "in Christ." Galatians 3:27, upon fair examination, is found to be no exception, for it has in view the same mystical union of all believers "in Christ" whether "Jew" or "Greek," "bond" or "free," "male" or "female" (v. 28).

4. To Expound Any Passage in the Bible the Portion Selected Must Be Logically Presented in Finished Sermonic Form with Illustration, Explanation, Argumentation, Exhortaton and Application

This is exposition proper and in its best sense, to which all the other preliminary steps — analysis, exegesis and interpretation — are preparatory and toward which they are aimed.

Exposition (from Latin ex, "out," and ponere, "to place") is the setting forth or laying open the sense or meaning of a passage. It is quite similar, as is obvious, to exegesis and is often used synonymously with it. But it is a larger concept and, although it includes exegesis, it goes beyond it, denoting "a more extended development and illustration of the sense, dealing more largely with other scriptures by comparison and contrast."[10]

Much so-called exposition is not logically presented and possesses no finished homiletical form. It is frequently a bewildering mass of conglomerate facts, that instead of laying open the meaning of a passage confuses the hearer. This type of expository perversion is to be studiously avoided. It may be based upon careful analysis of the book from which a passage is used. It may also be exegetically accurate and interpretationally sound. But it is abortive. It stops short of logical organization and lacks balanced illustration, orderly

[10] Milton Terry, *Biblical Hermeneutics* (New York, 1911), p. 19.

explanation, closely knit argumentation, pointed exhortation and relevant application to the needs of the hearers. It fails to qualify as preaching at all.

Although there are varieties of expository method that do not employ homiletical treatment,[11] these ought not to be the ideal of the expository preacher, at least not for formal preaching from the pulpit. He should guard the sacred desk for the best examples of expository work, which presupposes not only diligence in exegesis and soundness of interpretation but also the highest type of logical organization and artistic presentation of his material.

In dealing with Galatians 3:23-29 the following expository treatment is suggested:

OUR SPIRITUAL COMING OF AGE

INTRODUCTION:

1. Examples of progress: covered-wagon trails westward — later railroads; horse-and-buggy days — modern automobile, sailboat and modern ocean liner.
2. So there is progress in God's revealed ways with man. Examples: slaying of animals to cover nakedness of our sinning parents in Eden, pre-Mosaic and Mosaic sacrifices and ritual. Coming of Christ and His perfect sacrifice.
3. Example, of law and grace. Age of Moses and the Gospel age.

I. THE LEGAL AGE WAS A PERIOD OF SPIRITUAL CHILDHOOD (vv. 23, 24).

1. *A preparatory period* (23a).
   a. "Before *faith* came," i.e., previous to "the *gospel of Christ*" (Gal. 1:23; 3:25; Acts 6:7; Jude 3).
   b. Compare childhood as a preparatory period.
2. *A period of confinement* (v. 23b).
   a. O. T. believer "confined" under control of the Mosaic Law — "as if by a military guard" (*ephrouroumetha*), that we might not escape from its power.
   b. Compare childhood as a period of confinement.
3. *A period of restraint* (23c).
   a. O. T. believer "shut up" (*sugkleiomenoi*), "completely, with no way of escape," to the demands of the Law.
   b. Compare childhood as a period of disciplinary restraint.
4. *A period of spiritual immaturity* (v. 24).
   a. O. T. believer under a "child-tender" (the Law).
   b. Compare the Greek and Roman boy.

[11] See Chapters V and VI.

II. The Gospel Age Is a Period of Spiritual Adulthood (vv. 25, 26).
  1. A *perfected* period (25a).
    a. "But now faith *has come*."
    b. Compare the Gospel with adulthood.
  2. A period of spiritual maturity (25b).
    a. No longer under a "child-tender."
    b. Compare the Greek and Roman youth at his majority.
  3. A period of spiritual privilege (26).
    a. "*All* the *sons* (adult sons) of God by faith in Christ."
    b. Contrast status of *children* under the Law.
III. The Basis of Our Spiritual Adulthood in the Gospel Age Is Our Position in Christ (vv. 27-29).
  1. We are baptized into Christ" (27a).
    a. The Holy Spirit unites us mystically to Christ (Rom. 6:3, 4; Col. 2:10; Eph. 4:5; I Cor. 12:13).
    b. Compare all N. T. passages referring to our position "in Christ" (Eph. 1:3, 6, 7, 13, etc.).
  2. We have "put on Christ" (27b).
    a. The Holy Spirit gives us the status of adulthood.
    b. Compare the Greek and Roman youth exchanging the boyish tunic for the adult male *toga*.
  3. We are "one in Christ" (28).
    a. The Holy Spirit produces a unity transcending all human barriers and distinctions.
    b. Compare the barriers and distinctions under the Law (Rom. 9:4) between Israelites and non-Israelites, freemen and slaves, male and female.
  4. We are Christ's (29).
    a. Hence Abraham's spiritual progeny.
    b. Heirs of faith.
Conclusion:
  1. What a privilege is ours to live under the Gospel, to enjoy the benefits of adult sonship, of being "in Christ" by the Spirit's baptizing work, to come of age spiritually and be delivered from legalism, and all human distinctions of race and social standing, to be freed from rules and minute regulations that governed the O. T. believer as a *child* under the Law.
  2. What a blessing to have the enablement of the Holy Spirit to fulfill the weightier obligations as a citizen of a heavenly commonwealth (Phil. 3:20), to be clothed with Christ's own standing and merits, to be "accepted in the Beloved" (Eph. 1:7) rather than laboring to be accepted on the basis of works and personal merit.
  3. Are we "sons of God" by faith in Christ Jesus? If so, are we living up to our glorious position and privileges?

This, the sermonizing variety of expository message, is the highest type of expository work. The title of the sermon, its main divisions and subdivisions, and its subject matter are all drawn from the passage expounded. Accordingly, the treatment adheres in the closest manner possible to the text and seeks on the basis of thorough analysis and exegesis, together with sound interpretation, conscientiously to set forth in the clearest, most finished and logical form what the Holy Spirit intends to teach by this section.

In addition, it concerns itself only with salient features. It emphasizes what the passage itself emphasizes. By adhering resolutely to the logical argument of the text, it avoids featuring any details that would blur the definite impression to be made. The spiritual, as it should be, is kept in the supreme place of importance throughout. Temptation to sidetrack the spiritual meaning and be occupied unduly with the several interesting historical allusions the passage contains is overcome.

Finally, the spiritual message is employed in pointed illustration, exhortation and application to the needs of the hearers, whether they are saved or unsaved. Expository work should never become so absorbed in facts, even in Biblical truth, that it crowds out these vital elements of good preaching. People who attend upon a sermon want to be inspired, challenged and moved. They want their hearts warmed with heavenly fire as well as their heads filled with heavenly wisdom. It is the job of the expository preacher to do both, and his task is the most glorious that was ever committed by God to man.

GENERAL INDEX

A

Abel, 51
Abbott-Smith, G., 127
Abimelech, 191
Abomination of Desolation, 159
Abraham, 50, 51, 137-138, 161, 190, 203, 208, 210; as a type, 207-8
Academic training, 65-7
Accommodation, 119
Achaia, 25
Actions, as types, 209
Adam, 126; as a type of Christ, 204-5, 213
Adamic nature, 58
Adon, 125
Adonai, 125
Adonai Jehovah, 126
Advent of the Spirit, 58
Advocate, 121
Agapao, 127
Ahaz, 227
Aitema, 127
Akkadian, 123
Albright, W. F., 139
Allegorical interpretation, 118
Allegory, 159, 189-190
Allis, Oswald T., 68
Amillennialism, 21, 88, 217, tests of, 224-6; 230-35
Amos, 176
Anacoluthon, 146-8
Analysis, 238
Analytical method, 97
Analytical outlines, 239
Angels, fallen, 103
Angus, J., 202, 210, 213
Anthropology, 166

Anthropomorphisms, 116, 181
Anthropopathy, 181
Anthropopathisms, 116
Antitypes, 204, 206
Apologetic interpretation, 119
Apologetic study of the Bible, 20
Apologetics, 72
Aposiopesis, 184
Apostles, 62
Application, 250-2
Arabic, 123
Aramaic, 70, 123
Archeology, 17-18, 33, 71, 122, 125, 150-2
Argumentation, 250-2
Argumentum ad hominem, 112
Argumentum ad ignorantium, 112
Argumentum ad vericundiam, 112
Armageddon, 166, 220
Art, 33; of expository preaching, 83
'Asham, 126
Assonance, 181
Assurance, 101
Atonement, Day of, 208, 213
Aurochs, 123
Author, Biblical, 136-9
Authority, 24-7, 143, 167
'Aval, 126
'Avar, 126
'Aven, 126

B

Baal worship, 139, 180
Babylonian captivity, 220

Background material, 71
Bailey, Albert E., 137
Baptism, 248-9
Baptism of the Spirit, 88, 90, 113, 144
Baptismal regeneration, 144
Baptizo, 242, 248
Barthianism, 18, 76
Baumgartner, Walter, 124
Baxter, J. Sidlow, 239
Beardsley, Monroe C., 98, 110
Beast, number of, 192
Beast, superman, 214
Begging the question, 112
Ben, 122
Bengel, 197
Berkhof, L., 118, 136, 141, 143
Bible, 33-42; as a textual anthology, 33-4; context, 34; conference, 35-6; a unity, 36-7, 156-7; reading the, 41-42
Bible-centered ministry, 31
Bible college, 66
Bible institutes, 18
Bible knowledge, decrease of, 32
Bible study, 238
Biblical authority, 18, 81-2
Biblical backgrounds, 71-2, 227-8
Biblical illiterate, 34
Biblical introduction, 72
Biblical prophecy, 164

SCRIPTURAL INDEX

NOTES

NOTES

NOTES

NOTES

Notes